"Author Ed Silvoso has a habit of writing profound, life-changing books. The Body of Christ has gained so much through his life and ministry that I can't imagine where we would be without his instruction along with his testimonies of Kingdom breakthroughs. Yet *Ekklesia* may be the most important book he has ever written. As such, it is one of the greatest books of our lifetime. Contained in these pages are tried-and-true insights and experiences that will inspire the greatest skeptic and equip all who have a heart to see 'the kingdom of this world become the Kingdom of our God.' This book is simply brilliant, inspired, profound, and challenging. I encourage you to join me in reading *Ekklesia* for personal transformation, that we might be equipped to transform the cities and nations for His glory."

Bill Johnson, senior leader, Bethel Church, Redding, California;
author, *When Heaven Invades Earth* and *God Is Good*

"Ed Silvoso's newest book, *Ekklesia*, is not just an important book for church leaders to read and digest—it is an *extraordinarily* important book! God is moving us into a new season, one that is changing our paradigm from church-centered to Kingdom-centered. Silvoso helps us see the church as not just a congregation with a pastor where we gather in a building on Sunday mornings. Rather, the Church is Ekklesia, scattered throughout society carrying the Word and the works of the Kingdom. This change is a complex project, and there is no better road map toward seeing it accomplished than Ed Silvoso's *Ekklesia*. You will cherish this book!"

C. Peter Wagner (1930–2016), Global Spheres, Inc.

"Ed Silvoso has a way of writing groundbreaking books that start movements, and *Ekklesia* is no exception! This book is a message that reveals how to see Kingdom principles implemented in a masterful yet practical way! This is a nation-changing book!"

Cindy Jacobs, Generals International

"Ed Silvoso has created another masterpiece in *Ekklesia*. Ed takes a fresh look at Scripture to rediscover the Church as a people versus an institution and how that should impact the way we express the Gospel to every sphere of influence. He shows us what the Church is intended to be versus what it has become. We need a course correction, and Ed provides us the needed master plan to right the ship. Well done, Ed!"

Os Hillman, author, *TGIF: Today God Is First*;
president, Marketplace Leaders

"Finally! A book that clarifies the difference between the Church as Jesus *meant* it to be and the churches we see today. Tragically, the two aren't even similar. Today, we hear the word *church* and think of a building or a religious organization. Jesus, on the other hand, wasn't talking about either. He was talking about a gathering—a coming together of His followers, who would deny themselves, take up their crosses and follow Him. And following Him means becoming a disciple and making disciples. The power and simplicity of His call to '*disciple* all nations' has been obscured and diluted by the *manmade* institutionalization of Christianity. This book takes us back to the true callings of Christ. I enthusiastically recommend it to *all* who call themselves followers of the Lord Jesus Christ."

Steven K. Scott, author, *Jesus Speaks*
and *The Greatest Words Ever Spoken*

"For decades, Ed Silvoso has ranked among the Church's most inspiring catalytic leaders. He is a unique thinker and a brilliant communicator. *Ekklesia* is a true groundbreaker. It is a gift that will bring many to a profound view of the Gospel and the Kingdom. Having been his friend for years, I am especially grateful for his commitment to affirm pastors and engage local churches in his passionate vision of the future."

David Cannistraci, lead pastor, GateWay City Church,
San José, California

EKKLESIA

Books by Ed Silvoso

That None Should Perish
Prayer Evangelism
Women: God's Secret Weapon
Anointed for Business
Transformation
Ekklesia

EKKLESIA

REDISCOVERING
GOD'S INSTRUMENT
FOR GLOBAL
TRANSFORMATION

DR. ED SILVOSO

Chosen

a division of Baker Publishing Group
Minneapolis, Minnesota

© 2014, 2017 by Ed Silvoso

Published by Chosen Books
11400 Hampshire Avenue South
Bloomington, Minnesota 55438
www.chosenbooks.com

Chosen Books is a division of
Baker Publishing Group, Grand Rapids, Michigan

Paperback edition published 2017
ISBN 978-0-8007-9856-7

Printed in the United States of America

The Library of Congress has cataloged the hardcover edition as follows:
Names: Silvoso, Ed, author.
Title: Ekklesia : rediscovering God's instrument for global transformation / Ed Silvoso.
Description: Minneapolis, Minnesota : Chosen, 2017. | Includes bibliographical references.
Identifiers: LCCN 2016049392 | ISBN 9780800798444 (cloth : alk. paper)
Subjects: LCSH: Church.
Classification: LCC BV600.3 .S555 2017 | DDC 262—dc23
LC record available at https://lccn.loc.gov/2016049392

Cover design by Dan Pitts

18 19 20 21 22 23   7 6 5 4 3 2

To Ray Pinson, an anointed marketplace minister, dear friend and spiritual son who has faithfully and generously served as chairman of our board for over two decades. And to Ruth, the love of my life, who lovingly and patiently sat by me while I wrote, praying, advising and encouraging me.

This book is also dedicated to pastors and marketplace ministers, who together make up the enterprise that Jesus labeled "the Ekklesia." It is my fervent prayer and intense desire that the scriptural truths and inspiring prototypes presented in this book will strengthen their hands and rekindle their passion to see people and nations transformed *in this generation.*

Contents

Gratitude

I wish to express my deepest gratitude to everybody who walked alongside me in this rediscovery journey, in particular to Dave Thompson and Cindy Oliveira, who accompanied me through many long days and a few long nights to have this manuscript ready on time. I am deeply indebted to Roberto Beretta for his clarifying analysis of key Greek words, and to Greg Pagh for taking the point in helping with the *Ekklesia Group Guide*. I am also grateful to the following people, who all provided valuable contributions along the way. Some of you I quoted or mentioned in the book, some of you assisted me with review and feedback, and some of you encouraged me with words of affirmation and motivation:

John Arnott, Gaston Bader, Kim Bangs, Brian Beattie, Dick Bernal, Victor Bianco, Michael and Paulette Brown, Brian and Margaret Burton, Omar Cabrera Jr., Jane Campbell, Allen Cardines, Norberto Carlini, Barbara Chan, Y. K. Chan, Cal Chinen, Daniel Chinen, Sirus Chitsaz, Francisco Contreras, Loren Cunningham, Clifford Daugherty, Dick Eastman, King Flores, Daniel Ghinn, Ken Gott, Dave Gschwend, Ted and Sandra Hahs, David Hamilton, Bishop Bill Hamon, Jack Hayford, Rick and Rachel Heeren, Os Hillman, Tito Itojanovich, John Jackson, Cindy and Mike Jacobs, Beverly Jaime, Bill Johnson, Myles and Joyce Kawakami, Danny Kim, Trish Konieczny, Derk and Annita Maat, Melanie MacNaughton, Benjy and Jesica MacNaughton, Aldo and Roxana Martin, Bishop Vaughn McLaughlin, Kevin Mitchell, Bob

Mumford, Poncho Murguía, Norm Nason, Alex Noriega, Francis and Caroline Oda, Joseph Okia, Omar Olier, Juan Carlos Ortiz, George Otis Jr., Matt Pagh, Kathy Pinson, Geoff and Salina Poon, Graham Power, Chuck Proudfit, Miguel Angel Pujol, Jill Robson, Father Dimitri Sala, Sergio Scataglini, Ken and Marilyn Schuler, Steve Scott, Jackie Seeno, Jack and Alice Jane Serra, Chuck Starnes, Clifford Sullivan, Anthony Summers, Sue Thompson, Roy Tirtadji, Lloyd Turner, Daniel Valles, Kris Vallotton, Werner and Sheri Vavken, Diane Vermooten, Peter and Doris Wagner, Evelyn and Karl Wallace, Brent Walters, Myles Weiss, Dave Wendorff, Ross and Lynne Whitehill, Pastor Wong Po Ling, Patnie Woo, and Baha Yahyagil.

Introduction

Questions That Brought This Book into Being

If the Church is so important, why did Jesus mention it only twice in the gospels?

And why is there neither a command nor instructions in the Bible on how to plant one?

These are intriguing questions that beg new questions, such as how was the New Testament Church able not just to survive, but also to radically transform the hostile social and political environs into which it was born? How did it set in motion a process that impacted nations in a relatively short time, *without buildings, professional clergy, religious freedom or social status*?

And why, in comparison, does it appear that the Church's influence on social matters today is progressively diminishing? How can this be the case if Jesus assured His followers of two dynamic truths: that when He is lifted up, all men will be drawn to Him, and that we will do greater works than He did? Could it be that in our generation the fullness of the *real* Jesus has yet to be discovered, as well as the actual depth of our call as ministers?

Why are we not experiencing the evangelistic growth reported in the gospels, where everybody was "forcing his way" into the Kingdom

(Luke 16:16)? Could it be that instead of preaching the Gospel of the Kingdom, we are preaching the Law and the Prophets?

Why does there seem to be a major disconnect between what we read in the book of Acts and what we see nowadays? Why don't we see God performing extraordinary miracles, as He did through the hands of Paul while Paul was manufacturing tents—miracles that resulted in everybody who lived in Asia hearing the word of the Lord (see Acts 19:10)? That was over a million people evangelized by a movement anchored in a tent-making shop!

How was it that Paul planted churches with such capable *local* leadership that their rapid expansion soon left him with no more room to minister between Jerusalem and modern-day Croatia—all of Asia Minor? (see Romans 15:19).

Why is it that when Jesus comes to judge the nations, those who thought they were "in" will end up "out," and vice versa?

More intriguingly, why were those who appealed Jesus' decision on the basis that they had cast out demons, prophesied and performed miracles told, "Depart from me, you who practice lawlessness" (Matthew 7:23)?

Does that mean that miracles, prophecies and deliverance are wrong? Since it is impossible to contemplate such a possibility because the New Testament's narrative testifies to the validity of those ministries, how do we reconcile that with what we do in church today? And what about all the other discrepancies we see between the New Testament Church and the Church of today?

Could it be that we have confined to four walls once a week what is designed to be a 24/7 people movement out in the marketplace, transforming our cities and nations? And could it be that we have restricted ministry to professionally trained specialists, instead of ministry being the work of all the saints?

The Church Jesus launched is meant to be expansive, like salt, water, light or leaven—metaphors He used to describe the Kingdom of God—none of which is effective if contained or controlled. Salt left in a shaker is useless. Stale water turns putrid. Light that is blocked results in darkness. Leaven in a container remains inert.

Jesus was very clear when He introduced the Church. He stated unequivocally that the Gates of Hades would not prevail against it. There is no question that those Gates are deeply entrenched in our cities and nations—where we work, live, go to school. *But so is the Church!* In fact, the Church is the only institution on earth that has a branch in every city and a representative in every neighborhood. So why is there an impression that it is losing?

The issue is not so much what we are doing wrong, but rather what is missing that is keeping Jesus' stated objectives from materializing? As we know, the enemy of the "best" is not so much the "worst," which is usually very evident to us. Rather, the enemy is the "good," because by being so satisfying, it deprives us of hunger for the "much more" that in this case God has in store.

If that is the case, what is missing and how can we find it?

The Ekklesia, Jesus' Church, was never meant to resemble a prisoner-of-war camp waiting to be liberated. On the contrary! God has a hope and a future for each one of its members. His plans are for good and not for evil. Furthermore, the Bible states with no ambiguity whatsoever that the saints, the Church, will overcome the devil and his demons here on earth (see Revelation 12:11). Not to believe this means not to preach it, and not to preach it means to resign ourselves to mere subsistence. This would not only be tragic, but would constitute a dereliction of spiritual duty.

The Ekklesia that Jesus is building is equipped (as the old hymn states) with a story to tell, not just to individuals but also to the nations, that will turn their hearts to the Lord. And more than that, the Ekklesia is specifically empowered to disciple and to transform them. In the worldwide movement Transform Our World that I had the privilege of founding with my wife, Ruth, we have been blessed with some of the most promising prototypes of societal transformation. Businesses, schools and governments, injected with the leaven of the Kingdom of God, are experiencing what until now was conceived as possible only inside the four walls of the Church. These models look like a church, walk like a church and do the things that a church does, *but in the marketplace.* Could it be that they are churches indeed?

These challenging questions, combined with these and other extraordinary experiences that I will expand on later, have led me into the most stimulating Bible research I have ever been on: a comparative survey of scriptural phenomena and contemporary examples to rediscover the Church as Jesus *really* designed it to be. This book is the result.

I offer answers here not as the final word—since so much is still in process—but as field notes and observations submitted with a humility forced on me by the magnitude of the task and the awareness of my own limitations. This is why I have titled chapters dealing with key doctrinal issues as "A *Fuller* Understanding of . . ."

What I share in the following pages is meant to be revolutionary, but not rebellious. When I address the shortcomings of the modern-day Church, I do so with the utmost respect for its leaders and members. I also do it with the unshakable conviction that Jesus is still building His Church, because I know that "He who began a good work in you [us] will perfect it until the day of Christ Jesus" (Philippians 1:6).

To that effect, I aspire to see replicated today the metrics that characterized the Ekklesia (Church) in the book of Acts (see Acts 2:41–47; 5:12): (1) members being devoted to their leaders' teaching; (2) individual and corporate prosperity to provide for every need inside and outside their circles; (3) daily additions (numerical growth) happening; (4) ongoing and expanding favor with outsiders, especially those in authority in their city; and (5) signs and wonders being performed at the modern equivalent of Solomon's Portico—that is, in the public arena.

The biblical principles, validating testimonies and case studies in this book will inspire you and lead you to a victorious *lifestyle* in your own journey, in your family and in your sphere of influence. This progression will enrich you with faith to believe that not just individuals, but also nations will be saved (see Revelation 7:9; 21:24–27). And you will enter into a fascinating partnership with God to take His transforming power and presence everywhere, every day of your life.

For this to happen in a sustainable and expandable way, I have striven to offer a biblical rationale, validated by contemporary examples, so that pastors can find their Aquilas and Priscillas, and marketplace ministers can find their Pauls. Once this happens, the former can serve as equippers "a la Ephesians 4" for the latter to take the presence of God, already resident in them, to the heart of the city—the marketplace—24/7.

Turn the page and join me on this journey. You will never be the same, but better yet, the world will never be the same!

1

Church: A Radical Proposition

From "Something Wrong" to "Something More"

Jesus did not state, "I will build My Temple" or "I will build My synagogue," the two most prominent Jewish religious institutions at the time. Instead, He chose a secular entity first developed by the Greeks when He said, "I will build My Ekklesia." Why? The answer is fascinating, challenging and empowering.

Nowadays, when we hear the word *church*, we usually picture a solemn building with a cross on top, a pulpit, clergy, a choir, a worship leader and members.

I do not put such notions down, because they reflect cherished expressions of how and where most Christians teach or practice their faith today. During the days when Jesus walked this earth, however, *Ekklesia*—the Greek word translated into English as "church"—*was not religious in nature or connotation at all*. In fact, by the time He first uttered the word in the gospel of Matthew, it had been in use for centuries in both the Greek and Roman empires to refer to a secular institution operating in the marketplace in a governmental capacity.

When Jesus chose the word *Ekklesia* to introduce His redemptive agency, no one among His disciples would have conceived it as redeemable—as we will see later—since the existing *ekklesia* embodied a foreign stronghold. (Note that when I use the term *ekklesia* with a lowercase *e*, it refers to the secular institution. When I capitalize the term, I am referring to Jesus' *Ekklesia* of Matthew 16:18.) Granted, the term *Ekklesia* is present in the Septuagint (Greek) translation of the Old Testament to describe religious assemblies, but Jesus' usage was related to the secular Greek version. So, how did this secular institution that Jesus was referencing evolve into the religious one we are so familiar with today? And more important yet, once the *Ekklesia* became Jesus' redemptive agency, how did it mutate from the pivotal, pace-setting role in society that we read about in the Scriptures into its seemingly less relevant and more ethereal role of today?

A Different Kind of Church

The New Testament examples of church are vastly different from the contemporary notion that it is a place where members go, usually once a week. Back then, church always referred to *people*, never to *buildings*, and it was made up of individuals who operated 24/7 "from house to house" all over town as a transforming organism, not as a static institution (Acts 2:46; 5:42). Its objective was the transformation of people *and of society*, rather than acting as a transfer station for saved souls bound for heaven.

In fact, the New Testament Church was so vibrant and expansive that it overcame the powerful political and religious establishments bent on stamping it out since its very inception. Its vitality is attested to by the fact that in a matter of weeks it filled Jerusalem—the city that crucified its founder—with its doctrine (see Acts 5:28), leading many thousands in just a few days to join its ranks by publicly confessing that Jesus was indeed the Son of God.

Its capacity for growth was so dynamic that two years after Paul planted the Ekklesia in Ephesus, "all who lived in [the Roman province of] Asia heard the word of the Lord" (Acts 19:10), no small accomplishment since the population of that region exceeded a million people.

And not long afterward, Paul was able to state with certitude that "from Jerusalem and round about as far as Illyricum I have fully preached the gospel" (Romans 15:19). That was a surface area of around 300,000 square miles—leading Paul to set his evangelistic eyes on Spain, a place that stood some 3,600 miles by land from Jerusalem, the birthplace of Christianity (see verses 18–24).

What makes this stunningly remarkable is that Jesus' Ekklesia accomplished all of this without military or governmental support. It was instead a massive *people movement* that swept region after region victoriously as the counterculture to the existing status quo.

The magnitude of the Church's expansion in such a relatively short time is hard to imagine, much less conceive as the norm in our contemporary environs, since it was accomplished without seminaries, campuses, full-time staff or professional ministers. Furthermore, with the exception of some epistles that circulated regionally, it did not have the New Testament epistles and had only occasional access to Old Testament writings. Yet it was so healthy and powerful that rather than being an item on someone else's agenda, the Ekklesia was the agenda setter!

A Much-Needed Reality Check

These observations beg additional questions: Where is the influence of the Church today in the midst of the social, economic, political and moral upheaval that is wreaking havoc in the world? And how is it doing relative to the victorious climax that Revelation 21:24–27 describes, where, led by their rulers, a procession of *saved nations*—not just saved people— will bring their honor and glory as a wedding present to Jesus? In light of all this, I believe it is both fair *and necessary* to admit that there is something missing that we have not tapped into yet. If so, what is it?

I don't despise, nor is it my intention to put down, the Church as we know it today. Ministers are among the most giving and sacrificial people on earth, folks whose lives are dedicated to helping others week after week. I am unconditionally committed to the Church as it is, both as a faithful member and a leader. This is why no one can join our ministry team unless they are full-fledged members of a local church.

I will never demean or disqualify the Church, but I would rather constructively point out that to fulfill the mission that Jesus assigned it, it must recover what worked so well back then and reinject what is missing into its mainstream.

There is something missing that we have not tapped into yet. If so, what is it?

This is why, instead of the word *Church*, with its rich religious and traditional connotations, I have chosen the one used in the original manuscripts—*Ekklesia*—for this quest to rediscover the meaning and function of the entity that Jesus stated will both prevail against the Gates of Hades and cause not just individuals but also *nations* and their *rulers* to be saved. Furthermore, instead of spelling it *ecclesia*, I have deliberately used *Ekklesia* because most readers are bound to associate the former spelling with *ecclesiastical*, which is used to describe traditional religious activities.

Jesus' Intriguing Silence about the Church

One would assume that during His years of public ministry, Jesus must have spent considerable time teaching about the Church, specifically about its nature and also how to plant and grow one. Get ready to be surprised, because as far as the four gospels are concerned, Jesus used the word translated "church" in our Bibles *only three times* (see Matthew 16:18; 18:17). That is the extent of His *recorded* teaching on the subject in the gospels.

Most Christian leaders, myself included, acknowledge the key role church planting has in fulfilling the Great Commission. It is perplexing that in the Scriptures, however, there is neither a command nor instructions on how to plant a church. This does not signify that churches were not planted, because in New Testament times they were established all over the interconnected world. Nor could it mean that the Church is not essential, because Paul described it as "the household of God . . . the pillar and support of the truth" (1 Timothy 3:15). Furthermore, after planting quite a few churches, he taught extensively on how to govern them. Nevertheless, the questions remain, why did Jesus speak so little about the Church, and why did neither He nor His apostles give *specific* instructions on how to plant a church?

The manner in which church elders were chosen and appointed in biblical times challenges us even further. Today, we consider epistles like those written to the Philippians and Thessalonians prime timber with which to build the theological furniture of the Church. But Paul, who planted those churches, spent less than a week in Philippi and not quite three weeks in Thessalonica. Yet by the time he left town, he had established dynamic churches in both cities, *with capable local leadership in place.*

Nowadays, we are so meticulous about planting a church, and even more so about appointing elders, that it usually takes years. I have no objection to being thorough about this, since in a passage dealing with the government of the Church Paul admonished us, "Do not lay hands upon anyone too hastily" (1 Timothy 5:22). But the fact remains that not only was the premier New Testament church planter able to do it, complete with competent leadership, in a much shorter time than it takes us today, but also that the congregations under these local leaders' oversight became models for us to emulate.

> *When Jesus introduced the Ekklesia, His intention all along was to co-opt an existing secular concept and impregnate it with His Kingdom DNA.*

This thought-provoking contrast between what Paul did so well and what we try to emulate with much less success triggers another challenging question: What kind of churches did Paul plant? For this I found the answer in the Church's *secular roots*, which opened the door to see, in an unanticipated way, what Jesus had in mind when He introduced the Ekklesia. In fact, I was surprised to discover that His intention all along was to co-opt an existing secular concept and impregnate it with His Kingdom DNA.

Understanding the roots and function of the secular ekklesia—which predated Jesus' use of the term—is crucial for us to rediscover the Church as it was really meant to be.

The Genesis of the Ekklesia

At the time of Jesus' birth and all through His life on earth, there were three main institutions in Israel: the Temple, the synagogue and the ekklesia. It is usually assumed that all three were religious bodies, but only the Temple and the synagogue fit that description. The ekklesia was not religious at all, since it was first developed as a ruling assembly of citizens in the Grecian democracy to govern its city-states. It consisted of men eighteen years or older who had done two years of military service; in essence, people substantially committed to their city-state.

In a broader sense, ekklesia also came to mean an assembly of citizens duly convened. When the more hierarchical Romans replaced the Greeks in the imperial scene, the Romans assimilated the concept.[1] Consequently, the general public in Jesus' day understood ekklesia to mean both the secular institution and the governmental system it represented.

We find an example of the Hellenistic ekklesia in the book of Acts, when Paul's associates Gaius and Aristarchus were dragged to the theater in Ephesus (a Roman colony) in response to a complaint brought by the local union of silversmiths. The word that is translated *assembly* in this instance is the same one rendered *church* elsewhere in the New Testament (see Acts 19:32, 39). Here ekklesia refers to the crowd twice, and a third time to the court itself, showing that the term was employed to describe a body of people assembled to conduct governmental business. In fact, when the town clerk "dismissed the assembly [ekklesia]" amidst warnings of illegality (Acts 19:41), the same noun translated *assembly* in that verse is translated *church* 112 times elsewhere in the New Testament. This assembly model is precisely the one that Jesus chose to emulate conceptually, as we will see in greater detail later.[2]

It is most revealing that Jesus did not say, "I will build My Temple" or "I will build My synagogue"—the two premier Jewish religious institutions. If He were thinking along those lines, He could have said, "I will restore and even surpass the former glory of the Temple so that heads of state will journey to Jerusalem, as the Queen of Sheba did, until every world ruler has bent his or her knee before the God worshiped here." He could have also said, "I will build My own worldwide network of synagogues to make the Gospel available to people in every nation." The synagogue was the religious place where Jews met on the Sabbath to read the Scriptures and to pray. Like the Temple, a building was essential to the synagogue's function.

When the moment came to introduce His transformational agency, Jesus selected neither one. Instead, He announced that He would build *His Ekklesia*—choosing a term that, in the Roman Empire in general and also in subjugated Israel, described a governmental institution.

The Lord did not discard everything that went on in the Temple or the synagogue, but assimilated significant components from both institutions into His Ekklesia. From the Temple He kept the indwelling presence of God, and from the synagogue the central role of the Scriptures and the fellowship of its members.

Where the Temple and the synagogue differ with Jesus' Ekklesia, however, is in the areas of constitution, location and mobility. The Temple and the synagogue were static institutions that functioned in buildings that members had to go to on specified occasions, whereas the Ekklesia was a *building-less* mobile people movement designed to operate 24/7 in the marketplace for the purpose of having an impact on everybody and everything.

> *The Ekklesia was a building-less mobile people movement designed to operate 24/7 in the marketplace for the purpose of having an impact on everybody and everything.*

The *Conventus*: A Fascinating Caveat

The Greek and Roman versions of the ekklesia appeared in different forms and sizes, all of which are relevant to the subject at hand. But one format is especially notable: the *Conventus Civium Romanorum*, or *conventus* for short. According to Sir William Ramsay, when a group of Roman citizens as small as two or three gathered anywhere in the world, it constituted the *conventus* as a local expression of Rome. Even though geography separated them from the capital of the empire and the emperor, their coming together as fellow citizens automatically brought the power and presence of Rome into their midst. This was indeed the Roman ekklesia in a microcosm.[3]

We see an expression of this in Acts 16, when the Roman magistrates panicked at the realization that they had beaten and thrown in prison a fellow citizen (Paul) without the due process accorded to Romans. Later on, another centurion and his commander exhibited similar concerns after finding out that Paul, who they were about to punish, was also a Roman citizen (see Acts 22:24–29). Evidently, when two or more Roman citizens connected, the laws (and protection) of the emperor were in their midst.

This is relevant to our discussion because in Matthew 18, after describing the authority entrusted to His deputies as the Ekklesia to bind and release for the will of God to be done on earth, Jesus stated that this was possible because "where two or three have gathered together in My name, I am there in their midst" (verse 20). That is exactly what the *conventus* did for the emperor. Jesus made His authority available to His Ekklesia in the same manner, but in a much greater dimension when He stipulated that "whatever you bind *on earth* shall have been bound *in heaven*; and whatever you loose *on earth* shall have been loosed *in heaven*" (Matthew 18:18, emphasis added).

> To *the people in the Roman Empire, including Israel, the ekklesia was as familiar a concept as the state assembly is to those living in a democracy.*

By selecting the ekklesia model over the Temple or the synagogue, Jesus chose an agency better suited to succeed everywhere—not just in Israel, where He ministered extensively, but also in the pagan societies where He would send His disciples. His ultimate objective was not to reproduce or expand religious institutions. It was to see nations discipled by inserting the leaven of His Kingdom into their social fiber through His Ekklesia.

Once we understand that Jesus chose a concept with which His disciples and their contemporaries were already familiar in the secular arena, we can then see why He taught so few times about it: There was no need to explain what everybody already knew. It was unnecessary to teach the obvious. To the people in the Roman Empire, including Israel, the ekklesia was as familiar a concept as the state assembly is to those living in a democracy, or the management team is to the employees in a corporation. There was no need for Jesus, or for the New Testament writers later on, to describe for their audiences what was already known as a decision-making, society-impacting people institution.

On the other hand, it *was* essential for Jesus to teach extensively about the Kingdom of God, or its equivalent, the Kingdom of heaven, as the new factor in the equation—so much so that He made reference to the Kingdom over a hundred times.

Turning Tables into Pulpits

The super-rapid growth of the Ekklesia in the New Testament was possible because Jesus made it ride on social tracks *already in existence*—namely, meals. This is present in the first description of the *assembly* (Ekklesia) of His followers right after Pentecost, where they were seen "*continually* devoting themselves to the apostles' teaching and to fellowship, to the breaking of bread [eating] and to prayer" (Acts 2:42, emphasis added). This was not a one-time or sporadic occurrence, since one of the most common examples of a church meeting in the New Testament is believers partaking of food, to which the addition of the doctrine of the apostles—to ascertain and to obey the will of God—upgraded it from a mere meal into an assembly. Those mealtimes constituted an inclusive forum (unlike the Temple or the synagogue), thus inserting the Ekklesia into everyday secular life instead of isolating it from it.

By making the Ekklesia run on existing social tracks (mealtimes), Jesus turned tables into pulpits and homes into assembly halls into which strangers were welcome, rendering them prime candidates for evangelism. No wonder His disciples' archenemies accused them, just a few weeks after Pentecost, of having "filled Jerusalem with your doctrine" (Acts 5:28 NKJV). This was so, *not* because all of Jerusalem was trying to attend a church service, but because the Ekklesia had thoroughly permeated the city, so much so that people lined up their sick on sidewalks, awaiting the shadow of Peter to heal them, something that turned Jerusalem into a citywide campus for the Ekklesia (see Acts 5:15–16).

This turned out to be the case—first, because Jesus did not confine the gathering of His followers to buildings or subject them to a rigid schedule of centralized meetings. Instead, it was people who constituted His Ekklesia (wherever and whenever as few as two or three gathered, with His manifest presence in their midst). And second, because Jesus' Ekklesia was not meant to be a sterile, sanitized holding tank into which His disciples were to store in isolation converts fished out of a turbulent and doomed sea, to await the arrival of a refrigerator ship for transfer to a heavenly port for final processing. Instead, His Ekklesia, whether in the embryonic expression of the *conventus* or in a more expansive version, was designed as the vehicle to inject the leaven of the Kingdom of God into the dough of society so that first people, and then cities and eventually nations, would be discipled (see Acts 1:8; 5:28; 19:10; Romans 15:22–24; Revelation 21:24–25).

> *Jesus designed His Ekklesia to make its presence, power and culture known, but with a revolutionary caveat that gave it the upper hand.*

In the same manner that Rome made its presence, power and culture felt in the far reaches of its empire, Jesus designed His Ekklesia to make its presence, power and culture known, but with a revolutionary caveat that gave it the upper hand: It would have the authority to legislate in both the visible and invisible realms so that the Gates of Hades could not prevail in either realm.

At the heart of every cry for revival today, there is always a deep longing to find the way to the majestic, all-powerful Ekklesia that Jesus launched, free from any form of restraint or containment and overflowing with power. This is the journey we are on. Allow me to share with you next where we are now and how we got this far.

2

Transformation Is a Journey

From Dawn to Full Day

> Transformation is a process. Like the feeble light at the crack of dawn, it is meant to grow brighter and brighter. But the "dawn" does not happen, and the path remains untraveled, until one begins taking steps of obedience in the right direction.

Transformation is a process that shifts paradigms so that we can see what we have not seen before, which allows us to do what we have not done yet. And for this, we must be open to change.

I am not talking about altering any of the anchoring tenets of our faith such as the deity of Christ, the essence of the Atonement, the character of God, the infallibility of the Scriptures, or the centrality of the Church as the Body of Christ. Those are immutable, and as such they can never change. When it comes to the scope of the Atonement and the role of the Church as God's transformational agent on earth, however, what are we missing that prevents us from seeing the will of God be done on earth?

My own journey in this regard, along with that of Ruth and our children, has been inspired and framed by the principle found in Proverbs 4:18: "The path of the righteous is like the light of dawn, that shines brighter and brighter until the full day." It began in a most dramatic way when, at the age of 34, I was told by my doctors that I had a maximum of two years to live. Cognizant that time was short, Ruth and I, along with our daughters Karina, Marilyn, Evelyn and Jesica (ages 10, 8, 4 and 2 at the time), chose to dedicate the 40-acre property our weekend home in Argentina sat on to build a prayer chapel. The site eventually became a training center, but the centerpiece was the chapel. We were motivated to do this by the realization that within a 100-mile radius there were 109 towns and villages without an evangelical witness.

Because time was running out and my medical condition was rapidly devouring my health and our resources, we focused on prayer. Little did we know that this would be the kernel that would produce a most bountiful harvest, one beyond anything we could ever have imagined. In the process, we learned that prayer and evangelism are two sides of the same coin. That realization gave birth to what now is known all over the world as *prayer evangelism*. In addition, God miraculously healed me, expanded our vision, allowed us to set in motion a process that resulted in each one of those towns being evangelized,[1] and gave us a passion to see cities (not just people or small towns) evangelized.

> *In the process, we learned that prayer and evangelism are two sides of the same coin.*

Resistencia: Learning "That None Should Perish"

This is what led us next to Resistencia, a larger city in northern Argentina, with the determination to reach it for Christ. We were such novices faith-wise that we did not dare use the word *transformation*. Instead, we chose "city reaching." But very much like the moment of absolute darkness that precedes the break of dawn, we sensed that light was about to insinuate itself over the still obscure horizon in Resistencia.

We critically needed that hope, because Resistencia was one of the driest of spiritual deserts. Beginning with its name, which in Spanish means "opposition," it represented a monumental spiritual stronghold. Only 5,143 evangelical believers out of a population of 400,000 attended 70 small churches, 68 of which were the result of church splits! The city was immersed in witchcraft, and demonic altars defiled its sidewalks. In addition, the cult of Saint Death, the chief principality over the region, was widespread.

At first we were able to partner with only seven pastors, but gradually others joined in to cover the entire city with prayer through the establishment of "houses of light" in 635 neighborhoods.[2] We knew from our pioneering experience in my hometown that prayer was the place to begin, even if we did not know what else to do to reach an entire city for Christ. The resulting citywide network of houses of light enabled local believers, in a relatively short time, to pray regularly for the 400,000 inhabitants and to see miracles and salvations occurring *in the marketplace* rather than just in evangelical gatherings, as they were used to.

The resulting citywide network of houses of light enabled local believers, in a relatively short time, to pray regularly for the 400,000 inhabitants.

As a result, significant numbers of people came to Christ. This set the stage for a series of neighborhood evangelistic rallies that culminated with a major citywide crusade in which unprecedented numbers received Christ. In fact, the initial harvest of almost 7,000 new church members was larger than the combined membership of all the churches at the time, a figure that grew by almost 100 percent the following year. It has kept doubling even until today, when over 100,000 people in the city, and many more in the region, are reportedly born again.

The mayor, judges, police officers, lawyers and doctors of Resistencia, most of whom had never set foot inside an evangelical church, welcomed the Kingdom of God into their spheres of influence. As an integral part of the city-reaching thrust, community water tanks to dispense fresh water were built in poor neighborhoods. The regional hospital was also blessed with the donation of much-needed medical equipment.

What we experienced went beyond the customary results of a traditional crusade. The "doctrine of the apostles a la Acts 5:28" literally filled the city as the Gospel became the subject of favorable conversations in sidewalk cafés, at football matches, on radio and TV programs, and in parks and plazas.

This cascade of unusual breakthroughs, and the resulting exceptional church growth, inspired my first book, *That None Should Perish*, in which I describe the foundational principles behind it all.[3] In fact, I will be telling you a little bit about four of my other books, too, because their progression theologically parallels our praxis on the field as the new transformational paradigm emerged. I hope this will serve to show you how we discovered things backed by Scripture as the light shone brighter and brighter on our journey. The light that broke over the horizon at this early point illuminated a major milestone: Prayer evangelism can be effectively used to reach an entire city, and as a result, the Church can experience extraordinary growth.

Before long, other communities asked for help, and world-class evangelical leaders like Peter and Doris Wagner, Omar and Marfa Cabrera, Eduardo Lorenzo, Jack Hayford, Cindy and Mike Jacobs, Dick Eastman, Paul Cedar and Bill Bright, to name a few, lent their support and endorsement to the principles we were implementing.

Discovering Biblical Methodology

When numerous new city-reaching efforts happened as a result of Resistencia, I wrote my second volume, *Prayer Evangelism*.[4] This book explains why the rapid and lasting outcomes we were seeing were biblical, and it didactically points out the striking contrast between Jesus' widely differing emotions recorded in the gospel of Luke.

In Luke 9:41, Jesus reached a very low point. Visibly frustrated, He reprimanded His apostles by saying, "You unbelieving and perverted generation. How long shall I be with you and put up with you?" This uncharacteristic outburst was triggered by the preponderance of demonic activity and His disciples' inability to cast out the demons. But worse yet, Jesus was frustrated because their treatment of the lost revealed they did not know what spirit they were of (see Luke 9:55). The level of demonic activity was so intense, and the resulting spiritual atmosphere was so foul, that even Jesus was now buffeted by disappointment due to the toll it was taking on His apostles.

In Luke 10, however, something happened that turned everything around. Jesus sent out a new batch of disciples, traditionally referred to as "the seventy," to the towns and villages He was about to visit. They reported that every demon they came in touch with had submitted to them (see verse 17). This was such good news that Jesus "rejoiced *greatly* in the Holy Spirit"—a most significant statement since this is the only place in the gospels where He is portrayed rejoicing (verse 21, emphasis added). The reason for this spectacular turnaround, as Jesus put it, was that Satan fell down from heaven like lightning (see Luke 10:18). This was definitely a major breakthrough since not only the demons, but also Satan, had been brought down.

> *It is possible to change the spiritual climate over a city; it is biblical to meet the felt needs of unbelievers.*

The key was the four-step strategy Jesus had entrusted to the seventy in Luke 10:5–9: First, *bless* the lost; next, *fellowship* with them, *minister* to them, and then *proclaim* that "the kingdom of God has come near to you" (verse 9). In essence, this is what the "houses of light" in Resistencia had done. In our ministry experience, a full working understanding of these principles is indispensable to transform the marketplace and cities, something that I will explain in depth in chapter 16.

The ever-growing light of dawn illuminated two important new milestones. First, it is possible to change the spiritual climate over a city. Second, it is biblical to meet the felt needs of unbelievers without demanding that they first receive Christ. The latter provided theological justification for us to show sinners compassion without compromising God's holiness by putting them in touch with His mercy through prayers that ministered to their *felt* needs—so they would access His saving grace out of gratitude for such prayers.

Light at Home and in the Marketplace

The legendary missionary C. T. Studd said, "The light that shines farthest shines brightest at home." With the Resistencia prototype becoming known and new cities being reached, I was prompted to write *Women—God's Secret Weapon*,[5] to underscore the biblical role of women and the vital relationship of mutual honor and respect God designed so that both genders, walking in harmony, could reflect the fullness of God's image at home and the light of that dynamic shine far into the cities and beyond.

The light of dawn had illuminated how vitally important it was to incorporate gender reconciliation into the rapidly evolving transformation continuum. If we ignored that principle, it was bound to disable the effectiveness of prayer, which is *the* driver for transformation: "You husbands . . . show her [your wife] honor as a fellow heir of the grace of life, *so that your prayers will not be hindered*" (1 Peter 3:7, emphasis added).

Our new experiences in the public arena soon put us in touch with the anointing on the traditionally called "laypeople" that was producing remarkable transformational inroads into the marketplace. This led me to delve into the Scriptures to highlight that so-called laypeople are in reality full-time ministers called by God to do exploits in the marketplace. This set the stage for my next book, *Anointed for Business*.[6] In that book, I highlight biblical truths that provide these "laypeople" with a jersey, so to speak, to be able to join the ministerial team with biblical legitimacy.

Once these rediscovered ministers learned how to carry the power and the presence of God into the workplace, they became "mobile arks of the covenant," as my associate Rick Heeren likes to say. And as a result, they came to love weekdays as much as they already loved Sundays.

Myles and Joyce Kawakami, in Hawaii, became pioneering examples of this new understanding when Myles responded to the Lord's request for half of his business. Having the Lord as his "Senior Business Partner" made conceptual sense to Myles, and even more so since his accountant had advised him that that particular year would end in a deficit. With the Lord in the partnership the projected debt miraculously turned into a surplus, and Myles began sowing the Lord's 51 percent into meeting the felt needs of their island, Maui. Under Joyce's inspiring leadership, Feed My Sheep was born—a nonprofit agency dedicated to addressing the needs of people living below the poverty level. Beginning with hunger, Feed My Sheep started meeting those needs, which eventually led to the salvation of many in the marketplace. With a user base of over 9,500 people, the agency provides over 100,000 meals every month,[7] which has practically made the island of Maui a hunger-free zone because of these marketplace ministers.

Paradigms for Changing the World

The increasing brightness of the light of dawn had shown us the scriptural centrality of the marketplace and the need for pulpit and marketplace ministers to work in partnership. This discovery created a "problem," however, that led us to the next milestone in this journey. Many pastors proceeded to envision marketplace ministry as another church-based activity, with additional meetings. But a church-based marketplace ministry is an oxymoron of sorts. It is as contradictory as proposing that hangars be built for orbiting satellites. The only place where marketplace ministry can take place is *in the marketplace*.

To address this inward pull into the church, those of us who were involved in this discovery continuum set ourselves on a journey to articulate the new paradigms that would bring pulpit ministers into partnership with marketplace ministers *in the cities*. This produced my fifth volume, *Transformation*,[8] which is structured around five pivotal paradigms that provide the biblical rationale for pulpit and marketplace ministers to work as full-fledged partners. I will discuss these paradigms in more detail in chapter 16, but let me mention them briefly here:

1. The Great Commission is about discipling nations and not just individuals. "[As you go] make disciples of all the nations" (Matthew 28:19).

2. The Atonement secured redemption not only for individuals, but also for the marketplace, which is the heart of the nation. "For the Son of Man has come to seek and to save that which was lost" (Luke 19:10; see also Ephesians 1:7–10; Colossians 1:19–20).

3. Labor is worship, and since all believers are ministers, they are to turn their jobs into places of worship to God and ministry to others. "Whatever you do, do your work heartily, as for the Lord rather than for men" (Colossians 3:23; see also Galatians 6:9–10; Ephesians 2:10).

4. Jesus is the One who builds His Church, not us. Our assignment is to use the keys of the Kingdom to lock and unlock the Gates of Hades in order for Him to build His Church where those Gates stand. "I will build My church. . . . I will give you the keys of the kingdom of heaven; and whatever you bind on earth shall have been bound in heaven, and whatever you loose on earth shall have been loosed in heaven" (Matthew 16:18–19).

5. The elimination of systemic poverty in its four dimensions— spiritual, relational, motivational and material—is the premier *social* indicator of transformation. "The Spirit of the Lord is upon Me, because He anointed Me to preach the gospel to the poor" (Luke 4:18; see also Acts 4:32–34; 20:35; Galatians 2:10; Revelation 21:24–27).

These five paradigms opened new and vast horizons for both pulpit and marketplace ministers to do in the marketplace what until then was only conceived as timidly possible inside a circle of believers. Such was the case for a pastor in the Philippines who, while doing double duty as a taxi driver, began to apply prayer evangelism and these paradigms with such outstanding results that eventually the mayor of his city came to the Lord and dedicated the city to God. Corruption was renounced, and a process was set in motion that turned City Hall into a transformation center where miracles came to be expected.

We observed similar outcomes in nations with no Christian history. For instance, Brian Burton, a British missionary in a Buddhist nation (Thailand), trained his fledgling congregation in these principles and set in motion a chain reaction that led to the provincial mayor[9] receiving Christ, inviting Jesus into his government, and appointing Pastor Brian as his "advisor for righteousness." In the process, seven million dollars in bribes were returned! Here, too, as in the Philippines, a government entity was turned into a transformation center.

Up until 2012, Ciudad Juárez, Mexico, was known as the murder capital of the world, with over 10,000 murders to its discredit in a five-year period, until the tide turned dramatically as a result of the bold application of these principles and paradigms. The mayor was so impressed that he requested "that churches increase their evangelistic activities because it is good for the city and it makes our job easier," and he instructed the 6,880 municipal workers to undergo transformation training!

These five paradigms opened new and vast horizons for both pulpit and marketplace ministers to do what they had not done before.

I will be unveiling the details of these and similar stories in the course of this book, but the reason for these early tastes of what is ahead is to provide a context for the challenge that these new developments posed for us. Undoubtedly, we were delighted to see government entities co-opted to do "church" things in the public arena with such groundbreaking results. But we found ourselves in need of divine reassurance, as Paul was after he began to do in the marketplace—with unprecedented returns—what he had done before with limited success in or around the synagogue (see Acts 18:9–10).

For us, when not just people, but also companies, schools and government agencies began to experience these new spiritual phenomena, a major compounding factor was that the Church as we knew it was not equipped to handle such a harvest. This was something new that was happening in the marketplace, in which the mainstay in the new converts' spiritual diet did not consist of sermons delivered from the pulpit, but mainly of prayer for miracles that led unbelievers to salvation and to dedicating their households to God, very much in the way Zaccheus did, to the astonishment of the religious elite (see Luke 19:2–8).

No One Dared Call It a Church

More challenging yet was what to do when a myriad of people in the marketplace came to Christ during work hours, without a direct connection to the established Church. This was the situation faced by one businesswoman who, after hearing the principles for marketplace transformation, dedicated her factory in China to the Lord and embraced her call to "pastor" this "congregation" of unsaved workers. Since traditional preaching was not an easy option in light of the restrictive Communist environment, I instructed her to build a much larger than average "Jesus chair," paint it shiny white to draw attention to it and place it in the factory dining hall. There at the chair, workers could seek Jesus' favor for personal needs. This suggestion was inspired by the time when I was a young CEO in a corporation greatly affected by systemic corruption. With no mentors to guide me, I would close my office door when I did not know what to do and kneel before a red chair that I had set aside exclusively for Jesus—hence the name "Jesus chair"—and there I would listen to His guidance.

A year later, we heard that thousands of Chinese workers raised under atheism had come to Jesus as a result of having Him answer the petitions they presented at the Jesus chair the businesswoman had set up. This was "complicated" by the fact that the traditional church was not able, and sadly in this case, not even motivated to incorporate these *unusually born* born-again believers. This factory—as well as similar cases in other parts of the world—smelled like a church, talked like a church and walked like a church, *but no one had yet dared call it a church*.

These unusual experiences led me to embark on the most exciting and revolutionary biblical research I have ever been involved in during my fifty years of ministry—to rediscover the Church as Jesus *really* meant it to be. I began searching the Scriptures to look for what we have missed in the Church's current expression. I wanted to find out what it would take for us to see the powerful and life-changing things that customarily take place inside the Church's four walls also happen in the public square. And that is what this book is all about.

Like the path of the righteous, transformation progresses in a way that resembles Proverbs 4:18's light of dawn, growing brighter and brighter with every step of obedience.

Light dispels darkness, which is exactly why Jesus defined the function of His Ekklesia as an operation of light against the spiritual darkness covering the world. He associated darkness with the Gates of Hades, which we are about to discuss in the next chapter.

3

A Fuller Understanding
of the Gates of Hades

From Enslaving Ignorance
to Liberating Understanding

When Jesus introduced His Ekklesia, He made reference to the Gates of Hades—more specifically, to the fact that His Ekklesia would prevail against them—something that the book of Acts chronicles. For the modern Church to emulate that, it must relearn the spiritual dimension of life in order to confront and defeat the demonic entrenchment in *both* the heavenlies and on earth.

What were the factors responsible for the phenomenal growth that took the Ekklesia from a small band of shell-shocked disciples locked up in a room, into every living room in Jerusalem, and from there to the entire interconnected world in a stunningly short span of time?

One key factor was the Church's thorough understanding of the Gates of Hades, something that Jesus specifically mentioned when He first introduced His Ekklesia. The setting was Caesarea Philippi, a town founded by the Romans. It was a major center of occult worship, as evidenced by three demonic centers: the Temple of Caesar, the temple of the god Pan, and *the Gates of Hades*. Yes, the Gates of Hades was actually a physical location, a cave where human and animal sacrifices were offered.[1]

Jesus deliberately chose the darkest spiritual place in Israel to unveil the two most fundamental revelations about Himself. First, His divinity—that He is the Christ (the Messiah), the Son of the living God. And second, His Ekklesia, which He designed to prevail against the forces of evil entrenched in government (Caesar), idolatry (the god Pan) and the devil himself (the Gates of Hades).

With His intentional choice of location and words, Jesus underlined that life on earth consists of both matter and spirit, and the latter is the realm where evil is entrenched and from where it exercises control over affairs on earth. This is not easy for the contemporary Church to grasp, particularly in the Western world, because it is not as aware of the *spirit realm* as the New Testament Ekklesia was.

Basically, we are talking about two different worldviews, and this is where the Enlightenment played a most destructive role. As a philosophical movement emerging in Europe in the seventeen hundreds, the Enlightenment was instrumental in blinding the Western world to the piritual dimension of life, because it enshrined *human reason as the supreme arbiter of truth*. This miscarriage of truth severely impacted the Church in the United States when the G.I. Bill later lured seminaries into "expanding" their curriculum by adding secular subjects so that they could qualify for government grants. As a result, the secularizing influences originating out of the Enlightenment made it harder to understand the biblical worldview concerning the spirit realm. Thus, thousands of Bible school and seminary graduates entered the ministry while being ignorant of the activity of the spirit world on earth and "in the heavenlies."[2]

This is most unfortunate, because we need to understand the spiritual dimension of life—and the demonic entrenchment therein, with its resulting effect in the natural realm—in order for the Ekklesia to advance effectively, since its mission is to uproot the demonic entrenchment in both realms. Operating in such conditions would be like the world's best soccer team showing up for the world championship game at the wrong stadium, or if at the right stadium, limiting itself to playing on only its half of the field and never daring to attack on the other team's half. In the first example, the world's best team will lose by default. In the second, even though it may play a superb defensive game (as the modern Church is known to do), it will have no chance of winning the championship.

History to the Rescue

I must confess that in this discovery journey I have often felt as if I were walking through a minefield, because what I saw in the Scriptures about the Ekklesia was not only different from, but too often, it was at odds with what we call the "Church" today. I have also been aware that the concepts and observations I am introducing challenge the traditional consensus on a most sensitive subject, and that by bringing up the secular roots of Jesus' Ekklesia and the nonreligious forums where it is meant to operate, I run the risk of being perceived as secularizing what is meant to be sacred—hence the minefield metaphor.

The world's best team showing up at the wrong stadium has no chance of winning the game.

Admittedly, the contrast between biblical and contemporary examples of the Church has been disturbing at times. If what we see in the Scriptures is the right way (and it definitely has to be since "it is written"), how could we have deviated so much? And when and why did we go wrong? Questions like these buffeted me, until a piece of information out of the annals of history came to the rescue. While the Enlightenment played a deceiving role, it was another major interference—the scheming of King James[3] and the Bible version that carries his name—that significantly contributed to relegating the modern Church to a weaker role than the Ekklesia of the New Testament. Let's look at some necessary background on how this came about.

When it comes to Bible translations, William Tyndale is considered the father of the British Bible. In 1522, he published the first English New Testament, making him the British equivalent of Martin Luther, who had done the same for the German-speaking people. Tyndale was a linguistics scholar who translated the Bible with meticulous accuracy from the original texts. He rendered the Greek word *ekklesia* as *assembly*, which is its correct meaning. Subsequent English translations, including the General Bible, the Bishop's Bible and the Geneva Bible, did likewise. In fact, many scholars consider those translations amplifications of Tyndale's original work since the bulk of their content was taken from or shaped by his.

King James, however, was displeased with those translations being available to common folks, in particular the Geneva Bible's Explanatory Notes. His intolerance to opposition was a projection of his most ungodly character. He persecuted, incarcerated and executed his opponents, including Pilgrims and members of other dissident groups. The teaching those Notes contained on church government ran diametrically counter to his belief in the "divine right of kings," which ascribes absolute power to sovereigns to rule uncontested in every area of their reign.

The Anglican Church, of which King James was the head, was one of the main vehicles through which he channeled his royal authority. He did it through its episcopal[4] form of government, implementing his rule through the bishops he appointed. The notion that common folks could have an authoritative voice in religious matters constituted a real and present threat to him. To counter this, King James convened 47 scholars to produce a new version of the Bible that eventually became known as the King James "Authorized" Version.

Granted, new versions usually improve on previous ones, and this one was no exception—except that at the very outset King James placed fifteen directives on the scholars in charge of the project.[5] One of those directives specifically prohibited them from translating the Greek word *ekklesia* as *assembly* because it went counter to the Anglican Church's episcopal form of government. Instead, a different word was to be used: *church*. Clearly, King James's intention was to *keep* the government of the Church in his hands.

Etymologically speaking, *church* means "of the Lord," but it was the wrong translation for the Greek word *ekklesia*. To make matters worse, by that time the word *church* was perceived as meaning a building with clergy.

Once the Bible version bearing his name and carrying the allure of the Crown was published, it became *the* "Authorized" Version. The breadth and width of the British Empire turned it into the most used version in the English-speaking world, and it became a major influence on Bible translations into other languages.

> *Clearly, King James's intention was to keep the government of the Church in his hands.*

I am grateful for the way the King James Version has made, and continues to make, the Word of God available to English-speaking audiences. When we came to study in the United States, my first English Bible (which I still have) was a King James. I have no intention of casting negative aspersions on the edition that carries his name, but for the purpose of grasping why the notion of church nowadays is so dramatically different from the New Testament examples, it was necessary to bring up the role this unrighteous monarch played in the mistranslation of the Greek word *ekklesia*.

Mixing Church with State

Mixing the governance of the Church with the State is never good. This type of malicious intervention in the Church by rulers happened before King James, with Constantine and Charlemagne. Contrary to generalized perceptions, these two monarchs set back the genuine work of the Ekklesia enormously. Constantine was the first ruler to blend the cross with the sword, a blatant scriptural oxymoron.[6] Following a decisive victory that he attributed to divine intervention on his behalf, upon entering Rome he sought the favor of the Bishop of Rome by presenting him with a palace. Subsequently, as he evicted pagan priests from their temples, he turned the buildings over to their Christian counterparts, thus advancing the notion of centralized liturgical priestly led worship.

Even though he was not baptized until the day before his death, he had no qualms about convening a council of the Church[7] to rule on doctrinal matters shortly after he conquered Rome.

Charlemagne's case resulted in much more dire institutional consequences. He was crowned emperor of the Romans by Pope Leo III on Christmas Day in AD 800 at Old St. Peter's Basilica, but this was not a union made in heaven since these two characters were anything but godly. Pope Leo III was almost killed by relatives of his predecessor, Pope Adrian, and had to flee Rome to seek protection from Charlemagne, king of the Franks. When Roman emissaries came to press their case against Leo, Charlemagne offhandedly dismissed their credible accusations of blatant immorality against his protégé and had his soldiers escort Leo to Rome, where he retook control of Church affairs with their backing. Soon afterward, Charlemagne himself came to Rome, held a council with representatives of both parties, had Leo exonerated and then confirmed as pope, and had his opponents exiled. A few days later, Leo crowned Charlemagne emperor.[8] It was definitely an evil quid pro quo.

Hanging Hades' Gates in God's Building?

This illicit marriage of a spiritual institution and a temporal government has always arrested the intended impact of the Ekklesia, because, as stated earlier, the Ekklesia is meant to be expansive, like salt, water, light or leaven.

The gory fights and intrigues for control of the empire and the "Holy" Roman Church produced some of the darkest pages in history. Fortunately, many pious Catholics redirected their energy and resources toward monasteries and frontline evangelistic missions that resulted in the expansion of Christianity into new territories, which took place in spite of the official Church in Rome. It was in those outposts distant from Rome that the most eloquent Catholic exponents of Christianity emerged, and it was their missionary work (such as that of Saint Francis of Assisi) that converted the pagans.[9]

On the Protestant side of the equation, the great British missionary movements were not birthed out of the Anglican Church (which was headed by the Crown), but in dissident groups such as the Pilgrims, the Plymouth Brethren, the Presbyterians, the Baptists, The Salvation Army and the Methodists, to name a few. The same is true of missionaries alighting from continental Europe who were sent out not by state-sanctioned religious bodies, but by grassroots nonconformist churches.[10]

This illicit marriage of a spiritual institution and a temporal government has always been counterproductive for the Church.

Closer to home, the global evangelistic tsunami released by the Azusa Street revival in Los Angeles at the beginning of the twentieth century was not rooted in the traditional mainline denominations. Instead, a decentralized wave of evangelists turned darkness into light in distant lands through bold preaching confirmed by signs and wonders. Because they pioneered missionary work in countries where their organizational brand did not yet exist, they had to start where the apostles did in the book of Acts—in the marketplace, in the public square, on street corners and gathering in homes, while at times suffering brutal persecution by both the religious and secular establishments. Nowhere was this more apparent than in the "house church" movement in China.

Like the Ekklesia in the New Testament, these expressions held a respectful (and on occasion, adversarial) relationship with the secular powers. And when persecuted, rather than caving in or seeking compromising accommodations, they courageously resisted and grew, proving once and again that "the blood of the martyrs is the seed of the Church."[11] They knew that it was wrong to hang the Gates of Hades in God's building.

What Are Those Gates of Hades?

The Gates of Hades represent Satan's domain, run by demonic deputies who enforce his control or influence over specific regions in society through governments and culture molders such as education, the arts and entertainment, commerce and so on (see Colossians 1:13; Acts 26:18). Paul describes them as "rulers . . . powers . . . world forces of this darkness" and "*spiritual forces* of wickedness in the *heavenly places*" (Ephesians 6:12, emphasis added).

Terms such as *spiritual forces* and *heavenly places* can easily mislead us to conclude that it is an ethereal reign. But the overriding context in the book of Ephesians, where this teaching is found, is that it is the Ekklesia's mission to heal unreconciled *human* realities that exist in the *earthly realm*. Ephesians describes ethnic divisions in chapter 2, religious disunity in chapter 3, ministerial competition in chapter 4, discord between genders in chapter 5, and family strife and marketplace injustice in chapter 6.

These social gaps reflect how the spirit realm determines the state of affairs on earth, since the devil himself is identified as the leader of this amalgam of spirit rulers (see Ephesians 4:27; 6:11). And this is why, after identifying these gaps as the work of Satan, Paul proceeds to teach that the Ekklesia is empowered and expected to fight against the rulers of this darkness in both the spiritual and human spheres (see Romans 16:20; Ephesians 4:25–32; 6:12).

This interplay between the two is also found in the Lord's Prayer. We are very familiar with its majestic closing words: "For yours is the *Kingdom*, the *power* and the *glory*, forever and ever, Amen." These words exalt God's jurisdiction over the seen and unseen realms. Yet those same words were uttered previously by Satan in a different setting, and with the opposite intent:

> And he [Satan] led Him up and showed Him all the *kingdoms* of the world in a moment of time. And the devil said to Him, "I will give you all this domain [*power*] and its *glory*; for it has been handed over to me, and I give it to whomever I wish."
>
> Luke 4:5–6, emphasis added

In the case of the third and final temptation, Jesus did not rebut Satan's claim of being over the kingdoms of the earth, because they were indeed *handed over to him* through Adam and Eve's disobedience.

He obtained them through deception, of course, but his claim could not be challenged yet, since God had given Adam and Eve dominion (stewardship) over His creation. Those kingdoms had to be recovered legally in order to void Satan's claim, but that would be the result of a process first initiated by Jesus on the cross and then completed by His Ekklesia (as I will explain in greater detail later on). In such a context, it is essential to understand that the struggle against principalities and powers is not an ethereal one, because it is the Ekklesia's mission on earth to reclaim those kingdoms for God.

> *The struggle against principalities and powers is not an ethereal one. It has to do with the Ekklesia's mission on earth.*

I like to picture it as the equivalent of a third strike in baseball, after which the batter is out. Satan is the batter, and he has two strikes against him already. The first strike took place when he and his demons were cast out of God's presence. Here are the passages I consider to be the record of his eviction from the first heaven: "How you have fallen from heaven, O star of the morning, son of the dawn" (Isaiah 14:12). "Your heart was lifted up because of your beauty; you corrupted your wisdom by reason of your splendor. I cast you to the ground" (Ezekiel 28:17).

The second strike happened when Michael and his angels dislodged them from the second heaven: "And there was war in heaven, Michael and his angels waging war with the dragon. The dragon and his angels waged war, and they were not strong enough, and there was no longer a place found for them in heaven" (Revelation 12:7–8).

That second eviction set the stage for Satan's upcoming and final defeat, the third strike: "And the great dragon was thrown down, the serpent of old who is called the devil and Satan, who deceives the whole world; he was thrown down to the earth, and his angels were thrown down with him" (Revelation 12:9). "And they [the saints, the Ekklesia] overcame him [the devil and his forces] because of the blood of the Lamb and because of the word of their testimony, and they did not love their life even when faced with death" (Revelation 12:11).

This struggle is real and ongoing, but the outcome is already predetermined—the Gates of Hades will not prevail. For this, the Ekklesia must show up on the right field, the one where those Gates are entrenched. This is at the very center of the cry, "Your Kingdom come, *Your will be done on earth* as it is (already done) in heaven."

The Charge against the Gates

Let's go back now to the Ephesians grid mentioned earlier. After showing how to bridge those dreadful social gaps, Paul next exhorts the saints that constitute the Ekklesia in Ephesus to put on the full armor of God so that they can stand firm against those evil forces. The fact that Paul instructs them to take a defensive position (stand firm) and describes the devil in an offensive stance (firing "arrows") seems to suggest that the Gates of Hades in that particular region had collapsed already, because a dislodged devil was firing from a distance (see Acts 19:9–11).

The results on earth from dealing with the spiritual forces of wickedness were amazing: "All who lived in Asia [the Roman province where Ephesus was located] heard the word of the Lord, both Jews and Greeks" (Acts 19:10). Ephesus was a metropolis where the Ekklesia had debunked the demon-based economy (see Acts 19:23–29).

To my knowledge, no other religion, before or since, has been able to bridge those gaps successfully. This was possible because the Ekklesia knew something that we seem to have lost sight of: All the devil has been left with are gates for which he no longer has the keys, because Jesus took them away: "I am alive forevermore, and I have the keys of death and of Hades" (Revelation 1:18). And I suggest that Jesus turned them into the keys of the Kingdom for His Ekklesia, so that we could use them to set free what the enemy had used to hold captive. He told us,

> I will build My church [Ekklesia], and the gates of Hades shall not prevail against it. And I will give you the keys of the kingdom of heaven, and whatever you bind on earth will be bound in heaven, and whatever you loose on earth will be loosed in heaven.[12]
>
> Matthew 16:18–19 NKJV

The Gates of Hades are a reality in both the heavenly and the earthly realms. Jesus designed and empowered His Ekklesia to confront and defeat those Gates *in both realms*. The result is a message that is not merely preached with words, but is put on visible display by deeds. That new message is "the Gospel of the Kingdom," which is the subject of the next chapter.

4

A Fuller Understanding of the Gospel

*From the Law and the Prophets
to the Gospel of the Kingdom*

In Luke 16:16, we learn that everyone was "forcing his way" into the Kingdom. In John 12:32, Jesus said, "And I, if I am lifted up from the earth, will draw all men to Myself." If Jesus is so irresistible and the Gospel is good news, could the refusal of people to receive it today be the result of our preaching something less?

One of the most fascinating statements that Jesus made is found in Luke 16:16: "The Law and the Prophets were proclaimed until John; since that time the gospel of the kingdom of God has been preached, and everyone is forcing his way into it." This is fascinating because it states that *everyone* was *forcing* his way into God's Kingdom on earth, and we have never seen anything like that.

Was this meant to be a one-time occurrence? Did it happen only because Jesus was around? Not really, because we can see His disciples emulating Him with very similar results throughout the book of Acts (see Acts 2:43–47; 5:14–16; 8:12; 13:44, 49; 17:4; 18:8, 10; 19:11, 20).

Furthermore, an even greater positive response to the disciples' message was the expected outcome, since Jesus stated that His followers would perform greater works than Him (see John 14:12). Also, Jesus' statement in John 12:32 implied that when He was lifted up—a future event at the time He stated it—all men would be drawn to Him. Finally, at the end of human history entire nations are reported as being saved as a result of His disciples' work (see Revelation 21:24–27).

This reference to "everyone forcing his way into the Kingdom," therefore, cannot be summarily dismissed as a one-time thing, nor can we attribute it solely to the *physical* presence of Jesus on earth. We had better take an in-depth look at it, because the implications are essential for the successful rediscovery of the Ekklesia today.

A Shift in the Proclamation

We find that the key to this phenomenon of people forcing their way into the Kingdom lies in understanding the difference between the Law and the Prophets and the Gospel of the Kingdom. What triggered such extraordinary results was a shift in proclamation from the former to the latter, which established "the new normal."

Having said that, I hasten to add how important it is that we do not dichotomize the Law and the Prophets and the Kingdom of God, because of the anti-Semitism it can justify if we do not place things in their proper context. Toward that end, Mordecai "Myles" Weiss, a friend and someone who honors me as his spiritual father, has greatly enlightened us. The bulk of what I write in the next few paragraphs comes from his wise input. His insights will help us avoid setting into opposition two scriptural dynamics that are so intrinsically connected that they constitute the backbone of the Old and New Testaments.

Original Hebrew	Greek	English through Greek	English from Hebrew
Yeshua	Iesous	Jesus	Joshua
Miriam	Marias	Mary	Miriam
Yehuda	Iudas	Jude/Judas	Judah
Mashiach	Christos	Christ	Messiah

When first-century Jews like Saul (Paul) went to Greek-speaking nations to preach about Yeshua the Messiah, they would refer to Him as *Iesous the Christos*. To their pagan hearers, this was clearly a Jewish-Hebraic concept because they expressed it using the Greek translation for the Hebrew words (as shown in the language comparison table above). This left no doubt that what they were expressing were not pagan, Greek or Roman concepts. Since Jesus was presented as the Jewish Messiah, people had no difficulty seeing the Hebraic roots of the new Christian faith. Furthermore, the followers of Jesus became known as *Christians* because they believed Jesus to be the Messiah (Christos) prophesied about in the Hebrew Bible (see Acts 11:26).

Tragically, over the centuries its Jewish roots have been all but ethnically cleansed from "Christianity," and today Jesus is no longer seen and presented as the Jewish Messiah, but as the founder of a religion foreign to the Jews.

A New Beginning

Why do I offer this clarification in the context of a discussion on the relationship between the Law and the Prophets and the Gospel of the Kingdom? Because the latter marks a new beginning, which by definition makes the former old. But *old* in this case does not mean *irrelevant*.

Everything taught in the Law and the Prophets points by direct reference, implication or inference to the advent of the Messiah. The first Passover—with its instructions on how to sacrifice a lamb and how to mark Israelite houses with its blood, all the way up to the detailed ceremonial practices observed first in the Tabernacle and subsequently in the Temple in the Old Testament—presages the advent of the Messiah. Once that advent happened, it became the central theme in the New Testament.

The Law and the Prophets therefore constitutes the foundation on which the Gospel of the Kingdom is erected. Walls without a foundation cannot stand, and foundations that do not support walls betray their purpose. Both are essential, which is why it is vital to understand what each one represents and contributes.

By contrasting the two in Luke 16:16, Jesus highlighted an evolution in the message that people were hearing. The Law and the Prophets was proclaimed up until John the Baptist, marking a season that came to an end to make way for the new message: the Gospel of the Kingdom.

> *When the Church as we know it today fails to make the transition . . . to the Gospel of the Kingdom, it ends up preaching a message that is relevant only to the past.*

It is not possible to proclaim the Gospel of the Kingdom using the old paradigms, because the Law and the Prophets announced in the *past* that something was going to happen in the *future*, whereas the Gospel of the Kingdom focuses on the *present*—the here and now. Granted, the fullness of God's Kingdom will not come until our Lord's return in glory, but its insertion into the fiber of society by the Ekklesia—like leaven placed in the dough—sets in motion a process that culminates in that fullness.

Danger: Contemporary Legalism Ahead

When the Church as we know it today fails to make the transition from the Law and the Prophets to the Gospel of the Kingdom, it ends up preaching a message that is relevant only to the past (Christ died on the cross to redeem us) and the future (He will return in glory), but it fails to present its relevance for today. This, in turn, can easily give room to legalism and to falling out of sync with God's timing.

Let me expand on this. Contemporary legalism, like the legalism practiced by the Pharisees, leads us to focus on the forms: the temple (building), the liturgy, the traditions and the creeds. Falling out of sync with God's timing paralyzes us spiritually because it causes us to relegate our expectations to something that we believe will happen only in the future, when in reality it is already here. The consequence of all this is inactive believers who hover around a temple and live innocuously inside a religious system, at best. Or at worst, they become prisoners in a doctrinal POW camp, hoping to be liberated when their Commander in Chief returns.

Right after John the Baptist's ministry came to an end, Jesus announced the advent of the Kingdom: "Now after John had been taken into custody, Jesus came into Galilee, preaching the gospel of God, and saying, '*The time is fulfilled, and the kingdom of God is at hand*; repent and believe in the gospel'" (Mark 1:14–15, emphasis added). Jesus' Gospel from the very beginning consisted in the proclamation of God's Kingdom as being present *now* in the midst of *people*.

Consequently, His Ekklesia is not the Ekklesia of the Law and the Prophets, which can only remind us of what He did in the past and what He will do in the future. That outlook would leave us with just the temple, the forms and a resignation to wait for better days. Not at all! Jesus' intention is that the Ekklesia's proclamation of the Gospel of the Kingdom would confront the Gates of Hades now, *in the present*, until those gates collapse so that people, and eventually nations, are transformed.

The "New" Message

It is evident that a new season requiring a new message was at hand when Jesus exhorted His disciples to "lift up your eyes and look on the fields, that they are white for harvest" (John 4:35). The Gospel of the Kingdom was that new message.

The timing and context for Jesus' instructions are the key to getting the full meaning of His pronouncement, since they were uttered right after His theological exchange with a Samaritan woman in which part of their discussion included the topic of the Temple and its rituals. The Law and the Prophets established that worship should take place in the Temple. The subject came up, but Jesus moved past that when He declared, "But an hour is coming, and now is, when the true worshipers will worship the Father in spirit and truth" (John 4:23). This resulted in the Samaritan woman eventually believing that He was the Messiah, and causing many in her city to believe as well. The result was so profound that Jesus did what was culturally unacceptable to the Jews: He spent two days with the Samaritans, who ended up acknowledging that He was the Savior *of the world* (see John 4:40–42). Interestingly enough, nowhere in the gospels is it recorded that anyone else confessed Jesus as such!

On the other hand, John the Baptist found himself struggling unexpectedly with this tension between the old and the new, which is why he sent messengers to ask Jesus, "Are you the one who is to *come*, or should we *expect* someone else?" (Matthew 11:3 NIV, emphasis added). His query reflects the heart of the Old Testament message. But instead of letting Old Testament types and prophecies breed passivity, John was pushing through the fog created by his own doubts, striving to see if, by any chance, what had been anticipated for so long had indeed arrived, as he had proclaimed at Jesus' baptism. John's query is revealing, because there was a question within his questions. He was asking if Jesus was the right one, and if this was the right time, and he reflected his dilemma in the two words he used: *come* and *expect*.

Jesus addressed both of John's questions: "Go and report to John what you hear and see: the blind receive sight, and the lame walk, the lepers are cleansed and the deaf hear, the dead are raised up, and the poor have the gospel preached to them" (Matthew 11:4–5). He built His answer on what John's messengers were able to *see and hear, then and there*. Who is the One who was to come? Jesus. When? Now. How can we know that? By what He is doing *in our midst today*. Therefore, the Kingdom of God has come!

> *The Law and the Prophets can be summarized in one phrase: "He will come." The Gospel of the Kingdom is expressed in this: "He is here!"*

This has profound and radical implications for the content and the results of the Ekklesia's message today. On the content side, the message must be the introduction to the living Christ who is in the Ekklesia's midst to change lives *now*. On the results side, that message must be validated by miracles that benefit the hearer—"the blind receive sight, and the lame walk . . . the deaf hear," to quote Jesus

Himself. Such a manifest presence of the Messiah, and the validation of the message by miracles, is what became the norm for the Ekklesia when Jesus' disciples "went out and preached everywhere, while the *Lord worked with them*, and confirmed the word by the signs that followed" (Mark 16:20, emphasis added).

The Law and the Prophets can be summarized in one phrase: "He will come." The Gospel of the Kingdom is expressed in this: "He is here!" That truth snatches us out of a passive "escapism" mindset and puts us on a path of personal victory and transformation. And once the message of the Gospel of the Kingdom is rediscovered, institutions, corporations, cities and even nations are able to experience transformation through the Ekklesia's proclamation of the Gospel of the Kingdom in the public square, as we will see in the next chapter.

5

A Fuller Understanding of Proclamation

From Words to Deeds

> The Scriptures describe the Kingdom of God as "righteousness, peace and joy"—elements that must be proclaimed by deeds, not just words, because they are meant to make right what is wrong. An emerging expression of the Ekklesia in Vallejo, California, is demonstrating the biblical proclamation of the Gospel of the Kingdom.

In the New Testament it is evident that the Ekklesia and the Kingdom are two sides of the same coin. One of the reasons why we don't see them as such today is the prevalent teaching that this is exclusively the Church Age, which will be followed by the Kingdom Age sometime in the future. Even though it is true that the fullness of God's Kingdom is still in the future, that does not exclude the fact that it is also present today. In the New Testament, when the Kingdom became manifested, the Ekklesia was established, and wherever the Ekklesia was in operation, it put the Kingdom in evidence.

Since the Kingdom is the side we are least familiar with, we need to raise the question, what exactly is the Kingdom of God? As Paul explained to the Ekklesia in Rome, it consists of righteousness, peace and joy in the Holy Spirit (see Romans 14:17). The word *righteousness* at its most basic earthly level is the result of making right that which is wrong, and could easily be translated "justice." This clarification is necessary because we tend to see it exclusively as God's righteousness, with no relevance for the day-to-day situations we encounter. Certainly, His righteousness is *the* ultimate source, "For in it [the Gospel] the righteousness of God is revealed from faith to faith; as it is written, 'But the righteous man shall live by faith'" (Romans 1:17). It definitely transforms unrighteous sinners into saints.

That vertical dimension is not the only one, however. There is also a horizontal dimension. Paul uses the word *righteousness* 34 times in this epistle, the first time to explain how it impacts and transforms individuals. But the last use, in Romans 14:17, is the capstone in a long section on practical, "down-to-earth" applications throughout chapters 12–14 that show how people made righteous by Christ must connect with the unrighteous world to make right(eous) that which is wrong (or crooked), so that others may also obtain peace and joy.

This is the pattern we see in the New Testament: Once wrongs were righted by righteous deeds, it opened doors for divinely inspired peace and joy to replace human despair and sorrow. This was accomplished by tangible deeds (not just words) produced by divine power, because "the Kingdom of God does not consist in words but in power" (1 Corinthians 4:20).

Turning the Tables on Unrighteousness

A compelling biblical example is the case of Zaccheus. Could it be that Zaccheus, who was an important public official and as such should have had no problem obtaining a respectable place from which to observe Jesus, was subtly but painfully snubbed by his fellow citizens, who took advantage of his short stature? Perhaps Jesus, noticing that Zaccheus had been publicly humiliated, decided to right that wrong by staying at his house and subsequently by communicating to Zaccheus and his fellow Jews that he was also a son of Abraham (see Luke 19:3, 9). The resulting peace and joy led Zaccheus, in turn, to right his own wrongs and to bless the poor, enabling them to have peace and joy by the fruits of his newfound righteousness.

In Acts 16:22–34, we learn how unrighteousness was overcome in a dark dungeon in Philippi. There Paul and Silas, after being flogged, overcame evil with good and prevented a frantic jailer from committing suicide—an unrighteous impulse, engendered by despair, that was bound to wreak havoc on his family. As a result of this righteous deed the jailer was saved, setting him on a "Kingdom of God continuum." First, he got saved and immediately undid some wrongs by washing the wounds unjustly inflicted on Paul and Silas, and in the process he imparted peace and joy to them. Next, he and his household got baptized. And finally, he brought the apostles into his family quarters and set food before them, and everybody rejoiced greatly (see verses 31–34).

Unrighteousness, despair and sorrow constitute the lethal cocktail that the Gates of Hades dispense constantly to individuals and to society. Jesus empowered the Ekklesia to right those wrongs not just in the lives of its members, but also with transforming and catalytic deeds in the marketplace. And this is what it is doing today in the city of Vallejo, California, on the northern shore of the San Francisco Bay Area.

Vallejo—From Bankruptcy to Abundance

In 2008, Vallejo was the first large city in California to declare bankruptcy. As a result, unrighteousness, turmoil and sadness overtook the population because schools and public services went underfunded, unemployment rose and real estate values plummeted.

At the peak of the crisis, however, marketplace and pulpit ministers came together to bring the Kingdom of God to the city. For this, they gathered for prayer on the steps of City Hall. Mayor Osby Davis addressed them, saying, "Continue to pray. Pray regularly and pray consistently, but most importantly, I ask that you dedicate this city to God."

Right then and there they dedicated the city to God. Pastor Tony Summers reports the results: "From that moment on, hope for transformation was born, and since then we have seen signs all across the city."[1]

Michael Brown, owner of Michael's Transportation Services, recounted the beginning of all this in a documentary video. He talked about how he came into contact with the principles of transformation at a seminar in nearby Oakland:

> Ed was introducing his book *Anointed for Business*. When he spoke to the crowd that was there, everything that I was asking God during my fast, he answered one after the other. I had been asking, *God, what I do every day as a businessman, does it really matter?* The answers that Ed presented from the Scriptures answered my questions in conclusive terms: I am a minister of God to bring righteousness, peace and joy to the marketplace, and my company is my ministry.[2]

The realization that there was just as powerful an anointing for ministry in the marketplace as there was for pulpit ministry changed everything for Michael. He came to see that God was looking for people on earth to lend Him their hands, so their labor would become worship and they would become agents to benefit a city and a region (see Acts 19:10–11). This opened his eyes to see the first glimpses of the Ekklesia.

"God became Chairman of the Board, Jesus became my CEO, the Holy Spirit became my legal counsel."

It was a learning curve for everyone, just like the verse I quoted earlier from Proverbs 4:18 about the emerging light of dawn. Adriana Catledge, a member of his management team, recalls, "When Michael came to us and said something about transformation, that from now on the business belongs to God, we were not really sure what he was talking about—but the more we listened, the more we understood."

From that moment on, the corporate lifestyle of the company changed because, as Michael puts it, "God became Chairman of the Board,

Jesus became my CEO, the Holy Spirit became my legal counsel, and I became a good steward over God's work."

Proclaiming the Gospel of the Kingdom

These steps of faith became the cradle into which the coalition known as Transformation Vallejo was born.[3] To "pastor" the hurting city, its marketplace and pulpit ministers charted a course to bring together church, business, government and education in a thrust centered on prayer evangelism.

In a county where African American males constitute the highest percentage of students who fail to graduate, a program was launched that focused on these young men—not inside a church building, but at Peoples High School. Called the Emerging Gentlemen's Program, it nurtured positive character qualities and social skills. Transformation Vallejo also provided resources for the school's basketball teams, with great impact on students along the way. Tammy was one of them. "Mister Brown made me an offer that he would employ me if I stayed in school and graduated," she recounted. "I did, and I became valedictorian, and now I work at Michael's Transportation!"

"He told me he would employ me if I stayed in school," she recounted. "I did, and I became valedictorian!"

Scott Nalley, a pastor and member of the Transformation Vallejo team, founded Campus Transformation Clubs, which consist of student-led extracurricular gatherings that put deeds to prayers by helping youth at risk with personal and academic issues. The clubs also provide encouragement to other students, and as a result, violence in the schools has come down noticeably. One student put it this way: "Every time you come to a Campus Transformation Club, it tells you that you are not alone, that you have a 'family.'"

That feeling has spread all the way to the public school district offices. Superintendent Ramona Bishop described it this way:

If one of our schools needs something, we know that Pastor [Anthony] Summers, Michael's Transportation and Mr. [Michael] Brown always respond, and there are other things that I don't even know that happen. That's a true adopt-a-school process—where pastors, business communities, are saying, "We are now responsible for your success, and whatever you need, you call upon us; we'll help you get there."

Putting God's Power on Display

As societal wrongs (unrighteousness) in Vallejo were made right, peace and joy soon found residence in many lives there. But it is the fourth factor Paul listed when describing the Kingdom of God that differentiates all this from other social programs: *power*. Or more precisely, God's power having an impact on those who need it (see 1 Corinthians 4:20).

First in Michael's Transportation Services headquarters, and later on in an expanding circle, people experienced God's power in the form of miracles. One of the beneficiaries was a troubled young man who was also fighting an incurable disease—making him hopeless and more despondent with every day that passed. He confessed,

> I had given up on the Church, and I did not know at the time that Michael's Transportation was a ministry, a *business* ministry. As I started to go there, Michael would tell me, "Look, come over here every day if you need to. Just sit in here and we're going to pray for you." And that's exactly what they did!

The Ekklesia at Michael's Transportation prayed, and God healed him. The young man did not find the Ekklesia; the Ekklesia found him!

Transforming a city requires embracing everything and everyone in it. Transformation Vallejo has spearheaded the Transform Our World Network's *Adopt Your Street* initiative[4] to get every street, and everything on the streets, adopted in prayer. The city is being systematically prayer walked, and doorknob hangers let residents know that someone "has their back" in prayer. Business owners are receiving prayer and encouragement. The co-owner of the Hummingbird Bakery & Dessert Bar, Anastasia Domingue, beams as she says, "Since we've been adopted in prayer by Pastor Summers, we have grown—we have grown way beyond anything that we ever expected. He has equipped us to be marketplace ministers, ministering to anyone who comes into the store."

A modern renaissance has begun in Vallejo, visible evidence of which is a brand-new transfer station to serve the ferry service linking it to San Francisco, something made possible because the Ekklesia shattered in the heavenly places through deeds and prayers done on earth the hopelessness that was driving Vallejo over the cliff of despair. Many other evidences are rekindling a sense of purpose in the population, something Mayor Davis confirmed: "You can clearly see a big difference. There is a difference in the makeup of the city, in what it looks like physically. There is a difference in the attitude of the people; everybody has more hope."

When Transformation Vallejo was launched, we were not familiar with the Ekklesia vocabulary that we have today. Yet we can see in retrospect that it constituted the embryonic inception of the Ekklesia in the city, and it has emerged and moved out of the four walls of the traditional Church to take the Kingdom of God to the Gates of Hades *and bring them down.*

Why Is Social Relevance Lacking?

It is imperative that the Church attains greater social relevance in our cities through doing tangible deeds to make right what is socially wrong. Os Hillman brought home the importance of this through a study he quoted on his website.[5] He told of a British journalist who studied the impact of the Church on the local culture of the American city with the highest index of church attendance. The study found that taking into account crime, racism, poverty and other social factors, that city ranked among the lowest in the nation as far as quality of life. This conclusion shocked me, but I was even more shocked by the fact that when this journalist asked a group of pastors in that city to comment on the study, they replied, "Those things do not concern us. We are spiritual leaders."

Without a doubt, many people are going to heaven from that city, and this is something that we greatly value. But we should also be longing for the climactic finish described in Revelation 21 to happen, or at least to *begin* to happen, in our lifetime: nations, not just people, saved. Since God's promise, first uttered through Joel and later eloquently proclaimed by Peter on the Day of Pentecost, will undeniably come to pass, we must admit that we face pressing theological and structural challenges to live up to that outcome. One of those challenges has to do with the way we do proclamation. Something is missing, because people are not responding to our proclamation as the Scriptures state they should. I submit to you that we lack the deeds to demonstrate and validate the relevance of the words in the message we preach.

The deeds that accompany the message are what make it desirable and acceptable. Today, the Kingdom of God is being proclaimed in Vallejo by convincing deeds that constitute good news and not just good advice. This is the proclamation that the New Testament Ekklesia practiced, for which there is no alternative, since Jesus was very clear *and even severe* on this point: "Not everyone who says [words] to Me, 'Lord, Lord,' will enter the kingdom of heaven, but he who does [deeds] the will of My Father who is in heaven" (Matthew 7:21). And then He got very specific: "Many will say to Me on that day, 'Lord, Lord, did we not prophesy in Your name, and in Your name cast out demons, and in Your name perform many miracles?'" (verse 22). Evidently, ministry activities can become meaningless without deeds, because next Jesus stated, "And then I will declare to them, 'I never knew you; depart from Me, you who practice lawlessness'" (verse 23).

Deeds, Not Words, Constitute the Criteria

In the same fashion that faith without works is dead, proclamation without deeds is also dead. James was very direct about it: "Pure and undefiled religion in the sight of our God and Father is this: to visit orphans and widows in their distress, and to keep oneself unstained by the world" (James 1:27).

In fact, righteous deeds to correct wrongs are so intrinsically linked to the nature and the proclamation of the Kingdom of God that on the day when Jesus will judge the nations, the criteria for admission or rejection will be the provision of food for the hungry, water for the thirsty, lodging for the stranded, clothes for the naked, care for the sick and comfort for those in prison (see Matthew 25:35–36).

Going over these passages deepens the fear of God in my own heart, because those who thought they were in ended up out, and vice versa. Oh, may God grant us the grace to go beyond merely prophesying, casting out demons and performing miracles, to becoming *doers of the Word*.

How does one become a doer of the Word? The path to the answer begins with another question: Why would Jesus single out those who were performing three valid ministry activities as a preface to commanding those same performers to depart from Him?

Not because those activities are not legitimate, or because we should not be engaged in them. The reason is a deeper one. Those activities don't cost us anything. Prophesying, healing and casting out demons have this in common: All three are the result of a gift (a grace, a charisma) freely handed to us by God. No investment is required on our part, "For no prophecy was ever made by an act of human will, but men *moved by the Holy Spirit* spoke from God" (2 Peter 1:21, emphasis added). All we are is God's mouthpiece. The Holy Spirit is the one doing it. Demons are cast out in the name and by the power of Jesus (see Mark 16:17). We are just the channels, never the source. And miracles are categorized as one of the gifts of the Holy Spirit (see 1 Corinthians 12:10), for which we are the conduits. Such was the case when "God was performing extraordinary miracles by the hands of Paul" (Acts 19:11).

On the other hand, clothing the naked, feeding the hungry, ministering to the incarcerated and opening our homes to strangers all require a substantial *personal* investment on our part. Notice that Scripture does not say that those who were judged as *being out* should have given money so that someone else or some agency could clothe, feed or host those in need (which is not a bad thing to do in and of itself, of course). The indictment was issued because there was no *personal* involvement—sewing, cooking, hosting strangers, visiting prisoners—which brings up the fact that it is a matter of the heart and not the checkbook. Giving money without giving the heart is the issue.

What is happening in Vallejo is a small beginning compared to what still remains to be done, but "a cloud as small as a man's hand" is rising on the horizon, and it presages abundant rain (1 Kings 18:44). Functioning as the Ekklesia, the Transformation Vallejo team has taken the Kingdom of God to the city in such a way that a growing number of its inhabitants have come to realize that Jesus is in town, because the will of God is being done in the public square. The emerging Ekklesia is modeling the proclamation of the Gospel of the Kingdom with righteous deeds (justice). Preachers continue to preach from their pulpits and church members are being spiritually nurtured, but what is new is that now the Ekklesia in Vallejo is shattering hopelessness with life-giving deeds of righteousness, peace and joy. God's justice is producing social justice.

> *A growing number of Vallejo's inhabitants have come to realize that Jesus is in town, because the will of God is being done in the public square.*

This dimension of the proclamation of the Gospel is made possible when we understand the fullness of *everything* that happened on the cross, as we will see next.

6

A Fuller Understanding of the Cross

From an Icon of Death to a Fountain of Life

Jesus' death on the cross reached a stunning climax when He shouted, "It is finished!" But, what exactly was finished? The answer lies in comprehending not only what He did for us, but also what He did to the devil at the cross.

Jesus spelled out the Great Commission twice. In Mark 16:15, He sent us to "preach the gospel to all creation." This is the individual mandate. But in Matthew 28:19–20, He commanded us to "make disciples of all the nations." (Notice that Jesus did not say that we should make disciples *in* all the nations, but rather, *of* all the nations.) This is the corporate mandate. These two are complementary yet different dimensions of the Great Commission. Historically, and more so in the last two centuries, the Church has done a great job leading individuals to faith in Jesus. Yet in spite of the large numbers of new believers, very few nations are being discipled, if any at all. Apparently, leading people to Christ does not necessarily result in a nation being discipled, no matter how large the number of new disciples turns out to be.

A case in point is Guatemala, a beautiful country that reputedly has the highest percentage of born-again Christians in Latin America. Add to this that Guatemala has had two evangelical presidents who were very intentional about sharing their faith, coupled with some of the most dynamic megachurches and a nationwide network of Christian radio stations that saturate the land 24/7 with evangelism and Bible teaching, and it would seem we have the key elements for the transformation of a nation. Guatemala ranks among the bottom five nations of the Caribbean and Latin America, however, when it comes to security, economics and transparency in government. It ranks behind even Haiti, another beautiful nation, but one immersed in witchcraft.[1] Why?

I respectfully suggest that it is because the Church has not been as intentional about discipling the nation as it is about discipling individuals. Integrating these two dimensions of the Great Commission is the missing key, and how to do that is the central theme of this book. While joyfully celebrating its efforts in preaching to every creature, the Church must now discover and embrace the other side of the Great Commission—to disciple all nations.

Did Jesus really mean to disciple *nations*, or was He referring to ethnic groups instead of the politically organized entity that constitutes a nation? This is a relevant question, because the Greek word for *nations* used in Matthew 28:19 is *ethna*, which is also used to describe ethnic groups. Could it be that Jesus sent us to disciple ethnic groups so that once representatives from all of them have been saved, His return would occur?

Since the individual mandate in Mark 16:15 to preach to every creature is something that we all seem to agree on, let's examine the corporate side of the Great Commission in Matthew 28. The action verb Jesus used was not *to preach to*, but rather *to disciple* all nations. Nor did He qualify this command in any way, shape or form. He was emphatic: "Disciple all the nations."

Authority to Recover Everything Lost

Jesus prefaced His specific reference to discipling nations with the assertion that He has absolute authority both in heaven and on earth.

Authority in heaven was something He already possessed as the Word by whom and through whom all things were created (see Matthew 28:18; John 1:1–3). But He subsequently established His authority on earth when He gave Himself in ransom for all, as 1 Timothy 2:6 says, which touches on the salvation of individuals. Luke 19:10 expands on that by stating that He came "to seek and to save that which was lost." In other words, *everything* that was lost—not just lost individuals, but *that* which was lost.[2]

To ascertain the full dimension of what was lost, we need to revisit the moment when such loss occurred in the Garden of Eden. What is it that was lost? First, the eternal destiny of every human being because sin raised a wall of separation between God and man. Second, the relationship between man and woman since Adam and Eve's relationship ceased to be harmonious. But third—and this is key for the point under discussion here—the marketplace, which the Garden of Eden represented, was lost.

In my book *Anointed for Business*, I describe the marketplace as the combination of business, education and government. These are the three arteries through which the life of a city or a nation flow. Business was lost because an abundance of fruit had graciously been available in the Garden before, but after the Fall it would have to be earned by the sweat of man's brow. Education was damaged because God no longer came in the cool of the afternoon to instruct His creatures. And finally, government was defiled because rebellion entered the world. That unleashed such hostility that shortly afterward, the first homicide was reported—a forerunner of the tsunami of violence that eventually led to the Flood and continued to escalate afterward.

> *Did Jesus die for something more than people's souls? When He cried out, "It is finished!" what exactly is it that was finished?*

It is an accepted biblical truth that Jesus died to redeem people. But a different, albeit complementary, question needs to be asked: Did Jesus die for something more than people's souls? When He cried out, "It is finished!" what exactly is it that was finished?

The context for Luke 19:10 is the salvation of a despised marketplace leader—Zaccheus. It is most intriguing that such a greedy person would part with substantial portions of his wealth so suddenly by giving 50 percent of it to the poor and putting up the other half as collateral to make restitution for any wrongs he may have committed. Why would a sinner of such stature do something of this magnitude? Jesus revealed the reason when He declared, "Today salvation has come *to this house*" (verse 9, emphasis added). The term *house* in biblical days encompassed both family and workplace, since most people worked out of their homes. Jesus' words explained why it was possible that Zaccheus, a sinner who collected taxes for the hated Romans, would part with his wealth in such a restorative way. It is because salvation came to his house!

All Things Reconciled

Paul explains this wider scope of salvation in his letter to the Colossians: "For it was the Father's good pleasure for all the fullness to dwell in Him, and through Him to reconcile *all things* to Himself, having made peace through the blood of His cross; through Him, I say, *whether things on earth or things in heaven*" (Colossians 1:19–20, emphasis added). He confirmed it in his epistle to the Ephesians: "In Him we have *redemption* through His *blood*, the forgiveness of our trespasses, according to the riches of His *grace* . . . the summing up of *all things* in Christ, *things in the heavens and things on the earth*" (Ephesians 1:7, 10, emphasis added).

These two passages specify that *all things*, both in heaven and on earth, are reconciled with God through Jesus Christ. In fact, the mention of *redemption, blood* and *grace* is very confirming as well. In the United States, if I ask what comes to mind when I say coffee, bacon and eggs, by word association people will reply, "Breakfast!" Likewise, redemption, blood and grace can reflect only one thing: the Atonement. Its scope encompasses everything that was lost, both in heaven and on earth. Yes, Jesus paid the price to redeem everything, including nations.

Revelation 21 confirms the wider scope of salvation. The specific reference we find in verse 24 to kings (rulers) marching at the head of their nations shows that these are politically organized entities and not just representatives of ethnically homogeneous people groups. And the subsequent statement in verse 27 that "only those whose names are written in the Lamb's book of life" are part of that parade corroborates that these nations have experienced salvation.[3]

> *The idea that salvation also can be applied to cities and nations is just as challenging to us as it was to the disciples.*

Jesus' teaching on the judgment of nations in Matthew 25 further supports the concept of nations being saved. His disciples were well acquainted with the concept that the Messiah was going to restore (save) Israel. But the notion that other nations would also be beneficiaries of such redemption must have been overwhelming. This is relevant today because, like the disciples, we believe that the Lord brought salvation to us and even to our households. But the suggestion that such salvation can be extended to cities and nations is just as challenging to us as it was to them.

The Other Side of the Cross

As stated earlier, if we accept that *ethna* also means nations and that Jesus came to save everything that was lost, then we will conclude that He came to save more than just individuals. But in order to align ourselves fully with what God's Word states, we need a fuller understanding of what took place at the cross. We are very familiar with what Jesus did there *for us*: He paid the price for our redemption. Paul captures this in his letter to the Colossians: "When you were dead in your transgressions . . . He made you alive together with Him" (Colossians 2:13). Seeing Him forgive those who unfairly and cruelly hurt Him when He was in excruciating pain provides an unshakable assurance that no sin can ever be greater than the grace poured out to us at Calvary.

That is what Jesus did for us at the cross, but there is another dimension that shows what He did there *to the devil*. It is necessary for us to understand that dimension in order to obtain faith for discipling nations. Farther on, the same passage in Colossians from which I just quoted describes an often overlooked power encounter:

> When you were dead in your transgressions . . . He made you alive together with Him, having forgiven us all our transgressions, having canceled out the certificate of debt consisting of decrees against us, which was hostile to us; and He has taken it out of the way, having nailed it to the cross. When He had disarmed the rulers and authorities, He made a public display of them, having triumphed over them through Him.
>
> Colossians 2:13–15

Here, the devil is pictured brandishing a certificate of death as if it were a weapon aimed at Jesus while He is agonizing on the cross. This weapon is a legal document—a decree that was contrary to us. It is not hard to imagine the devil taunting Jesus, trying to add more pain by screaming, "I cannot touch You because You are sinless, but everybody else—from Adam all the way down to the last baby born today, and yes, even Your own mother—they belong to me, because according to the rules that Your Father stipulated, 'The soul that sins will surely die.' You are dying alone!"

In the precise moment when Jesus cried out, "My God, My God, why have You forsaken Me?" the devil saw his opportunity to deliver what he thought would be the fatal blow. He drew closer as Jesus struggled with the additional grief caused by being forsaken by God, but just when he was close enough, Jesus disarmed him and his underlings by taking the weapon away and nailing it on the cross with "FORGIVEN" inscribed on it, not with ink, but with His own blood.

But He did not stop there. He proceeded to make a public spectacle of the evil forces by shaming them. I like to imagine this unexpected turn of events for the devil this way:

> When Jesus nailed the decree on the cross, the devil protested stridently, "You cannot do that! It is against the rules. They cannot be forgiven!"
>
> At that moment, God the Father thundered from heaven, declaring, "I just changed the rules! There's a new one!"

> Angry and confused, the devil asked, "What new rule is that?"
>
> God thundered a second time, "*Grace* is its name!"
>
> Satan objected, "How come I never heard of that before?"
>
> And with satisfaction that echoed all the way to the remotest galaxy, God drove home the powerful truth: "You did not see it before because it was hidden in the blood of My sinless Son, waiting for you to foolishly cut Him open so that when the first drop of His precious blood was shed, everybody who had sinned would be forgiven. Sorry, devil. Game over!"

Satan ended up looking as foolish as a cocky quarterback whose team is ahead by five points on Super Bowl Sunday, in possession of the ball, and with only forty seconds left on the clock. All he needs to do is sit on the ball while time runs out, and the game is won. But he is too proud for that and decides to show off by throwing a pass that gets intercepted. The ball is run into the end zone, and his team loses the game he was so sure he could never lose!

Satan may have thought victory was within his grasp, but instead, Jesus defeated him and made a public spectacle of him and his principalities. Jesus won the fight to redeem everything that was lost, and the devil was publicly humiliated. God knows it. Jesus knows it. And most importantly, the devil knows it. The question is, do we know it?

The Full Scope of Victory

It is absolutely important to realize the full scope of what Jesus recovered at the cross, because unless we are convinced that the same precious blood that paid for our salvation has also made provision for nations to be saved, we will not walk in the authority required for total victory. We will settle for subsisting in a POW camp instead of taking the war to the enemy.

The cruelest slavery is the slavery inflicted by ignorance of the truth. Let me illustrate this with a compelling example from history. General Jonathan Wainwright was the only American general taken prisoner by the Japanese during World War II. His captors held him captive in a POW camp in remote Mongolia, where he grew progressively weak and feeble. He never compromised his honor, however, and he conducted himself with dignity while hoping for the Allies to win the war. Every time the Japanese commandant gave him an order, he had to obey. He was a prisoner of war waiting for his commander in chief to liberate him.

When President Roosevelt sent General Douglas MacArthur to Australia to organize the counteroffensive that eventually defeated Japan, MacArthur left Wainwright in charge in the besieged Philippines. MacArthur instructed him not to surrender, but the carnage caused by the Japanese was so atrocious that Wainwright reluctantly capitulated, leaving him with a deep sense of shame.

When the troops under MacArthur defeated Japan, a cablegram went out to all Japanese POW camps instructing the commandants to surrender to the highest-ranking Allied officers. Everybody complied except for the commandant in whose camp Wainwright was held captive. Because the general did not know the truth—that Japan had been defeated—he continued to behave like a POW. Every order from his captors lacked legitimacy, but not knowing that, he obeyed them.

> *Unless we are convinced that the same precious blood that paid for our salvation has also made provision for nations to be saved, we will not walk in authority and go for total victory.*

With no news about his former second-in-command, MacArthur dispatched a senior officer to assess the situation. The plane landed near the POW camp, where the American emissary walked up to the fence. When Wainwright approached, he saluted and announced, "General, Japan has been defeated!"

Wainwright returned the salute, then feebly leaning on his cane, he slowly walked to the commandant's office, opened the door, and without even raising his voice, he uttered the liberating truth: "My commander in chief has defeated your commander in chief; I am in charge here now!"

Immediately, the Japanese commandant surrendered to Wainwright, who took control without firing a single shot. Why? Because he had finally learned the truth, and the truth had set him free.

Let this chapter on the full dimension of the cross be the functional equivalent of the American army officer who comes up to the fence that is holding you captive inside a doctrinal POW camp, suppressed by faulty doctrines. Hear now the liberating truth: Our Commander in Chief, the Lord Jesus Christ, has defeated the devil and his demons. He has disarmed them and made a public display of them at the cross, and He has given us full authority over all the power of the evil one (see Luke 10:19). It is finished!

"My commander in chief has defeated your commander in chief; I am in charge here now!"

Anything less is satanic bewitchment designed to block you from comprehending the full scope of what took place at the cross. It has happened before, as we see in Paul's question to the Galatians: "You foolish Galatians, who has bewitched you, before whose eyes Jesus Christ was publicly portrayed as crucified?" (Galatians 3:1). But it does not have to happen again!

Jesus Claimed His Inheritance

I fervently pray that you will receive right now an empowering vision of Christ crucified that will help you capture the fullness of the scope of His triumph. The blood shed by our Lord paid the price not only to redeem our souls, but also to redeem everything that was lost: people, business, education and government. And there is nothing the devil can do to reverse it.

When Jesus cried, "It is finished!" it was not an agonizing gasp, but a triumphant shout proclaiming victory over the one who had boasted before that "this domain and its glory . . . has been handed over to me, and I give it to whomever I wish" (Luke 4:6).

Jesus did not contradict Satan back in the wilderness because Adam and Eve's disobedience did cede dominion over everything on earth to him. But at the cross, Jesus paid the price to redeem what was taken away from God's first children and their descendants. He gave Himself in ransom *for all*, and His blood was far more than sufficient to pay a price that can never be matched.

The Father had said to Jesus, "Ask of Me, and I will surely give the nations as Your inheritance" (Psalm 2:8). To that end, He redeemed them when He shouted, "It is finished!" while the heavens were flooded with celestial beings proclaiming, "The kingdom of the world has become the kingdom of our Lord and of His Christ" (Revelation 11:15).

This is why Jesus was able to state without any qualification, "All authority has been given to Me in heaven *and on earth*" (Matthew 28:18, emphasis added). Authority over the kingdoms on earth is the fruit of what He did *to the devil* and his minions at the cross.

There is no place for the contemporary Church to resemble a POW camp behind enemy lines. Even if in a weak and feeble condition (as General Wainwright was when he first heard the liberating truth), the Church today can and must walk in the authority emanating from this newly found truth, straight into the enemy's domain, and declare, "Our Commander in Chief has defeated your commander in chief."

Then it must proceed to reclaim as its inheritance "the very ends of the earth" as its possession (Psalm 2:8). This is what the Great Commission Jesus gave His Ekklesia in Matthew 28 is all about—reclaiming the *nations* He has redeemed, as we will see next.

7

A Fuller Understanding
of the Great Commission

From Saving Souls to Discipling Nations

> In Matthew 28:19–20, Jesus did not issue a Great Commission, but rather a Great Partnership, because He assured us that He would walk alongside us all the way to the end, and in so doing He turned a monumental task into a transformational lifestyle.

In the previous chapter I made a foundational point about the complementary relationship between the individual and corporate mandates of the Great Commission found in Mark 16:15 and Matthew 28:19–20. Of these two mandates, the commission to disciple the nations must have startled Jesus' disciples the most. Some of them were buffeted by doubts to begin with, for we read, "The eleven disciples proceeded to Galilee, to the mountain which Jesus had designated. And when they saw Him, they worshiped Him; but some were doubtful" (Matthew 28:16–17). Yet it was in the context of such evident human frailty that He chose to draw near to them to reassure them of His authority over whatever (on earth) may have caused their doubts.

It is not surprising, when we realize how young and inexperienced the disciples were at the time, that some were doubtful. The common assumption that Jesus' instruction was given to experienced leaders and may not apply to common folks like us does not stand up to closer scrutiny, since no one in that audience was older than 32.

I say this because Jesus began His public ministry at the age of 30 (see Luke 3:23). By the time He issued the Great Commission, He had been in ministry for three years. Based on John's references to Jesus' trips to Jerusalem for the Passover, He would have been 33 at that time. We also know that He was their Rabbi (see John 1:49). Since a rabbi's disciples are usually younger than he is, it follows that the age of the apostles ranged from the late teens (as in the case of John, perhaps) to the early thirties.

First-Century "Millennials"

In today's language, the disciples were "millennials," with the exception of John, who was even younger. Furthermore, none of them had yet traveled overseas or preached. They were novices in the purest sense of the term who, just moments before being commissioned, had descended from the heights of majestic worship to the mire of disabling doubts. This downward swing shows that the first recipients of the Great Commission had a lot in common with us today, since we are no strangers to buffeting doubts.

What did Jesus do when His disciples doubted? He drew nearer, and instead of rebuking them, He arrested their doubts by stating that He had all authority in heaven, and most importantly for the disciples He was about to send to nations, also on earth (see Matthew 28:18). Then He proceeded to send them to disciple nations, and for good measure, He reassuringly added that He would walk alongside them all the way to the end (verse 20).

> *A better choice of terms would be the Great Partnership, because of the resources Jesus is providing for us to fulfill the Great Commission.*

Jesus described the disciples' assignment in greater detail in Acts 1:8: "But you will receive power when the Holy Spirit has come upon you; and you shall be My witnesses both in Jerusalem, and in all Judea and Samaria, and even to the remotest part of the earth." He told them to begin in the city where they resided (Jerusalem), and next move on to a province (Judea), and then to a nation (Samaria), and after reaching that milestone, to keep on going until they had reached the ends of the earth.

I suggest that labeling this the *Great Commission* is not the best choice of terms, because such terminology places the responsibility entirely on us. A better choice of terms would be the *Great Partnership*, because of what Jesus is providing for us: all authority in heaven and on earth, and His presence alongside us until the task has been accomplished.

Who Should Be Discipled?

Two questions about fulfilling our commission or partnership still remain: *how* and *when*. The answers require a deeper look into what Jesus really meant. This is where an analysis of the Great Commission's sentence structure is helpful. Matthew 28:19 speaks of both discipling and baptizing nations. We will discuss baptizing later on, but for now, understanding the object of the command to disciple—the *who* we are to focus on—is foundational.

I am deeply indebted to Rev. Roberto Beretta, the senior pastor of La Iglesia de la Ciudad, a Baptist congregation in Mendoza, Argentina, for making available to me his research and text analysis on this subject. He consulted the Greek textbooks for a better understanding of the original manuscripts and meaning of the key words that constitute Matthew 28's Great Commission.[1] Look at the Greek-English table of those key words:

Πορευθέντες	*poreuthentes*	having gone
ουν	*oun*	therefore,
μαθητεύσατε	*mathēteusate*	disciple
πάντα	*panta*	all
τα	*ta*	the
ἔθνη	*ethnē*	nations,

This table indicates *whom* Jesus commanded us to disciple by show-ing that the direct object of the verb *disciple (mathēteusate)* is *nations (ethnes)*. In many translations, however, the rendition is ambiguous because we are erroneously taught that *make* is the verb, *disciples* is the object and *nations* the distributor. Reinforced by our traditional focus on people, this leads us to conclude that the passage states we are to make disciples of, and baptize, individuals instead of nations. But Jesus' instructions were specific and unambiguous: Make disciples *of* nations rather than make disciples *in* nations.

Nations are always present in God's master plan and works through-out history. The Bible mentions the words *nation* and *nations* a total of 589 times! In an embryonic sense, nations are present in God's command to Adam and Eve: "Be fruitful and multiply. Fill the earth and govern it" (Genesis 1:28 NLT). And they are certainly on display in the parade of saved nations in Revelation 21:24.

The promise God made to Abraham, the father of the faith, also makes clear that *nations* are the ultimate objective: "I will make you exceedingly fruitful, and I will make nations of you, and kings will come forth from you" (Genesis 17:6). "Abraham will surely become a great and mighty nation, and in him all the nations of the earth will be blessed" (Genesis 18:18).

This focus on the nations continues in the same manner with Isaac: "In your seed all the nations of the earth shall be blessed, because you have obeyed My voice" (Genesis 22:18). It also extends to Jacob: "God also said to him, 'I am

> *The vehicle that God designed to carry on the work of discipling nations is described as a holy nation.*

God Almighty; be fruitful and multiply; a nation and a company of nations shall come from you, and kings shall come forth from you'" (Genesis 35:11).

Furthermore, the vehicle that God designed to carry on the work of discipling nations is described as *a holy nation*: "But you are a cho-sen race, a royal priesthood, a holy nation, a people for God's own possession, so that you may proclaim the excellencies of Him who has called you out of darkness into His marvelous light" (1 Peter 2:9).

In other words, just as He chose the nation of Israel in the Old Testament to be a blessing to the nations of the earth, He also designated a New Testament equivalent to do the same—the Ekklesia.

Two Interwoven Dimensions

As we have seen, there are two dimensions of the Great Commission: a personal one that the Church is most cognizant of, and a corporate dimension involving nations that we have brought into focus here. The two are not disconnected; in fact, when it comes to the practical application, the first word in Matthew 28:19, *Go*, provides the key as to how interwoven these two are. That first word, translated in the table we just looked at from the Greek *poreuthentes*, literally means "having gone on the road," or more specifically, "going." It refers to moving from one place to another in everyday life, as in "as you go your own way."

This meaning reinforces the point that every believer is a minister and that labor is worship, and it defines the Great Commission as a lifestyle, not an occasional task or a special assignment. By the way Christians live—both at home and at work (see Colossians 3:23)—they are to bring transformation to every person, as well as to every sphere of the life of nations they encounter "on their way."[2]

We also find this dual dimension included in Mark 16:15 (NKJV): "And He said to them, 'Go into all the world and preach the gospel to every creature.'" While this is definitely a specific command to preach the Gospel to individuals, the text in the Greek uses the word *ktisis*, which literally means "all creation." This encompasses both creation in general and creatures, and in so doing highlights the fuller scope of the atoning work of Christ and consequently the broadest scope of the discipling mission entrusted to the Ekklesia.

In the Jewish culture, the expression "every creature" indicates that the whole creation is the object of redemption, both people and their environment, and also social systems.[3] And that is precisely everything that sin defiled and everything that the work of Christ redeemed.

Luke 19:10 confirms this interpretation. As I explained earlier, it specifies that the Son of Man came to seek and to save *that* which was lost. The Greek structure here, τὸ ἀπολωλός or *to apololos*, is an intentional and comprehensive reference to "that which has been lost." As we discussed in chapter 6, more than just mankind was lost at the Fall, and subsequently, more than just mankind was redeemed as a result of Jesus' atonement. Definitely, we can and must disciple the nations.

A Reality Check

This, of course, leads to the question, *how* do we disciple the nations? The answer is that we do it in the same way that Jesus discipled people. He brought the Kingdom of God to them, met their felt needs and, once their attention and gratitude had been secured, introduced them to principles that led to a healthy and meaningful life. Nations, and at a more embryonic level cities, schools and industries, also have felt needs. Once they see the Ekklesia meeting these felt needs, it will turn their hearts to God.

In a progressive status report on the disciples in the book of Acts, we can see their success at carrying out the *how* of the Great Commission. In Acts 5:28, we read that they achieved the first objective Jesus specified in His witnessing continuum in Acts 1:8, reaching a city as they filled Jerusalem with their doctrine. In Acts 19:10, we learn that they reached the second and third objectives, reaching a whole region: "all who lived in [the Roman province of] Asia heard the word of the Lord, both Jews and Greeks." Not too long afterward, in Romans 15 Paul stated that beginning in Jerusalem and round about as far as Illyricum, he had preached the Gospel so fully that he ran out of places, causing him to set his eyes on Spain, the farthest western nation in the then-civilized world (see verses 19, 23–24).

In a reality check on ourselves, we can see that the modern Church has definitely done a fair job evangelizing individuals, but we still have to embrace with equal conviction and determination the command to disciple nations. As I have stated before, something has to change, because in order to see results we have not yet seen, we must do what we have not yet done.

Pastor Norberto Carlini is one of the most successful and beloved apostolic leaders in Argentina. He planted a church in Rosario, Argentina, that gave birth to daughter churches all over the world. He is a father to multitudes of leaders. He has led tens of thousands to Christ. No one can question Norberto Carlini's commitment to the Church as we know it today. When I shared this material with him, however, he stated this:

> Ed, we need a new paradigm in order to see beyond our partial successes, no matter how impressive we think they are. Because in most if not all cases, our current religious structure and the theological mindset that built it stifle what is required to believe God for the "much more" that is so patently clear in the Scriptures and that you are so eloquently highlighting—that nations will be saved. I am afraid that we need to bring major changes for the new to be birthed. Basically, we need to love nations as much as we love people.

New Compassion for the World

When I became aware of the immensity of God's love for this world and I compared it to how little I cared for my nation, much less for other nations, I cried out to God in desperation to give me a new heart. He heard me, and I underwent heart surgery at the hands of the Great Physician, who implanted in my heart compassion for the nations.

As a result, I was able to begin to feel for nations what I already felt for sinners deformed and scarred by the work of the devil and sin. No matter how bad and ugly people look, I always believed that because Jesus paid the price, salvation was always an option for them. I now realize that the same precious blood that paid the price for sinners has also paid it for nations, and that nothing is beyond His reach. Understanding and embracing the commission to disciple nations is an issue of the heart.

After I shared these insights at a conference, some people in the audience felt this perspective was overenthusiastic. One said to me, "We are

Westerners, and as such, we are very cerebral folks. Facts, not emotions, are what determine our actions. We need proof of concept before we can commit to something new, especially so drastically new as discipling nations."

"Well," I asked, "is marriage a biblical ordinance?"

"Yes," they answered.

"On your wedding day, did you make a vow to be a good spouse?" I inquired.

Everybody answered affirmatively.

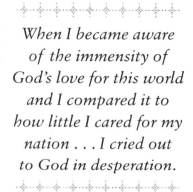

When I became aware of the immensity of God's love for this world and I compared it to how little I cared for my nation . . . I cried out to God in desperation.

Next I asked, "Were you serious about your vow?"

They gave the same affirmative answer.

"Okay," I said, "how much knowledge, or proof of concept, did you have about how to fulfill your role as a good spouse at the moment when you made that vow?"

The answer to that question was obvious. "Absolutely none," they replied, "because we still had not been pronounced husband and wife."

"So," I pressed further, "what drove you to make such a vow was the conviction of your heart, not your mind. You desired that person so much that you surrendered everything to be joined to him or her, and because you chose with your heart, your mind was directed to align with it."

The tipping point at a wedding ceremony is when the couple says, "I do." Everything else flows out of that. It is the same with discipling nations.

In the next chapter you will learn about three Christians who said "I do" when God asked them to give up everything to see their city transformed as a first step toward discipling their nation.

8

A Fuller Understanding
of Cooperation with God

From Contemplation to Partnership

"Without God we can't, but without us He won't." That maxim has inspired and energized the great missionary movements of the last two centuries, and this is why it is essential that today we say yes to God. Three riveting case studies eloquently illustrate the intriguing mystery of human cooperation with divine intentions.

Ricardo "King" Flores is a Christian who holds dual ministerial citizenship as CEO of an international financial transfer service in Manila, Philippines, and as a pulpit minister. When he was exposed to the principles of transformation, he immediately said yes to God. Soon afterward, he was working as a consultant to a relatively new believer who had just inherited eight businesses, one of which was a motel chain consisting of 1,600 rooms and employing 2,000 workers. Each room was used an average of five times a day by 3,000 prostitutes who, in cahoots with the management, were "processing" over 11,000 "clients."

King Flores's employer attended our Transformation Seminar and discovered the empowering and challenging biblical truths that he was a pastor in the marketplace, his employees were his disciples, his business was his ministry, and his clients were his congregation. He also embraced the scriptural principle that salvation should come to his corporation (household). Right after the seminar, he proclaimed, "The Kingdom of God has come to my business, and the Gates of Hades shall not prevail against it."

> *The boss gave them a novel assignment: "I will pay you not to preach."*

Instead of purging his staff of 2,000 "morally deficient" employees, he hired 30 pastors to "shepherd" them using prayer evangelism. Under King Flores's leadership, he gave them a novel assignment: "I will pay you *not* to preach." By this he was referring to prayer evangelism in its most elementary form: "talking to God about the lost before talking to the lost about God."[1] This process follows the four-step instruction Jesus gave us in Luke 10:2–9 for changing the spiritual climate: bless, fellowship, minister and then preach. Because Jesus listed preaching (proclaiming) at the end of the sequence, this business owner followed suit, telling the pastors not to preach right away, because they needed to cover the other steps first.

As an integral part of the many task forces required for running a motel chain, these pastors were now in a position to connect routinely with the employees, which allowed them to speak peace quietly over them. When doors opened up for fellowship, they struck up new friendships. As those friendships deepened, the employees began to share problems, and in turn the pastors—aka fellow workers—offered prayer. The answers to those prayers provided a compelling platform for proclaiming that the Kingdom of God had come near the employees in a convincing manner, as evidenced by the fact that in two years, 1,400 of the 2,000 employees had become believers.

In this newly improved spiritual climate, as soon as employees came to the Lord, they were taught to consider themselves ministers and to see their jobs as ministerial vehicles. Very soon, maids were cleaning rooms "heartily as unto the Lord," and inviting His presence to greet the new occupants. Cooks began to fix food "unto the glory of God." That and similar changes marked a radical turnaround, including establishing prayer chapels in each motel and recruiting intercessors. The most striking feature, however, was that employees at the front desk were informing guests during check-in that prayer for miracles was available for free upon request.

In essence, the motel chain became an Ekklesia, and one so effective that after eighteen months, thousands of clients had received the Lord, and many others were impacted by miraculous answers to prayer. What was formerly Exhibit A for the Gates of Hades became a hallmark of God's will on earth after His Ekklesia brought those gates down. What Jesus redeemed at the cross when He defeated the evil powers, His Ekklesia was now reclaiming for Him because of the scope of His Atonement.

Darkness can only be defined by its antonym. Darkness is the absence of light, which means that semidarkness is an oxymoron. When light is present, no matter how feebly, darkness ceases to be, because to exist darkness requires the total absence of light. This is why we are admonished not to despise small beginnings. If God is in the picture, it is bound to expand. And this is exactly what took place next. The transformation that began in the motel chain shattered the homogeneity of spiritual darkness over a vast area. Even though there was not a direct connection in the natural, the impact on the spirit realm (where the rulers of darkness were entrenched) was such that in short order the chief justice of the Supreme Court of that country invited Jesus into his heart and into the High Court. The commander in chief of the army followed suit and instructed every senior officer to undergo transformation training. One of those officers, after being appointed head of the Philippine National Police, directed the entire force (120,000-plus) to do the same.

> *In short order, the chief justice of the Supreme Court of that country invited Jesus into the High Court.*

Parañaque: Shattering Spiritual Darkness

The light that first broke through in the motel chain kept spreading to a city—Parañaque City, a suburb of Manila—when a municipal employee received the vision and anointing at one of our transformation seminars to claim it for Christ. Like the motel chain owner, she spoke the most powerful words, "Yes, Lord," and invited Jesus to come into her workplace, City Hall. That was a major challenge because she was just a clerical employee and the city was one billion pesos (approximately US$20 million) in debt as a result of endemic corruption. In fact, it was rated one of the worst cities in the nation.

Soon pastors began to pray on-site at City Hall, along with a growing number of intercessors. Before long, the spiritual climate had improved so much that the mayor came to Christ, corruption was publicly and officially renounced, employees found the courage to reject bribes as substantial as a BMW or a million pesos and church meetings were held regularly on-site before business hours. The city went from a one billion peso deficit to a one billion peso surplus, and crime decreased so much that 40 percent of the local prison cells remain unoccupied. The city council dedicated the city to God. In fact, the city's official seal now reads, "Parañaque City—Dedicated to God."[2]

To sum it up in one sentence, Jesus' Ekklesia co-opted the Gates of Hades' ekklesia, proclaimed the presence of the Gospel of the Kingdom through validating deeds and brought the Kingdom of God to hundreds of thousands of people. But this process was not launched until someone said yes to God and entered into a partnership with Him, revealing the importance of human cooperation with Him.

Tahiti: God Is Good for Government

Dr. Francis Oda, chairman of the renowned architectural firm Group 70 International, is also the chair of our Transform Our World Network. In 2005, the government of Tahiti, in French Polynesia, invited him to participate in a design competition for the urban waterfront of the capital city, Papeete. On the surface this was business, but in reality it was God's business because Francis Oda had said "Yes, Lord" when God called him to be a minister in the marketplace.

Upon arriving in Tahiti, he sought God in prayer for an opportunity to cooperate with Him. This opportunity did not take long to arise. During an official reception, French Polynesia's president asked Francis's opinion about what to do with a certain site on the waterfront. His answer, straight from the Holy Spirit, impressed the president so much that he asked Francis to make a presentation about it in three days' time.

Suddenly under an increased time and creativity crunch, Francis again said yes to the Lord and plunged into intercession, asking the Lord to download the details. To compound matters further, shortly before he was expected to present his work, an assistant to the president called to request Francis's opinion on how to solve another issue in the downtown area. The assistant intoned, "The president would appreciate it if you could have a solution."

Francis again "picked up" his direct line to the Creator as a marketplace minister whom He had deputized. And God again came through with a most practical insight about how to resolve the challenge and deliver all necessary drafts. What emerged for both projects was so extraordinary and riveting that the president, piqued with both elation and curiosity, inquired of Francis how he had come up with such brilliant concepts in such a short time.

Francis simply stated, "It was God."

As surprising as that sounded, it made sense to the president, because seven French engineers working on the second project for the previous six months had not come up with anything remotely close to what Francis was suggesting. The demonstration of God's desire and power to solve the president's challenges and dreams resulted in the president, his wife and the Tahitian architect who was collaborating with Francis all receiving the Lord. Francis was awarded the project, and on a subsequent visit to Tahiti he baptized all three of them in the president's swimming pool. After he laid hands on them, they were filled with the Holy Spirit.

Later, the government organized an international competition to design a large resort center for Tahiti. Out of 76 participants, Francis and his architectural firm, Group 70 International, were declared the winners. This is a $3 billion project in which all parties have a clear understanding that it is about much more than hotels, tourist facilities and airports. It is about blessing and discipling a nation through its economy.

Why is this happening? Because somebody said yes to God.

Ciudad Juárez: From Disgrace to Amazing Grace

Ciudad Juárez, Mexico, situated across the border from El Paso, Texas, was known as the murder capital of the world. The city's reputation was the result of a vicious war between drug cartels that spread to the general population. So many people were killed *every day* that 20 percent of the 1.5 million residents fled the city, leaving over 100,000 vacant homes and shops, in some of which criminals easily set up safe houses. Extortion and kidnappings ran rampant, with even policemen collecting ransom and protection money for the cartels. The economy plummeted as the city cowered in fear.

All of this was going on in spite of the faithful presence of hundreds of congregations valiantly doing good things in the city, but it was evident that "something else" and "something more" were needed. God directed Pastor Poncho Murguía to leave the growing church he had planted 29 years earlier, together with the newly completed $2 million facility that included a K–12 school and a pastors' college. Pastor Poncho was to fast and pray at the city entrance for 21 days. After saying yes to God and turning over his church to his second-in-command, he put up a tent and began the fast with the blessing of the city ministerial association.

Within a few days, a journalist came by to check on Poncho because he had heard that there was an angry person on a hunger strike. "Whom are you mad at? Why are you protesting?" he inquired.

Poncho replied, "I am neither angry, nor am I on a hunger strike. On the contrary, I'm fasting and praying for our city. I want to bring the blessing of God to Ciudad Juárez."

Puzzled, the journalist began to ask more questions. In particular, he wanted to know if God really spoke to Poncho. Once back at the office, he reported to his boss, "There's a weird guy over there who says he will not be eating for the next 21 days, just drinking water. He is not protesting against anyone, but is praying for God's favor to come to the city. He wants the government, the economy, education and everything else to improve. He says that God speaks to him."

Startled, his boss looked at him for a long time. Finally, he said, "Really? Well, this is what I want you to do: You go back every day and ask what God is telling him about the city, and we'll put it in the paper the next day!"

So every morning, the journalist came by and asked Poncho, "What is God saying?"

Poncho relayed the messages he was hearing from God, and they appeared in the newspaper the next day. Those fresh and anointed words of hope generated so much interest that a growing number of people came every day to Poncho's tent to ask for prayer. Drug addicts and prostitutes were among them, but also dignitaries and government officials. His tent became the miniature equivalent of an Old Testament city of refuge for people to run to and receive help. So many answers to prayer were recorded that at the end of the 21-day fast, more than 4,000 people gathered and Poncho was able to announce, by faith, the beginning of a new day for their troubled city.

"You go back every day and ask what God is telling him about the city, and we'll put it in the paper the next day!"

No sooner had he completed his fast than he received a call from the newly elected mayor, who asked for help in cleaning up El CERESO. At the time it was Mexico's worst prison, where "resident" drug lords, with the complicity of corrupted officials, directed the domestic and international drug trade without any restraint whatsoever. This was a highly coveted stronghold for the drug lords, because as the gateway for the North American Free Trade Agreement (NAFTA), Ciudad Juárez is the point of entry for billions of dollars in merchandise into the United States every year. For all practical purposes, the prison had become the command and control center for one of the city's most powerful cartels. (Two cartels were at war over the city, and one of them controlled the prison.)

If anything embodied the Gates of Hades on earth, it was El CERESO[3] Prison. It was originally designed to house a maximum of 1,100 inmates, but at that time it held 2,900. With such overcrowding it became unmanageable, and the cartel easily took over. Eighty percent of the robberies and violent crimes in the city were planned from inside the prison. The least expensive and best-quality drugs were sold right there. One-third of the inmates had the key to their own cell and were able to come and go as they pleased, generating $20,000 in daily profits from drug sales. In fact, residing in a cell inside El CERESO was the equivalent of owning a lease in a coveted shopping mall that typically went for a minimum of $1,000. According to Poncho, 93 percent of the inmates used drugs, and 60 percent of the guards were involved in bringing the drugs inside. Everybody was on the cartel's payroll: the guards, the janitors, the cooks and also the warden . . . especially the warden.

Cleaning up a prison was not an operation for which Poncho had been trained in seminary. But while attending our Transformation Conference in Argentina, he had seen that country's largest prison (Olmos Prison[4]) transformed to such degree that control was wrestled from crime syndicates, a church run by converted felons was established inside its walls, inmate-run 24-hour prayer chains were instituted, and recidivism rates were reduced from 85 percent down to 5 percent. Heartened by having seen this firsthand, Poncho knew that he needed to act accordingly, trusting in the God who had called him to believe Him for the city.

The mayor of Ciudad Juárez asked Poncho what he would need to accomplish this task. Poncho replied, "I want the chief of police and the chief of internal affairs reporting directly to me and sworn to secrecy to plan how to retake the prison by surprise." Immediately, the mayor agreed and told him to go for it.

In the small group of people who began to trust God for transformation—a functional *conventus* or a small Ekklesia—was a Spirit-led Christian lawyer who had served as a judge at the state level. Poncho immediately installed him as El CERESO's new warden. On his second

93

day at work, a mean-looking stranger walked into his office, placed a briefcase on his desk and cockily blurted, "Boss, here it is."

The new warden asked "what" was here.

"C'mon, don't pretend. You know how the game is played: Every week we will bring you a suitcase with $25,000. You just look the other way and everything will be okay."

Quickly and decisively, the man was informed that he could not buy the new warden with $25,000.

"Oh, you're one of those who plays hard to get. That's okay. How much do you want? We'll raise it to thirty."

Again, the warden said emphatically that such an amount did not even tickle him.

"Oh, you're one of the expensive ones? Well, okay, we'll give you forty."

Nope, the warden assured the man, $40,000 would not work either.

This was fast turning into a scene from *High Noon at the K (for Kingdom) Corral*. Tension was rapidly rising, and so were the stakes. The Christian warden knew that if he agreed, he would come under this particular cartel's control. His integrity, his communion with God and his walk with Christ would all fall by the wayside. On the other hand, if he kept saying no, the other party would say, "Okay, be prepared to suffer the consequences." And either he or someone in his family would be dead the next day. As a former judge, he was aware of how the drug lords operated.

Visibly irritated, the emissary from the cartel said, "Look, I don't know if you're hearing me. Take the money, because if you don't, you won't be able to withstand the pain that will come to you and your family. Look, man, we all have a price. Tell me what yours is. Let's stop haggling."

The warden insisted again that there was no possible way that the people this man represented would be able to pay the price he had in mind.

"What's your price?" shouted the emissary.

The warden responded with calm authority, "Look, if you have something more valuable than the blood that my Lord shed on the cross for my sins and yours, give it to me and I am all yours. If not, leave my office right now."

The emissary was completely caught off guard, not only by those words, but even more so by the conviction with which the warden spoke them. Visibly shaken, he muttered, "We don't want to mess with the Great Chief!" Then he grabbed the suitcase and left, never to come back again. (In Spanish *Lord* is *Señor*, which is used secularly to address God, but also a boss or a chief.)

Later on, when Poncho asked the warden how he came up with such an ultimatum, he replied, "It was the Holy Spirit. The Lord assured us that He would put the right words in our mouth when we are in difficult situations."

Those were definitely the right words, because the emissary was a member of Los Aztecas, a brutal gang of more than ten thousand members who consider themselves true Azteca Indians and who revere the Great Chief as god. And one taboo they will never break is challenging the Great Chief. If the new warden

> *"If you have something more valuable than the blood that my Lord shed on the cross for my sins and yours, give it to me and I am all yours."*

was under such a Great Chief, they figured they had better pull back. Amazing!

After securing strong intercessory support, Poncho led a midnight raid on the prison with a combined force of police, soldiers and a new batch of guards. They took over the prison and put it in total lockdown for thirty days. All corrupted officials were replaced. Inmates went through the drug withdrawal syndrome, but with the assistance of doctors and nurses as part of a newly instituted prison-wide rehabilitation program. In a short time the inmates began to get healthier, eat decent meals, gain weight and kick old habits, more so in the case of those who invited Jesus into their heart. Bribes and prostitution were eliminated. The congregation of believers inside the prison quickly grew to over 650 members.

In essence, God's Ekklesia co-opted the devil's ekklesia and turned it into a vortex for the Kingdom of God to bring down the Gates of Hades . . . with the government footing the bill.

All of this was a precursor for what was to happen in the city, because once their base of operations in El CERESO was shut down, the cartel moved into vacant homes and took over the marketplace, imposing a culture of death with ten or more murders a day. Those residents who were unable to leave town lived the combined horror of fearing for their lives while seeing people shot or hung from bridges as "the new normal." Any business that refused to pay protection money was given the 1-2-3 punch treatment: First, the cartels fired shots into the building from a passing car. Next, they set it on fire. Finally, they killed either the owner or a family member. Fear and hopelessness gripped the city.

Armed with the assurance that God could and indeed did want to reverse the situation, but knowing that human cooperation was required, Poncho and a new congregation that was learning how to walk in the paradigm of the Ekklesia said, "Yes, Lord." They reprogrammed their traditional indoor social church events—Christmas, Valentine's Day, Mother's Day, etc.—into outdoor celebrations in the sectors of the city where the highest number of deaths had occurred. It was a bold and courageous decision because of the lethal danger it exposed the congregation to, but the Gates of Hades could not withstand the assault as the Ekklesia exercised its authority "in heaven and on earth." The gloominess hanging over those places in the city was dispelled by worship music, prayers for healing and deliverance and the distribution of food and goods to the needy.

> No *wonder the press nicknamed Mr. Salas "God's Attorney General."*

That the momentum had shifted in favor of the Ekklesia was never more evident than when the governor of the state of Chihuahua chose attorney-at-law Dr. Carlos Salas to run the Justice Department as the new state attorney general. This disciple of Poncho dedicated the Justice Department to God on the day he was sworn in, and he proceeded to operate in the power of the Spirit, with strong intercessory backing. As a result of this "Yes, Lord," over a period of three years miracles resulted in the reclaiming one by one of the other state prisons, the capture of top-level criminals and the rescue of kidnapping victims. Where 98 percent of the criminals were previously being set free by a corrupt system, now they were all going to jail. No wonder the press nicknamed Mr. Salas "God's Attorney General."[5]

The Turning Point

According to Poncho, the turning point in the heavenly places over Ciudad Juárez occurred when he and a fellow Ekklesia pastor, Brian Burton from Phuket, Thailand (who has also seen his share of transformation miracles in the marketplace), said yes to God and went to a high place to adopt the city. Together, they declared, "Juárez, you are no longer an orphan city. You have been adopted by your Father in heaven, and by us."

Such an exercise is what is often described as a *prophetic act*, which I define as a spiritual action or declaration that draws a circle of truth around the devil. He intentionally refuses to stand on the truth because there is no truth in him . . . "for he is a liar and the father of lies" (John 8:44). We have seen that such an act becomes the precursor to the *bapto* event, as was the case here with Poncho.

"It sounds strange to say today that because we stood on a high place and made a declaration, things changed," Poncho explained, "but as we applied the five pivotal paradigms for transformation Ed taught us, and as we practiced prayer evangelism, we saw the power of God displayed like never before." Such is the authority Jesus has delegated to the Ekklesia.

As I reflected on this, I realized this was the functional equivalent of my own initial "Yes, Lord" moment many years earlier—the eviction notice we served in Arroyo Seco, Argentina, to the principalities and powers that had kept 109 towns and villages within a 100-mile radius of our newly built prayer chapel in spiritual darkness. "Cast your bread upon the waters, for you will find it after many days" (Ecclesiastes 11:1 NKJV).

Hit Men Up for Adoption?

The corresponding and decisive breakthrough on the ground in Ciudad Juárez came when sicarios (professional cartel hit men) began to come into God's Kingdom as a result of the Ekklesia adopting them in prayer. These extraordinary salvations did not occur right away. But the decision to adopt these men "sight unseen" was like leaven inserted in the dough. It took time, but it did the job.

It happened in an unplanned way. A Mexican inmate came to faith in a prison in the United States. Shortly afterward, the Holy Spirit directed him to minister to the cruelest criminal in the penal complex, a fellow national. Humanly speaking, this was a kamikaze mission because the other guy was running an evil system. But propelled by his first love and his accompanying childlike faith, this new believer also said, "Yes, Lord." Not long after, through a series of divine coincidences, he led him to the Lord.

Both men were released about the same time, but they went in opposite directions. The first one joined Poncho's congregation, where he grew spiritually. The other went to his hometown, where he reverted to his old ways and became the chief of eighty sicarios.

When the one now attending Poncho's church heard his pastor's charge to adopt sicarios, he also heard God say, *Go and find 'Juan' (not his real name), My son, who is not walking in the light, and pray for him.* Fully aware that he was risking his life, he made his way to the village where this Juan now had his command and control center. Surprised, the chief sicario asked him, "Why are you here?"

"Because God wants you back, and He sent me to pray for you."

There was so much authority in his words that the recipient was unable to deny his authenticity. Looking over his shoulder, Juan said, "Okay, but not here. I'm having a staff meeting with eight sicarios, and it won't be appropriate." He got that one right, because at that very moment they were plotting that night's killings.

The two men walked about two hundred yards away, and just when the Spirit-led Christian was about to lay hands on Juan to pray, they heard the distinctive noise of gunfire. Two cars packed with sicarios from the rival cartel had just driven up to the house and killed Juan's eight associates in a deadly shower of bullets.

What happened next is one of the most dramatic repentance and instant reconsecration stories I know of. The weight of what had just happened caved in on Juan, along with the realization of the risk his forgotten friend had taken to come find him. He consummated his vow to follow Jesus right there on the street.

How *Do* You Resign?

For Juan, next came the monumental problem of how to get out of the cartel, because there were only two ways to do so: prison or death. Facing the real consequences of his decision, he went to see his boss, automatic rifle under his arm.

Juan placed the AK-47 in his boss's hands and said, "I can no longer do what I've been doing. I know there is no way out. *Jálele, no más!*" (Spanish for "Pull the trigger, no fooling around!")

Shocked, his boss asked, "Why? You're an up-and-coming leader. You shouldn't throw all that away. Think it over."

"I've become a Christian, and I know the rules of our game," Juan replied. "I've thought it through already, and there's no turning back. *Jálele, no más.*"

At that moment, the Holy Spirit intervened so powerfully that what had never happened before in the cartel took place. With piercing eyes, his boss looked at him and yelled, "I will make an exception for the first and only time! You can go and be a Christian, but you'd better behave like one, because if you ever backslide, *I will personally track you down, and I will kill you mercilessly!*"

That was definitely a most convincing way to ensure that this new believer would remain faithful to the Lord. And it worked. From that day on, the two former sicarios now turned believers became the point of inception for other criminals to get saved, setting in motion a systematic depletion of key players on Satan's team.

Today, Ciudad Juárez is one of the safest cities in Mexico. Many cartel bosses have been captured. Homicides have decreased by 80 percent, extortions by 90 percent and kidnappings by 100 percent, according to Mr. Salas. People who had fled in terror have returned in hope. The economy has rebounded. Latin America's top children's museum under Poncho's leadership is bringing hope and joy to the fifteen thousand kids who have been orphaned by the violence.[6]

The then-mayor of the city, Mr. Escobar, told us, "I used to need ten to fifteen guards whenever I went out. Now, I walk with my family in complete peace. This is why I have called on the churches to increase their evangelistic activities—because it's good for our city!"

Homicides have decreased by 80 percent, extortions by 90 percent and kidnappings by 100 percent. People who had fled in terror have returned in hope.

Poncho and his team have also developed a program called *Avanza sin Tranza* (Thrive without Bribes). The plan is designed to train 6,880 municipal workers in transformation principles, as well as members of the various chambers of commerce.

Transformation becomes credible when the secular media notices and reports it. This is the case in Ciudad Juárez, because the *New York Times*,[7] the *LA Times* and *National Geographic*[8] have all published articles testifying to the city's radical transformation. And a city that was once listed as one of the most undesirable cities to visit is now being touted as a very attractive tourist destination.[9]

Two Hindering Factors

The testimonies in this chapter confirm the validity of the sweeping verdict that was won the day Jesus proclaimed on the cross, "It is finished!" He certified that He had accomplished the redemption of everything that was lost. As a result, no matter what Satan has taken over—whether a government institution, a prison or a motel chain—the Gates of Hades cannot prevail there when God's children say "Yes, Lord" and operate as the Ekklesia armed with jurisdiction to bind and to release.

This catalytic chain of transformational events, in which men and women said yes to God and in response He moved mightily, is as encouraging as it is intriguing. God, who is almighty, can do anything, anywhere, anytime He chooses. For reasons that defy human comprehension, however, this side of eternity He chooses and waits for our cooperation to do it. Fascinating!

I submit that the reason we are reluctant to see ourselves as God's partners is due to one of two factors. The first one is excessive humility, and the second is an ignorance of how special we are in God's eyes by undervaluing ourselves. Let's tackle them in that order.

Those whom God uses are genuinely humble people, because He "resists the proud, but gives grace to the humble" (James 4:6 NKJV). The devil knows that those who are humble will not easily succumb to pride, so he tempts them with *excessive* humility. Pride overshoots, and excessive humility undershoots. Both miss the mark and end up preventing people from being used by God for extraordinary exploits. "Who am I but a rotten sinner spared by God's unmerited grace?" is the motto of those with excessive humility.

As pious as this sounds, it obscures the fact that we are also "His workmanship, created in Christ Jesus for good works, which God prepared beforehand so that we would walk in them" (Ephesians 2:10). Our salvation is only by grace, but once saved, we are to serve God by doing those good works. Failure to do so has consequences, because excessive humility can also be a screen for laziness (see Matthew 25:26) or pride in disguise.

Jesus said, "You are My friends *if* you do what I command you" (John 15:14, emphasis added). Our obedience is required because of the intended benefit to *others*: "that you would go and bear fruit, and that your fruit would remain, so that whatever you ask of the Father in My name He may give to you" (verse 16).

Consider for a moment all the fruit that would not have materialized if the players in these stories had disqualified themselves from partnering with God. It would be tragic, because at the end of the day it is not about us, but about God, and God is about people and the world they live in. This is why "From everyone who has been given much, much will be required" (Luke 12:48).

The second factor that can hinder our partnership with God is undervaluing ourselves due to a spiritual inferiority complex. Let me explain this in the context of the two great commandments: "You shall love the Lord your God with all your heart, and with all your soul, and with all your mind," and "you shall love your neighbor as yourself" (Mark 12:30–31).

Even though two commandments are explicitly identified here, there is a third one embedded in them—the command to love ourselves. This is of vital importance because we can only love our neighbors as much as we love ourselves.

Why should we love ourselves? Fundamentally because God loves us, and not just now that we are Christians; He loved us when we were yet sinners. So we must be lovable if He loved us when we were at our worst (see Romans 5:8). Once we understand this vertical dimension, we can respond in like manner: "We love, because He first loved us" (1 John 4:19).

What the Devil Resents

It is this unimpeded, vertical two-way flow of love between God and us that creates in us the capacity to love others into His Kingdom, and this is *the* thing the devil will oppose vehemently.

How? Through deception. He is described as the accuser of the brethren, which by definition means that he is *constantly* bringing up *before God* every sin we commit. For us to believe this deception, he has to convince us that he is able to accuse us constantly in God's presence.

If we do not love ourselves, we cannot love our neighbors.

There is no basis whatsoever for his claim, however. The devil is no longer in a position to do so because "the great dragon was thrown down, the serpent of old who is called the devil and Satan, who deceives the whole world; *he was thrown down to the earth*, and his angels were thrown down with him" (Revelation 12:9, emphasis added).

The heavenly beings celebrated this, "Now the salvation, and the power, and the kingdom of our God and the authority of His Christ have come, for the accuser of our brethren has been thrown down, he who accuses them before our God day and night" (Revelation 12:10).

Since the devil has no legal grounds to accuse us in God's presence, all he can do is accuse us *in our own mind* by telling us an insidious lie.

He gets us to think that he is constantly bringing up our every wrong deed before God, and he convinces us that God is ready to punish us—until Jesus shows the scars on His hands and tells the Father, "My blood paid for their sins."

There is no scriptural basis whatsoever for this scenario. It is a total lie, since the devil is no longer allowed in God's presence, and God does not need to be reminded of what Jesus did for us. The next verse in Revelation 12 provides the key to victory over this lie: "And they overcame him because of the blood of the Lamb and because of the word of their testimony, and they did not love their life even when faced with death" (verse 11).

In practical terms, this means that all our sins have been atoned for—yesterday's sins, today's sins and even tomorrow's sins. They are already forgiven. There is not a single transgression that the accuser can bring up against us before God, who is the ultimate Judge. "Who will bring a charge against God's elect? God is the one who justifies" (Romans 8:33). We overcome our accuser.

We must next give testimony (the word of our testimony) to ourselves of this truth in order for our beliefs to align with God's Word, and we must give the same testimony to the devil as a rebuttal of his unfounded charges. When our beliefs align with God's Word and not with the devil's lies, we can joyfully sing with Paul,

> For I am convinced that neither death, nor life, nor angels, nor principalities, nor things present, nor things to come, nor powers, nor height, nor depth, nor any other created thing, will be able to separate us from the love of God, which is in Christ Jesus our Lord.
>
> Romans 8:38–39

But we should not stop there. We must also despise our life in order to counterattack and defeat the devil (see again Revelation 12:11), because it is not just about us experiencing spiritual freedom, but also about those who are still under his domain.

The devil also uses what Goliath tried against David—intimidation—by reciting a litany of tribulations, distress, persecution, peril and even death that will overtake us if we take up the divine assignment. He knows that without us, God has chosen not to do the work assigned to us. This upstreams to the earlier statement, "Without God we can't, but without us He won't." This is why the devil uses everything in his book of tricks to intimidate us.

A young William Carey, the founder of the modern missionary movement, was publicly rebuked by a senior leader, who stated, "Young man, sit down; when God is pleased to convert the heathen world, he will do it without your help or mine."[10]

Carey dodged that fiery dart and proceeded to despise his life in order to pursue the heavenly vision he had received, and he became the father of the modern-day missionary movement. Today hundreds of millions of former heathens have come to Christ (myself included) because Carey realized that his partnership was essential for God's will to be done on earth.

Both Parañaque City and Ciudad Juárez are on a path to fully becoming God's cities, and Tahiti has been injected with the leaven of the Kingdom, all because transformational believers have set in motion a process by which righteousness is replacing unrighteousness by the Ekklesia reclaiming what Jesus already redeemed at the cross. But something more is happening. As the institutions and people begin to be discipled, the cities and the nations are progressively being "immersed" in Jesus' teachings, which leads us to a more challenging issue: how to baptize a nation. If we agree that we must disciple nations, then according to Matthew 28:19 we must also baptize them, since the two commands are intrinsically linked. If this is so, *just how do we baptize a nation?*

To fully understand that, in the next chapter we will discuss personal baptism and the baptism of the Holy Spirit in-depth, as a staging area from which to learn how to disciple nations. Get ready to be challenged and empowered!

9

A Fuller Understanding
of New Testament Baptisms

From Religious Ceremonies to Power Encounters

> Skewed assumptions related to water baptism and to the
> baptism in the Holy Spirit have created major walls of divi-
> sion and impeded the contemporary Church from embrac-
> ing her full mission. A closer look at three different kinds
> of baptisms in the New Testament will point the way to "a
> more excellent biblical way."

For the past two thousand years, Christian baptism has been the subject
of intense theological debates over its value, its form of administration
and who should receive it. Those discussions have been instructive, but
more often than not, they have failed to take into consideration the
deeper meaning of baptism that, as we shall see, goes far beyond its form
of administration. We need to look beyond the method or the means
of baptism and focus on the experience that the baptism represents.
Our upcoming discussion in chapters 10 and 11 will be centered on the
subject of baptizing nations and not just individuals, but we need to

address both of these to find the significance of each. In that context, first I will address personal baptisms.

So far, we have looked at evidence that the Great Commission, as stated in Matthew 28:19–20, involves discipling nations and not just individuals. We have also seen that, according to the syntax of the verse, we are instructed to baptize nations as well. If this is so, then exactly how do we go about it?

To answer that, let's proceed from the known—the water baptism of people—to the still unknown, the baptism of nations. Unfortunately, faulty assumptions relating to the water baptism of people have obscured the meaning of Jesus' commission to baptize nations, causing us to assume that water is also involved. To provide an ample biblical framework that will bring us a fuller understanding in this area, in this chapter we will look at the three kinds of baptisms the New Testament mentions—a baptism of repentance like John the Baptist did, baptism in the name of Jesus and the baptism in the Holy Spirit.

We need to look beyond the method or the means of baptism and focus on the experience that the baptism represents.

Baptisms already existed in the Old Testament, albeit not called by that name, and involved a ritual cleansing or purification of people or things. One example is the case of the Syrian general Naaman, whom Elisha told to dip seven times in the Jordan to be cured of his leprosy (see 2 Kings 5:1–14). The ministry of John the Baptist is a clear example of this type of baptism of repentance.

In fact, according to Jesus, John's ministry marked the end of an era between the Old Covenant and the New Covenant (see Matthew 11:13–15).[1] Jesus restated this important shift in Luke 16:16: "The Law and the Prophets were proclaimed until John; since that time the gospel of the kingdom of God has been preached, and everyone is forcing his way into it" (a concept we discussed in-depth in chapter 4).

John himself declared, "I baptize you with water for repentance, but He who is coming after me is mightier than I, and I am not fit to remove his sandals; He will *baptize you with the Holy Spirit and fire*" (Matthew 3:11, emphasis added; see also Mark 1:8; Luke 3:16). John's declaration indicates that the essence of Old Covenant baptisms was for the repentance of sin, and the essence of New Covenant baptisms is the baptism in the Holy Spirit for power.

It follows, then, that it was for this reason Jesus ordered His disciples, "not to leave Jerusalem, but to wait for what the Father had promised, 'Which,' He said, 'you heard of from Me; for John baptized with water, but you will be *baptized with the Holy Spirit* not many days from now'" (Acts 1:4–5, emphasis added).

Jesus' instructions make a deliberate distinction between John's water baptism and the baptism in the Holy Spirit, a demarcation that has escaped most of us until now. He is referring to John's baptism as the climax of the old, and to the baptism in the Holy Spirit announced here, as the beginning of the new. The new is meant to fulfill what was announced in the old.

Distinct, Yet Inseparable Baptisms

Before we go any further, let me underscore for clarity the distinctions between the three baptisms I am referring to from the New Testament. The first is the water baptism John the Baptist administered, which was a baptism of repentance that preceded any kind of baptism in Jesus' name. It was the climax of the Old Covenant.

The second is the baptism "in the name of Jesus," and this one has happened in two different dispensations—before and after the cross. Before the cross, the individual being baptized was acknowledging Jesus as the Messiah, in anticipation of what was to take place at the cross. After the cross, or more precisely after Pentecost, as seen in various passages in the book of Acts, this baptism signified an individual's public confession of Jesus *as his or her Savior.*

The third is the baptism in the Holy Spirit. Unfortunately, today the subject of the "baptism in the Holy Spirit" represents a major discordant issue between charismatic and more traditional believers that goes beyond speaking or not speaking in tongues. This is why I beg you to bear with me throughout this chapter, because I will attempt to show "a more excellent biblical way" to enable both camps to see the baptism by the Holy Spirit as a uniting, not a dividing, topic.

Here is a challenging new insight I wish to offer: When the second baptism (in water in Jesus' name) is administered without the third baptism (in the Holy Spirit) taking place in the same time frame, the second baptism then reverts back to the pre-cross baptism because the new believers are not given the power that comes with baptism in the Holy Spirit. We see an example of this in Samaria in Acts 8, where such a baptism was done "simply" (only, exclusively) in the name of Jesus, without the accompanying baptism in the Holy Spirit. I will talk more about this up ahead, but the point I want to make here is that the modern Church, generally speaking, has reverted back to that second baptism "simply" in Jesus' name when leaving out the baptism in the Holy Spirit *at the time of water baptism*. This results in the church being filled with baptized members who have been *convinced* but not necessarily *converted*. My central message in this chapter is that we need to reverse that pattern and help new believers go beyond baptismal ceremonies to a Holy Spirit *power* encounter.

The verses I have quoted so far indicate that God will baptize believers by pouring on them the Holy Spirit. That provides the power encounter. Such an outpouring does not exclude people being baptized in water in Jesus' name, but it shows that water baptism is the *material* reflection of a spiritual experience. As such, water baptism is no longer meant merely to signify repentance, as was John's baptism, but to manifest salvation symbolically.

As the apostle Paul wrote in Romans 6:4, "We have been buried with Him [Christ] through [water] baptism into death, so that as Christ was raised [by the power of the Spirit] from the dead through the glory of the Father, so we too might walk in newness of life" (for which we need the Holy Spirit). Paul goes so far as to state in Romans 8:9–11,

> If anyone does not have the Spirit of Christ, he does not belong to Him.
> . . . But if the Spirit of Him who raised Jesus from the dead dwells in

you, He who raised Christ Jesus from the dead will also give life to your mortal bodies through His Spirit who dwells in you.

So then, water baptism in the name of Jesus (death of the old), as seen in the New Testament, and baptism in the Holy Spirit (resurrection life and power), as also practiced by the Ekklesia, are inextricably linked. In fact, they are inseparable. The interplay between them is affirmed throughout the New Testament. For instance, the narrative in Acts 2:38–41 is very confirming as it describes the first New Covenant baptisms: "Peter said to them, '*Repent*, and each of you *be baptized* in the name of Jesus Christ for the forgiveness of your sins; and you will *receive the gift of the Holy Spirit*'" (emphasis added).

In Acts 19:1–6, we read about certain disciples Paul came upon who had experienced the baptism of John, *but neither the baptism in the name of Jesus nor the baptism in the Holy Spirit*. This is such a clarifying example that it is worth looking at the entire passage:

> Paul passed through the upper country and came to Ephesus, and found some disciples. He said to them, "Did you receive the Holy Spirit when you believed?" And they said to him, "No, we have not even heard whether there is a Holy Spirit." And he said, "Into what then were you baptized?" And they said, "Into John's baptism." Paul said, "John baptized with the baptism of repentance, telling the people to believe in Him who was coming after him, that is, in Jesus." When they heard this, they were baptized in the name of the Lord Jesus. And when Paul had laid his hands upon them, the Holy Spirit came on them, and they began speaking with tongues and prophesying.

Paul makes a key correlation here between receiving the Holy Spirit and water baptism in the name of Jesus. To assess these disciples' spiritual condition, Paul inquires what kind of baptism they had received. After they acknowledge their ignorance of the Holy Spirit, he remedies their one-sided experience right away by baptizing them in water in the name of Jesus and laying his hands on them for the Holy Spirit to come on them. Again, water and Spirit baptism are shown as two sides of the same coin.

Not a Destination, But a Doorway

In Romans 8, Paul affirms the absolute centrality and necessity of the Holy Spirit:

> But if anyone does not have the Spirit of Christ, he does not belong to Him. . . . For all who are being led by the Spirit of God, these are sons of God. For you have not received a spirit of slavery leading to fear again, but you have received a spirit of adoption as sons by which we cry out, "Abba! Father!" The Spirit Himself testifies with our spirit that we are children of God, and if children, heirs also, heirs of God and fellow heirs with Christ.
>
> Romans 8:9, 14–17

Let's not miss in this passage how the Spirit is responsible for everything pertaining to our new life: for our salvation, for leading us, for empowering us to overcome fear, for intimacy to address God as Father, and for assuring us of our eternal inheritance. Wow! Death of the old nature is wonderful, but without the new life of the Spirit, the message becomes focused on the stick of death without the carrot of new life.

The cross is not a destination, but a doorway that enables us to walk out the Gospel message in the power of the Holy Spirit.

The cross is not a destination, but a doorway. It makes it possible to be seated with Christ in heavenly realms (see Ephesians 2:6) and to walk out the Gospel message in the power of the Holy Spirit. This is possible because the same Spirit that raised Christ Jesus from the dead is now at work in us, so ours becomes a message of life—a life filled with power. Unbelievers will receive this message of new life and power better than they will receive a message limited to the death to our sinful nature. And an essential part of that message has to be that the Holy Spirit will make them partakers of Jesus' resurrection power, which will take them from death to life.

In other words, our confession of faith in Jesus and death to the old nature, which customarily is done prior to being water baptized in His name, has to be followed immediately by the baptism with the Holy Spirit in order for the life that replaces death to become evident. Notice how Jesus linked the two baptisms in John 7:39: "This He spoke of the Spirit, whom those who believed in Him were to receive." It is a combination we also see on the Day of Pentecost with the first converts, when Peter admonished them, "Be baptized in the name of Jesus Christ for the forgiveness of your sins; and you will receive the gift of the Holy Spirit" (Acts 2:38).

My Struggle with Baptismal Expectations

My experience with water baptism may shed light on this interplay between water baptism and Holy Spirit baptism. The day I went into the waters, I expected that something extraordinary was going to happen when I came up. I remember the night before, imagining what that would be like. I already knew the Lord. The fear of death was no longer tormenting me, but I was still besieged by the hold that the flesh and the world, and perhaps to a degree the devil, had on me. There were areas where I was still struggling, and too often tasting the bitterness of defeat.

In preparation, I read the passage describing Jesus' baptism, eager for a similar experience. I even hoped to hear a voice from heaven, have the Holy Spirit descend on me, and have all my burdens left in the baptismal pool. But I did not experience any of that. It was a major disappointment. I felt that a very burdened "dry" Ed went in, and nothing more than a "wet" Ed came out. The change I had hoped for did not happen.

At that time, I had been a believer for three months. But because I worked and studied simultaneously, I was able to attend church only once a week, which constituted a spiritual oasis and was always an uplifting experience. The worship, the music, the corporate prayers, the fellowship and the teaching of the Word were like fresh water poured on my parched soul. I often felt like a soccer ball that had to be reinflated every Sunday. But I also knew from past experiences that on Monday, a deflating process would begin that would end up with me crawling into church a week later, desperate for another pumping up. The systemic evil that pervaded my school, and more so my workplace, persistently ate away at the infusion of power I received in church. This relegated me to living in a spiritual seesaw where repentance and forgiveness continually alternated over my emotional horizon. It was as if church was a feast served to a starving prisoner *inside his cell.*

This struggle was devouring me inside. Before becoming a Christian, I had lived in sin, with nothing better to compare it to since I had no awareness that there was a better way. This changed when I experienced God's forgiveness and I savored the abundant life, even if sporadically. Now I had something to compare it to, but my inability to possess the abundant life permanently made me echo Paul's words, "For the good that I want, I do not do, but I practice the very evil that I do not want. . . . Wretched man that I am! Who will set me free from the body of this death?" (Romans 7:19, 24).

This reached a crushing point on the night of February 14, 1959, while I lay in bed feeling overwhelmed by such powerlessness. In my desperation I cried out to God for power to overcome, and He led me to Acts 1:8, where Jesus promised that we should receive power when the Holy Spirit comes upon us.

> *I felt God literally "pushing me under" in my own bed, and when I came up . . . I was dripping with joy, power, peace and righteousness.*

My cry was as sincere as it was desperate. I was begging God to baptize me with the Holy Spirit. And at 2:42 a.m. on that unforgettable night, I felt God literally "pushing me under" in my own bed, and when I came up my soul was flooded with His presence and I was dripping with joy, power, peace and righteousness. Everything that had consumed me before had been burned by divine fire. That night I was baptized with *the Holy Spirit and fire.*

I ran into my parents' bedroom and woke them up with the exciting news. I could not wait for the morning to come, and when it did, I rode my bike around and witnessed to all my unsaved relatives. The first day I went back to school I preached to everybody. At work, where cussing and dirty stories constantly polluted the atmosphere and crushed my spirit, I was now able to look people in the eye and tell them about the redeeming power of Christ. It was not too long afterward that I led my first co-worker to Christ. On weekends, I stood fearlessly on street corners and preached to unreceptive and often cruel audiences. Dodging tomatoes, rotten eggs and stones was not uncommon, and when one of those hit me, I counted it a supreme privilege. Gone was the fearful teenager; a strong young man had replaced him.

Those positive feelings had happened before. On November 16, 1958, while attending my first evangelical meeting in a storefront church, divine light had flooded my dark heart. Joy pushed back my gloominess. Assurance replaced fear. Forgiveness swept away past sins. All as a result of having invited Jesus into my heart (see John 1:12). As I walked home, I remember gazing at the bright Southern Cone sky. Every star seemed to be blinking a smile at me. I had never felt that kind of joy before, and I was afraid that if I fell asleep it would be gone in the morning. So I sat on the edge of my bed and fended off sleep, to "ride it while it lasted." Finally, around 4:00 a.m. I conked out. When I woke up the joy was still there, but as the days went by, it progressively lost its vibrancy as the struggles with my sinful flesh reemerged.

In retrospect, I wonder what would have happened if the night I received Jesus as my Lord and Savior, I had been baptized *both* in the Holy Spirit and in water? It would have definitely followed a biblical pattern since this is what the book of Acts reports.

Working in Tandem

I realize that the question I just mentioned is bound to raise protest among people who put themselves firmly into camps that have differing perspectives on the baptism in the Holy Spirit. One of these camps teaches that the baptism in the Holy Spirit is a "second blessing" that must be accompanied by a specific manifestation of the Holy Spirit. The other camp believes that nowadays God's power is found in the written Word, and as a result they consider themselves already baptized by the Holy Spirit into the Body of Christ on the day they believed. But I wish to suggest that there is ample room to see these two perspectives working in tandem, as modeled by the New Testament Ekklesia.

Mark 16:20 states, "And they [the disciples] went out and preached [the word] everywhere, while the Lord worked with them, and confirmed *the word* by *the signs* that followed" (emphasis added). This passage is pace setting for the rest of the New Testament since it describes what took place through the Ekklesia right after Jesus issued the Great Commission. Here we see the word preached, together with or accompanied by the Spirit confirming such word through signs and wonders. To experience this today, we need to see the baptism of the Holy Spirit not as something that took place only in our past, but as something that we need permanently going forward.

Pentecostal and charismatic Christians are known to say, "I received the baptism by the Holy Spirit, with the evidence of speaking in tongues, X number of years ago." Conservatives readily state, "I was baptized by the Holy Spirit into the Body of Christ when I first believed." Both groups are right as far as the "biblicality" of their experiences. But both describe it as something in the past, when in the Scriptures it is given to propel us into the future.

This is evident in Acts 1:8, where Jesus stated that the power emanating from this type of baptism is to be used for being His witnesses (discipling) in Jerusalem (a city), Judea (a region), Samaria (a nation) and the rest of the nations. It is true that when first received, this baptism is for personal edification, but that is not meant to be "it." The *main* reason is to have power for discipling cities and nations.

This split between Pentecostals/charismatics and cessationists is most unfortunate, and its root is in the not-too-distant past. It goes back to a misdirection involving the printing of a certain edition of the Bible, similar to what happened with the King James Version. In 1906, the Azusa Street Revival brought an awareness of the power and gifts of the Holy Spirit and launched the missionary movement mentioned in chapter 3. A few years later, in 1909, the *Scofield Reference Bible* was published with teaching notes on dispensationalism and cessationism; that is, that the miraculous gifts and manifestations of the Spirit had ceased with the end of the apostolic age.

Those in the newly birthed Pentecostal movement were very skeptical of seminaries at the time, because seminaries were opposed to the manifestations of the Spirit. Since there was little literature produced by Pentecostal authors at the time, the movement ended up getting much of its general theology from the Scofield notes. This created a bipolar doctrinal approach since the newly minted Pentecostals learned their theology from a cessationist while practicing the gifts of the Spirit that Scofield taught had ceased. On the other hand, the conservative camp used Scofield dispensationalism to justify their anti-Pentecostal position.

This is why it has been suggested that Pentecostal theology is Scofield theology with one chapter added on how to speak in tongues, emphasizing the need for the Holy Spirit. And conservative theology is Scofield theology with ten chapters on why we *should not* be speaking in tongues, but instead should be stressing the absolute sufficiency of the Word.

This doctrinal split should no longer divide us. The power of the Word is in reality the work of the Spirit, the only One who convinces and leads us into all truth. The power of the Spirit is equally essential, and both camps need the strength that the other brings to the mix, because we all need the baptism of the Holy Spirit, as described in the Word, to become like Jesus, who has only one Body. Furthermore, it is the Holy Spirit who is charged with teaching us the Word and reminding us of all that Jesus taught (see John 14:26; 16:13–14). For the first three centuries the Ekklesia got the Word from the Holy Spirit directly since the New Testament was not compiled until AD 321, and even then, it was not available in the language of the people but in either Greek or Latin, a limitation made greater by the fact that the majority of the people were not able to read or write. Today we are most blessed to have easy access to the written Word, a privilege not available to Christians until the Bible societies were established, of which the British Bible Society was the pacesetter, but not until 1804! This access is the reason for the revivals that have swept the world since then. Nevertheless, it is necessary to remind ourselves that without the power of the Spirit, the written Word is severely reduced in its effectiveness, hence the absolute necessity of being Spirit led, both in our study and practice of the written Word.

Quite candidly, I dare to suggest that by allowing this unscriptural division between the written Word and the confirming manifestations of the Spirit, we have succumbed to a "less excellent way" where faulty positions cause the center to cave in. Taken to an extreme, either we observe manifestations that are not rooted in the Word, or we hear the written Word preached without any confirming signs by the Spirit. The former leaves us stranded in *emotion-land*, and the latter in *intellect-land*. We should never dichotomize those two, because as God's creatures we have both a brain and a heart. We must see the Ekklesia as a Body made up of different members that, "being fitted and held together by what *every joint supplies*, according to the proper working of each individual part, *causes the growth of the body* for the building up of itself in love" (Ephesians 4:16, emphasis added).

> *By allowing this unscriptural division between the Word and the confirming manifestations of the Spirit, we have succumbed to a "less excellent way."*

The way Peter officiated on Pentecost Day in regard to how both water baptism and Holy Spirit baptism must operate in tandem should be the norm, and not the exception. When the people heard Peter's message, "they were pierced to the heart, and said to Peter and the rest of the apostles, 'Brethren, what shall we do?'" (Acts 2:37).

Peter's reply presents both water baptism and Holy Spirit baptism as an indivisible unit: "Repent, and each of you *be baptized* in the name of Jesus Christ for the forgiveness of your sins; *and you will receive the gift of the Holy Spirit*" (Acts 2:38, emphasis added). As a response to the preaching of the Word, water and Holy Spirit baptisms should be considered inseparable!

The Symbiotic Connection

The reason we may not see this symbiotic connection between water baptism and baptism in the Holy Spirit is because we do not follow a well-documented New Testament *standard* practice: baptizing converts as soon as they believe in Jesus. The thirteen instances of water baptism recorded in the book of Acts all happened with no waiting period (see Acts 8:12, 13, 36, 38; 9:18; 10:47, 48; 11:16; 16:15, 33; 18:8; 19:5; 22:16). In this regard, Ananias instructed Paul in no uncertain terms: "*Now why do you delay?* Get up and be baptized, and wash away your sins, calling on His name" (Acts 22:16, emphasis added).

Today, generally speaking, water baptism requires that the candidates undergo extensive preparation before being deemed "ready." In the New Testament there is no precedent for such a wait. Why was the New Testament Ekklesia able to baptize new converts right away and end up with stronger members? Because water baptism was indelibly connected to a Holy Spirit power encounter in the context of a salvation experience. Conversion was the result of divine intervention by which the new believer was *literally* transferred from the domain of Satan to the Kingdom of God (see Acts 26:18). Such a transition was certified by the baptism of the Holy Spirit that incorporated and sealed them into the Body of Christ, the Church—the Ekklesia as we call it here (see Ephesians 4:30).

Such a power encounter by the Spirit of God convinces and convicts, causing the sinner to respond by publicly laying down his or her life, as symbolized by water baptism. This laying down is the prerequisite to new life in the Spirit, but of itself reflects our death, not our resurrected life in (the risen) Christ. Water baptism relates more to our death to the old than to the infusion of new life that is imparted by the baptism of the Holy Spirit. That is why both must be seen as interconnected and working in tandem.

A Precedent Worth Studying

In a precedent worth studying, Ananias outlines the same steps for Paul in Acts 9:

> "Brother Saul, the Lord Jesus, who appeared to you on the road by which you were coming, has sent me so that you may regain your sight and be filled with the Holy Spirit." And immediately there fell from his eyes something like scales, and he regained his sight, and he got up and was baptized.
>
> Acts 9:17–18

Note the reference to water baptism and baptism in the Holy Spirit working in tandem. It is also important to highlight that "immediately he [Paul] began to proclaim Jesus in the synagogues, saying, 'He is the Son of God'" (Acts 9:20). There was no waiting period after water baptism. Paul began to minister right away, and the implication is that such was the result of being filled with the Holy Spirit right after his conversion. Why is it that today, new believers (generally speaking) are not able, or perhaps are not expected, to follow this path, since it is so patent in the Scriptures?

I respectfully suggest that this may have to do with the practice of an intermediate baptism between John's baptism and the baptism in the Holy Spirit. It is mentioned in the book of Acts and is described as being baptized *simply* in the name of Jesus. We will look at this more closely, but it was the adverb *simply* that caught my attention when I was researching this subject (see Acts 8:16). Please bear with me, and keep in mind that I am candidly sharing my notes on a journey that is taking us into new territory. Whether you agree with what I am about to share or not, it definitely will challenge you.

We know that Jesus, through His disciples, baptized in water, as John did (see John 3:22; 4:1). It was not the baptism with the Holy Spirit, however, as Jesus made clear in John 7:38–39. The baptism His disciples administered in the gospels was a baptism to acknowledge Him as the Messiah, which was also the baptism Philip used when many Samaritans who had believed were "simply baptized in Jesus' name" without receiving the baptism of the Holy Spirit (see Acts 8:4–16). Those Samaritans had seen and experienced signs and wonders similar to those who previously had believed before His atoning death that Jesus was the Messiah (see John 4:40–42; 9:38). But it took the subsequent remedial visit by Peter and John for them to experience the baptism of the Holy Spirit.

It is fascinating how the word and the Spirit are mentioned as mutually complementary in the account of their visit: "Now when the apostles in Jerusalem heard that Samaria had received the *word* of God, they sent them Peter and John, who came down and prayed for them that they might receive the *Holy Spirit*" (Acts 8:14–15, emphasis added).

Evidently, the baptism in the Holy Spirit was the proof, the litmus test and the evidence of salvation. We see it also in the case of Cornelius. Peter at first was skeptical, even antagonistic, about being under a Gentile roof. When the Holy Spirit fell upon those listening to the word he was preaching, he and his Jewish associates concluded, "Surely no one can refuse the water for these to be baptized who have received the Holy Spirit just as we did, can he?" (Acts 10:47).

After Pentecost, the Ekklesia practiced water baptism in the name of Jesus, *but with the addition of—or working in tandem with—baptism in the Holy Spirit.* If individual water baptisms were done to the exclusion of baptism in the Holy Spirit, the situation required remedial action such as the one undertaken by Peter and John in Samaria. If the Church today were to recover this "lost" dimension of these baptisms working in tandem, the *convinced* would become the *converted.* (We will talk more about that in a moment.)

Later on, Paul made a confirming statement to the Corinthians when he described his ministry:

> For I determined to know nothing among you except Jesus Christ, and Him crucified . . . and my message and my preaching were not in persuasive words of wisdom, but in *demonstration of the Spirit and of power*, so that your faith would not rest on the wisdom of men, but on the power of God.
>
> 1 Corinthians 2:2, 4–5, emphasis added

Power versus Wisdom

Paul stated that the sum of his message was Christ crucified. Christ and the cross constitute the heart of the Gospel. But is that all he preached? No, but that was the foundation for *everything else* he taught afterward. In this same epistle, he explains how this plays out: "but we preach Christ crucified . . . Christ the *power* of God and the *wisdom* of God" (1 Corinthians 1:23–24, emphasis added).

The key is found in the words *power* and *wisdom*, and the order in which they are listed. The sequence in which words are presented in the

Bible is as essential as the order of the factors in an algebraic equation. Such order cannot be altered without altering the result. New converts in the New Testament Ekklesia experienced first God's *power* to set them free from the domain of Satan and baptize them in the Holy Spirit, and then that power gave them access to His *wisdom* to become progressively Christlike. The first is an event, while the second is a process.

Today, we seem to lead not so much with power but with wisdom, which in many cases is not so much wisdom as it is human knowledge or human doctrine. And in the worst cases, it is nothing more than a hollow, "feel good" motivational talk. This leads people to have a positive opinion about Jesus, but not a life-changing conviction. An opinion is what we think about something and is subject to revision. A conviction is what determines our behavior. The requirement that converts must attain "wisdom" before they are deemed ready to be baptized may account for the longer wait for baptism nowadays.

> *Today, we seem to lead not so much with power but with wisdom. . . . This leads people to have a positive opinion about Jesus, but not a life-changing conviction.*

It does not appear that the early Church had such a waiting period, because in the New Testament the gateway to salvation was consistently a power encounter, like in the people movements reported by missionaries in the last century, or what fuels the explosive church growth in the developing nations today. Power encounters cause sinners to turn from darkness to light, and from the domain of Satan to the Kingdom of God. Lacking the vast religious infrastructure we have in the West, they are immediately introduced to the Holy Spirit and His power so that when they return to their homes and jobs, they do it fully persuaded that greater is He who is now in them than the one who is in the world. And they expect the Holy Spirit to lead them because, as Jesus said, He is "the Helper, the Holy Spirit, whom the Father will send in My name, He will teach you all things, and bring to your remembrance all that I said to you" (John 14:26).

It causes me to wonder if perhaps many of those who get baptized and lack spiritual power are not in the same boat as the Samaritans before Peter and John laid hands on them to receive the baptism of the Holy Spirit. They believe that Jesus is the Messiah who by His death paid the price for their sins. But they have not yet experienced the "much more" that His life is capable of giving us: "For if while we were enemies we were reconciled to God through the death of His Son, *much more*, having been reconciled, we shall be saved *by His life*" (Romans 5:10, emphasis added). The context for the salvation referenced here is having power to exult in tribulations. This introduces the new believer to a continuum of perseverance, proven character and hope:

> We also exult in our tribulations, knowing that tribulation brings about perseverance; and perseverance, proven character; and proven character, hope; and hope does not disappoint, because the love of God has been poured out within our hearts through the Holy Spirit who was given to us.
>
> Romans 5:3–5

Paul stated as much about the indispensable need for power when he wrote in 1 Corinthians 2:4 that his preaching was "in demonstration of the Spirit and of power," a dynamic we also see when we read in Hebrews 2:3–4 that the word that was spoken "was confirmed to us by those who heard, God also testifying with them, both by signs and wonders and by various miracles and by gifts of the Holy Spirit according to His own will."

Convinced versus Converted

I respectfully submit that the reason we do not baptize new believers right away may stem from our bent toward informing prospective believers about the Gospel without the *power* component Paul referred to as the entry point. Or if they do get to believe in Jesus, and even if they are baptized in water, they have not been baptized by the Holy Spirit with power.

121

Rather than leading new believers to come into contact with the power of the cross and the resurrection in a supernatural way, we inform them about such power and get them on a journey to find it. As a result, they end up more *convinced* than *converted*. Baptizing them in such a state—without them having experienced the "power of the Holy Spirit"—may qualify them as members of a local fellowship, but they will not be transformational members of His Ekklesia.

> *Baptizing them in such a state . . . may qualify them as members of a local fellowship, but they will not be transformational members of His Ekklesia.*

When Peter had to report his unusual experience at Cornelius' house to a skeptical Jewish audience in Jerusalem, he won them over by explaining it this way: "As I began to speak, the Holy Spirit fell upon them just as He did upon us at the beginning" (Acts 11:15). It was the power of the Holy Spirit that gave credence to Peter's words, first at Cornelius' house and then in Jerusalem.

The water baptism of new believers in Jesus' name covers fundamental aspects of our personal experience of faith: It is a public witness and a sign of obedience. It testifies to others of our spiritual conversion, showing in a symbolic way what it means to be united by faith to the death and burial of Christ, and through His resurrection to newness of life evidenced by the baptism of the Holy Spirit. Water baptism mirrors in the visible realm what it means to be immersed in the Holy Spirit in the invisible one.

How does that relate to the baptism of nations? Well, turn the page!

10

A New Understanding of Baptizing Nations

From Dipping to Dripping

If the Great Commission in Matthew 28:18–20 is about discipling nations, then it is also about "baptizing" nations. How are we to go about that? Enter a captivating study of the word *baptizontes* and the secret to its meaning that comes straight from a pickle jar.

Discipling a nation is similar to discipling individuals. It involves bringing the Kingdom of God to a nation's doorstep so it will have an opportunity to enter in. That is why the Scriptures present the Kingdom as being like leaven. When leaven is inserted into dough, the dough does not rise immediately. Rather, the leaven sets in motion a process that in due time produces the change, once the leaven has permeated the dough. This metaphor also illustrates how to baptize a nation, as we will see from a study of the word *baptizing (baptizontes)*, and more specifically, the two Greek words from which this participle is derived.

First, we need to realize that the English term *baptize* is a transliteration. Bible translators had access to words for dipping or dyeing, but none that expressed satisfactorily the much broader meaning of the Greek word *baptizo*. This was an issue for Jerome when he produced the Latin Vulgate version of the Bible. Lacking one word in Latin to render "dip and submerge in tandem," he came up with a transliteration, *baptize*, that regrettably is inadequate in expressing the full idea, because the meaning of *baptizo* is broader than a ritual washing. Unfortunately, from there the word *baptize* passed into other languages with this diluted meaning.

Baptizontes is the participle form of *baptizo*,[1] a word that means "to submerge (as in a sunken vessel)." *Baptizo* was used to describe a process that resulted in a permanent change of state or condition. It in turn derives from *bapto*,[2] which primarily means "to dip, to immerse."

When the word *baptizo* appears in the New Testament, it is generally followed by one of three prepositions—all of them indicating an influence that alters a previous condition:

eis—communicates movement or direction of entry, indicates that something goes in, but does not come out

epi—meaning "on or overlapping," indicates to be covered; something resting on something else

en—signifies "by" or "with." In this case, the subject becomes the passive recipient of the baptism; in the case under discussion, it is generally applied to the Holy Spirit as the agent.

The point here is that the Greek words *bapto* and *baptizo* are complementary concepts that need to be combined in order for us to grasp the full scope of the word *baptizonte*.

Lessons from the Practice of Pickling

I was greatly blessed in this discovery journey by the privilege Ruth and I had of spending personal time with Loren Cunningham, the legendary founder and leader of Youth with a Mission (YWAM), while we were ministering in Amsterdam. We felt immensely honored to sit across from someone whom God is using to accomplish so much, yet who still displays genuine and effervescent humility and wisdom.

While we were together, I ran by Loren my notes on the Ekklesia, and he greatly encouraged me about them. When it came to the issue of baptizing nations, I was pleasantly surprised that Loren had also been on the same journey of discovery and pointed me to a most clarifying illustration concerning a Greek poet that, interestingly enough, my colleague Roberto Beretta also found in his research.

> The clearest example that shows the meaning of baptizo is a text from the Greek poet and physician Nicander, who lived about 200 B.C. It is a recipe for making pickles and is helpful because it uses both words. Nicander says that in order to make a pickle, the vegetable should first be 'dipped' (bapto) into boiling water and then 'baptised' (baptizo) [submerged] in the vinegar solution. Both verbs concern the immersing of vegetables in a solution. But the first is temporary [bapto]. The second, the act of baptising the vegetable, produces a permanent change [baptizo].[3]

The dipping of the cucumber in hot water softens its skin, making it receptive to the vinegar into which it is submerged later. Without the former dip, the unsoftened skin would prevent or delay its transformation into a pickle. This is why in the case of an individual, the initial power encounter (*bapto*) by the Holy Spirit must be followed by a permanent submersion (*baptizo*) in the Word (the teachings of Jesus). The same is true for nations. I wonder if the divisions we see today in the Body of Christ on the subject of the Holy Spirit are not caused by antagonistic schools of thought focusing primarily on one of these aspects at the expense of the other. This, in turn, prevents us from understanding how to disciple nations.

Generally speaking, this may account for why non-Pentecostals are less prone to believe in supernatural manifestations, since the skin of their soul may not have been softened initially by a power encounter, but more by a cerebral approach to the Gospel. And it may account for why Pentecostals seem to be in recurring need of "touches from God" to rekindle what the submersion in God's Word is designed to produce. Both approaches are valid when integrated, like two sides of the same coin. But they are not valid as antagonistic approaches to each other; hence the need for the unity of faith that is required to protect the Ekklesia from being tossed by the winds of doctrine (see Ephesians 4:13–14). This is just a thought, albeit a provoking one, aimed at complementing the point I made in the previous chapter about the need for finding "a more excellent way" when it comes to the baptism of the Holy Spirit.

Baptizing a Nation Is a Process

Allow me to linger on this insight regarding baptism, because it is essential for a proper understanding of the Great Commission's text.

What I want to point out is this: In the case of a believer, it is the baptism of the Spirit that produces a change of status by simultaneously initiating and overseeing a process of transformation based on applying the teachings of Christ to one's life. It is the same process when it comes to a nation. The new status can be achieved through the *means* of baptism (*baptizo*), by which a nation is put under a transforming power (agent) that changes its character or condition on a permanent basis.

The baptism of nations is a process and not a one-time event.

When we extrapolate this to the command to baptize nations, *baptizing* them cannot mean the actual dipping or spraying with water, because the baptism of nations is a process and not a one-time event. Also, it means connecting the nations to a transforming agent—the teachings of Jesus (as we will soon see).

The "pickling" (*baptizontes*) of our own heart, as individual believers, is a process of submersion in the Word that becomes complete over time. In the same way, when the Kingdom of God infuses a nation, a similar process for societal transformation is set in motion.

There is also an additional dimension that has to do with ownership. The word *onoma* in the Greek text means "name, authority or character." Thus, baptizing the nations "in the name (*onoma*) of the Father, the Son and the Holy Spirit" means bringing them under the authority or character of the Triune God, introducing a process of permanent change as a result of being exposed to (and submerged in) the teachings of Christ. This constitutes a foretaste of the final establishment of God's Kingdom.

According to W. E. Vine's *New Testament Word Pictures*, the phrase "baptizing them into the name" indicates that whoever (or whatever) was baptized now becomes closely linked to, or becomes the property of, the one in whose name he was baptized.[4]

What Goes In Does Not Come Out

Obviously, it is impossible to dip, sprinkle or spray water on an entire nation, and besides, there is no mention of water or ritual washings in Matthew 28:19–20. In fact, this passage uses the first preposition I mentioned above, *eis*, which indicates that something *went in to stay in permanently*. That eliminates water as the agent for the baptism of nations. To identify the agent, we must focus on the immediate context of the passage. When we do that, we are led to conclude that the substance into which the nations are to be submerged is the "teachings of Jesus."

The key is to realize that the passage is referring to a process, not an event, the goal of which is the discipling of nations. In our "going along the way" (a process), we are to make learners or disciples of nations by baptizing (*baptizontes*) them (a process). This begins with an initial dip (*bapto*) "in the name (*onoma*) of the Father, Son and Holy Spirit." (We will look at examples of that in the next chapter.) Then it "submerges" them (*baptizo*) in teachings (a process) whose standard of success is nations observing what Jesus had commanded. In essence, this is about the transformation of those nations.

In Hebrews 8 and 9, the Old Testament rituals are described as shadows or types of things to be fulfilled in Christ under a New Covenant. Moreover, Scripture states that the ceremonial requirements of the Old Testament have been abolished and replaced by a better covenant (see 2 Corinthians 3; Galatians 4; Hebrews 8). Through the baptism of the Holy Spirit into the Body of Christ, we are placed in a new position (positional holiness) where instantly God sees us as saints (set aside), adopted children and spiritually clean. But at the same time, it starts a process (sanctification) by which we are progressively molded into the image of His Son.

Sanctification as a process is somewhat like a contract in which the Spirit is a down payment in guarantee of future performance. This concept allows us to see that in Matthew 28:19–20 all the elements mentioned above involve a process. A nation—beginning with a city or any part of that nation—is first exposed to and impacted by the Spirit, usually through an eye-opening miracle or power encounter that validates with righteous deeds the proclamation of the message, as we discussed in chapter 5. The nation is then progressively submerged in the teachings of Jesus (see 2 Corinthians 1:22; 5:5; Ephesians 1:14).

"Baptism" on the Border in Hong Kong

A remarkable model of a transformation school started in 2010 at Ling Ying Public Primary School, on the border between Hong Kong and China. Three leaders dedicated the school to the Lord—Vincent Chu, the school principal; Anthony To, the school superintendent; and Hong Kong Transform Our World Network leader, Barbara Chan, who eventually was asked to join the school board. That was the *bapto* that began the *baptizo* process, and it resulted in the culture of the school being transformed. Teachers were taught the lifestyle of blessing and positive encouragement, which had a powerful impact on the students, many of whom came from across the border in China. Soon after the dedication, the government granted the school HK$35 million to build sixteen more classrooms.

From then on, miracles began to happen that showed that a transformation process was in place. Students from underprivileged families began to overcome the four aspects of poverty—spiritual, relational, motivational and material—to become students who excelled, many of them winning prizes at citywide competitions. The improved spiritual climate that provided such a favorable learning environment was so notable that in 2013, the Hong Kong secretary for education presented the school with the Hong Kong Award for the Most Outstanding Caring Campus.

Soon another transformational school board member, Eunice Lee, was invited to assist with infusing Kingdom values into the culture of the school, another step forward in the baptismal process. Many students came to know the Lord through teachers who ministered to them with love and prayer evangelism. The standard of English language taught at the school was so excellent that their teachers were invited by the Education Authority to give workshops on how to teach English for outstanding results. This is unheard of for a primary school in a place like this.

With prayer, the excellent work of the principal and superintendent, and the support of the Ekklesia members on the school board, the school is being continuously discipled (aka baptized) in the transformation process. It has become a showcase for Kingdom educational values, which are now impacting the community as well.

All this leads us to a concluding question: Who does the baptizing of the nations? The Ekklesia—which consists of believers like you and me. When and where do we do it? As we "go on our way," just as Barbara Chan, Michael Brown, King Flores, Poncho Murguía and Lydia, the businesswoman in Acts 16:14–15, have done. They opened the door of their city and nation through the proclamation of the Gospel of the Kingdom by deeds and actions (*bapto*) that set in motion a process of "submerging" them (*baptizo*), which has as its outcome putting the nations on course toward being discipled. In the coming chapter, I want to take you again to Ciudad Juárez through this new intellectual grid to get a clearer view of this amazing process in motion.

11

A Fuller Understanding
of *How* to Baptize a Nation

From the Sacrament to Societal Transformation

"Baptizing" a city or nation is a process that begins with
an event and continues by progressively saturating it with
the teachings of Jesus to improve its status. This is what
the ongoing scenario in Ciudad Juárez, Mexico, illustrates
most graphically.

The process of baptizing a nation according to Matthew 28:19 begins
with claiming it in the name of the Father, the Son and the Holy Spirit,
and then submerging it in the teachings of Jesus. This Trinitarian formula shows *for whom* it is being claimed, and the teachings of Jesus
define *into what* the nation is being immersed to progressively change
its condition—like the example in the previous chapter of the cucumber
that becomes a pickle after being submerged in vinegar.

How to baptize a nation will be easier to visualize if I illustrate it with a
contemporary example. Before we go into that story, however, let's pause
for a moment to reiterate that the "substance" (medium) into which a
nation—or a city—must be immersed is the teachings of Jesus. Doing

that requires much more than just academic lessons. Actually, it calls for *training*, which is the action of teaching someone a *new* skill or type of behavior.[1] Jesus was very specific about this: "teaching them [the nations] *to observe* all that I commanded you" (Matthew 28:20, emphasis added). The sheer volume of Jesus' teaching makes it obvious that this is most definitely a process (see John 21:25). Baptism involves both an event and a process, just as marriage is more than just the ring or the wedding ceremony.

As we know, the teachings of Jesus go counter to the unrighteousness that the devil imposes as normative in society. Once evil or unrighteousness is institutionalized, it becomes part of the culture, and culture is the prism through which life is lived and processed. Culture is the sum of ideas, customs and social behavior of a particular people or society.[2]

When wrong is seen as right, it becomes a systemic problem in society because at that moment, wrong (unrighteousness) is accepted as part of the culture, and people will say, "If everybody does it, it must not be that bad." Or if it is acknowledged as bad, they will justify it by stating, "Nothing can be done about it because it's part of the system." This is why baptizing a city or nation by progressively immersing it in the teachings of Jesus is absolutely necessary to dislodge and uproot the evil that is entrenched in the culture.

Thriving without Bribing

Now to the illustration. In Ciudad Juárez, as in so much of the world, corruption was intrinsic to the system, and as such it permeated everyday life. It was sanctioned as part of the culture by the popular maxim "El que no tranza no avanza," which in English translates "If you don't bribe, you won't thrive." But this city is now undergoing a Matthew 28 baptismal process that began when Poncho Murguía and his colleague from our Transform Our World Network, Brian Burton, claimed it in the name of the Father, the Son and the Holy Spirit. They courageously did this by going to the top of a hill overlooking the city at the height of the murder rampage, when more blood was being spilled than at any other time.

The city was *bapto*-ed on the day that it was claimed and adopted by Poncho and Brian. Next, it had to be *baptizo*-ed (immersed) in the teachings of Jesus to produce a permanent change of condition—in this case to revert the corrupted culture. To that end, the city had to be taught how to observe the teachings, or in other words, taught how to apply them.

As part of that process, Poncho brought up the need to uproot corruption. He did not get any pushback about that from the officials who had already invited Jesus into the government and into their lives. They knew *what* the problem was, but they did not know *how* to solve it. Poncho and his associates decided first to explain the *why*, because once the *why* is figured out, the *how* is easily determined. Why should corruption be uprooted? Because it is wrong, and what is wrong is also destructive. Corruption is not free. It definitely costs money, but worse yet, it also costs peace of mind and the self-respect of the parties involved, plus the cost to society as a whole. It is definitely not a good deal.

Instead of tackling head on the deeply ingrained "If you don't bribe, you won't thrive" culture with a religious-sounding slogan, the Ekklesia in Ciudad Juárez chose to co-opt it with something more appealing to turn it around. That is how they came up with "Thrive without Bribes." Because everybody wants to succeed (thrive), the new slogan proposed a positive and far more appealing alternative to the old one that was promising success by doing something wrong. Along with the new slogan came a twelve-lesson coaching program based on biblical principles that were articulated in secular language.

The mayor endorsed this new approach and instructed all municipal employees to go through the training. The presidents of the various chambers of commerce also bought in. So did the media as TV stations, radio stations and newspapers began to report on it. The initial interest was capitalized on in a public meeting to present the plan—a gathering attended by close to seven hundred influencers. Poncho and his team (the Ekklesia in Ciudad Juárez) made the presentation, which consisted of introducing the new concept, along with the training program to implement it. They invited participants to sign a pledge renouncing corruption. As part of the pledge, the participants agreed to wear a wristband with the slogan "Thrive without Bribes" on it and take the program to those in their sphere of influence.

I had the privilege of being present at that meeting to witness the most dramatic public *"bapto-baptizo"* combination that I have ever seen. It was like an evangelistic meeting, but without religiosity, with the Kingdom of God (righteousness, peace and joy) on full display. Key to its success was the fact that what was presented, albeit biblical, was expressed in secular language that this particular audience was able to understand. After explaining (preaching) the program (sermon), the people (sinners) were asked (invited) to make a choice (decision) to sign a pledge (commitment) that they were agreeing (confession) to be trained (discipled) to thrive without bribes (observe the teachings) and wear a wristband publicly testifying to their decision (baptism). It was an Ekklesia meeting!

> *I witnessed the most dramatic public "bapto-baptizo" combination that I have ever seen. It was like an evangelistic meeting, but without religiosity.*

The first ones to "come forward" to sign the pledge were the presidents of the various chambers of commerce. This set in motion a chain reaction that, in a matter of minutes, resulted in the entire assembly coming to the "altar" to do the same. The local media was covering the event, and a popular anchorwoman interviewed me. She was visibly touched by what she "felt" (the Holy Spirit) as she witnessed what she called "this unusual, but much-needed" event.

Since then, most city employees have been trained in *Avanza sin Tranza*, and a process has been set in motion to train the various chambers of commerce. Today, in City Hall there are official signs warning the public that bribes will not be accepted, and if offered, they will be reported and those offering them will be prosecuted.[3] And this movement is spreading quickly to other cities in Mexico.

Passing the Test in the Schools

A subsequent development in the form of a *bapto* event happened in public education. In Greater Ciudad Juárez there are close to a thousand schools. Poncho and his team requested permission from the Department of Education to introduce transformation in ten schools, from where they would then scale it to the other schools. The state sub-secretary of education told them, "I will only give you one."

Poncho asked, "Why only one?"

She replied, "Try it in the worst of the worst, and if you can make a difference there, I will consider giving you others. But let me warn you, every NGO [non-governmental organization] you can think of has already been to this place, and nothing has changed."

Basically, she was saying, "Prepare to fail."

According to Poncho, what made this school so extremely challenging was that the students "bought" their passing grades one of two ways. Students whose fathers were involved in criminal activities—drug dealing, extortion, etc.—would make an appointment with a teacher to "discuss" their child's grades. A dad would casually put his gun on the teacher's desk at the beginning of an unusual parent-teacher meeting and ask matter-of-factly, "How is my kid doing?"

I imagine that the teacher would be compelled to say something like, "Oh, he's a genius! His grades couldn't be any better," or "What grade would you like him to have?"

Not all the kids had fathers with the criminal muscle to do that for them, but they were paying money to get the same advantages some other way. How did those students get the money? Tragically, through the most perverted manifestation of the Gates of Hades in a high school anyone can imagine. They set up an "oral sex assembly line" on campus. They convinced (or coerced) young girl students to sign up and lined them up in adjacent closets—like a local version of the Amsterdam red-light district. The student "clients" would stand in line, pay a fee (which was shared with the girls performing those hideous and degrading acts), be serviced and move on.

Discipline had also broken down completely since teachers were bullied regularly, or bribed and extorted. If they did not cooperate, they were physically hurt. On top of that, gangs were extracting protection money from students. No wonder the school had become absolutely impossible to manage.

After securing adequate intercession, the Ekklesia approached these Gates of Hades with the keys of the Kingdom "to bind and to release." They arranged with the school district to transport the three thousand students to a nearby arena for a schoolwide assembly. The featured speaker was a Christian who in his youth had been so cruelly bullied, abused and betrayed by friends, schoolmates and even teachers that he tried to commit suicide more than once. Drug dealers had murdered his dad when he was very young, a tragedy that rendered him even more vulnerable. Going to school was hellish for him, to put it mildly.

This man shared his compelling story with the assembled students, connecting at the level of their pain and frustration. They began to see in him someone who knew what they were going through. Once he had established enough credibility and empathy, he told the students that if they did not have love and support at home, the school was the next best place to get it since teachers could be substitute parents. He said that this was why the devil had created such an ugly conflict between students and teachers—a gap made worse every time they abused or bullied a teacher. He then challenged them to make a decision to bridge that gap for their own good.

He climaxed his presentation by explaining to the students that the stadium lights would be turned off to give them a moment of privacy to make such a decision. Flowing powerfully in the anointing of the Holy Spirit, he gently said, "If you have hurt, bullied or disrespected a teacher, ask God for forgiveness so you can get a clean slate."

While the lights were off, all the teachers were directed to form a circle on the floor of the arena. When the lights came back on, the speaker told the audience, "If you have asked forgiveness for hurting a teacher, I want you to come down and embrace that teacher, or teachers."

Poncho and his team were in fervent prayer. If the Ekklesia was going to prevail over the Gates of Hades, this was the moment for a breakthrough. Also, the sub-secretary of education was there, watching and taking notes. The Word had been preached boldly. Would God now confirm it with some sort of sign or wonder?

The next moments felt like an eternity. No one moved at first. Suddenly, a young girl stood and made her way down from the bleachers, visibly moved, with tears rolling down her cheeks. She made a beeline for one of the teachers. When she got in front of her, she asked for forgiveness. The teacher broke down, they embraced and that became the tipping point for what followed next. First a handful, then a group, and finally droves of students made it to the floor to embrace the teachers. Tears rolling down the students' cheeks would merge with the tears on the teachers' faces. Eventually, over half of the students were on the floor, with groups of twenty or thirty forming hubs around each of the teachers. It was a revival meeting!

The next moments felt like an eternity since no one moved at first. Suddenly, a young girl came down from the bleachers.

The sub-secretary of education ran up to Poncho, and at first he did not recognize her because her makeup and mascara had been smeared by the torrent of tears flowing out of her eyes. She said with visible emotion, "This is what we need. This is what all our schools need. I'm going to call my supervisor and give him my recommendation to open the doors to you!"

Batting a Thousand

Poncho did not get the ten schools he originally wanted. He got an open door to all one thousand instead! Why? Why not! When the Gospel of the Kingdom (righteousness, peace and joy) is proclaimed with deeds and signs and wonders (power) to validate the proclamation, everyone forces his way into it.

This set the stage for developing a training course on values for the students, similar to the ones for businesses. Once in place, this course will constitute a *baptizo* (submersion) because it is based on the teachings of Jesus. It will serve as the baptismal agent into which to submerge the schools.

Cognizant that the command goes beyond teaching, to specify that the learners should observe (obey) Jesus' teachings, Poncho and his team plan to add field exercises to help students internalize the principles they are taught. To that end, these students will be equipped to "minister" to the community by taking care of the elderly, repairing run-down homes, arranging for medical services for the infirm and providing others with food and friendship. When they do such ministry, then the *baptizonte* (process) will be in place.

Ciudad Juárez is experiencing a *baptizo* in its schools, government and business institutions through a process by which the "cucumber" that yesterday was the murder capital of the world is now being progressively submerged in the transforming dye of God's Kingdom so that its status will be changed to the safest city in Mexico.

> *When the Gospel of the Kingdom is proclaimed with deeds and signs and wonders to validate the proclamation, everyone forces his way into it.*

Making the Application

Let's now apply *baptizontes*, the participle that describes the process of baptizing a city or nation, to the various facets of this case study. The initial *bapto* took place when the Ekklesia took control of El CERESO prison (the story reported in chapter 8) and Poncho and Brian, commissioned by the Ekklesia, subsequently went to the mountain to adopt the city.

As a result, the mayor and leading officials also got *bapto*-ed (immersed, as in dipping). Once their eyes were opened to the proximity of the Kingdom of God in their midst, they entered into it. And that got the mayor *baptizo*-ed (submerged) into the teachings of Jesus. Subsequently, *baptizontes* was the acceptance by City Hall and the various chambers of commerce of *Avanza sin Tranza* (Thrive without Bribes) and its twelve-lesson program to teach biblical values (Jesus' teachings) using nonreligious language.

Because the *Avanza sin Tranza* program reflects Jesus' teachings of righteousness, joy and peace, it constitutes the functional equivalent in a biblical sense of the vinegar in Nicander's pickling recipe, which I mentioned in chapter 10. A nation, or a city in this case, is immersed in this "vinegar" to change it permanently by reminding its people of what Jesus taught.

Is it biblical to disciple cities or nations and to baptize them by immersing them in the teachings of Jesus? After this in-depth study of Matthew 28:19–20, with these contemporary examples serving as evidence, we offer as the answer a resounding "Yes!"

12

A Fuller Understanding of the Ekklesia's Social Agenda

From the Pew to the City Square

The first-century Ekklesia introduced a radical and revolutionary social agenda that launched a process that literally changed the world. With the subsequent institutionalization of the Church, however, what was a lifestyle that implemented Jesus' agenda became programs of good deeds that fall short of transforming society.

It is most unfortunate that when the split between liberal and conservative believers took place in the last century, the liberals kept the social agenda and the conservatives kept the Scriptures, generally speaking. This resulted in one stream speaking up for social justice, without an accompanying emphasis on a personal relationship with God through Jesus Christ, and the other stream being very Bible centered, particularly when it comes to the point of being born again, yet being dismissive of the social aspects of the Gospel for fear of the so-called social gospel. These two streams ended up opposing rather than complementing each other.

God's justice is not fully manifested until it becomes social justice, something that is impossible to achieve without God's power. The key is in embracing a position where we are Word-based on ethics and Spirit-empowered on social issues. In fact, the New Testament Ekklesia modeled this very well.

The teachings of Jesus that the first-century Ekklesia modeled constitute what is now known as Christian ethics. No other philosophy has come close to matching it. In fact, the modern world is built on it because Christian values and ethics have no rival in either the secular or the religious arena.

There are four major social evils that the Ekklesia tackled successfully: systemic poverty, slavery, female servitude and the degradation of the family. Let's discuss them in that order.

Both Heavenly Minded and Earthly Good

Jesus' Ekklesia was never meant to be so heavenly minded as to become earthly irrelevant. On the contrary! It is a spiritual entity vested with governmental jurisdiction on earth to change world systems for the better.

We find this in the Lord's Prayer, where we are instructed to pray for the will of God in heaven also to be done on earth (see Matthew 6:10). We know there is no pain or sorrow in heaven, and we use that belief to evangelize. We have no hesitation about extolling valuable and ethereal expressions of the will of God such as peace, joy and forgiveness as the remedy for despair, sadness and guilt. But what about freedom from poverty since there is no poverty in heaven? Why don't we address that in our evangelistic endeavors?

Poverty was a front-and-center priority issue for Jesus. In His first recorded speech, He boldly declared, "The Spirit of the Lord is upon Me, because He anointed me to preach the gospel to the poor" (Luke 4:18). Unfortunately, the words *preach* and *gospel* can easily obscure the real meaning of His message because we associate them with the ethereal. We conclude, or at least we assume, that Jesus came to preach to the poor about heaven, where their earthly misery will come to an end.

But Jesus was *literally* announcing "Good News" to the poor. What would represent good news to the hungry? Food. And to the naked? Clothes. And to the poor? Wealth. Let's keep in mind that He is the Messiah who came to atone for the sins of man, in order to eliminate *all* of sin's consequences.

Why would poverty take center stage in Jesus' message? Because it was the first *tangible* social manifestation of the Gates of Hades on earth after the Fall of man. When God first created the world, poverty did not exist. But once sin entered the world, the ground no longer yielded a harvest abundantly and freely; man would have to trade the sweat of his brow for the fruit of the ground. As a visual reminder of this, God introduced thistles and thorns. Every time Adam and his descendants saw a thorn or a thistle, they were painfully reminded that poverty was the re-

> *Jesus' Ekklesia is the spiritual entity vested with governmental jurisdiction on earth to change world systems for the better.*

sult of their sin and that the only way to mitigate it was to trade the sweat of their brow for the fruit of the land. When Jesus carried the cross through La Via Dolorosa, the marketplace of Jerusalem, however, He wore a crown of thorns on his brow—in essence, His first drops of blood were touching the first emblem of poverty.

Jesus' promise to the poor was an integral part of the Ekklesia's agenda in Jerusalem later, "for there was not a needy person among them" (Acts 4:34). Not even those ranking lowest on the social scale, the widows of the Hellenistic Jews, were left in need (see Acts 6:1–6).

Later on, we see that caring for the poor was among the central requirements for Paul and Barnabas, in order for James, Peter and John (the leaders in Jerusalem) to acknowledge them as fellow apostles. "They only asked us to remember the poor," reported Paul, "the very thing I also was eager to do" (Galatians 2:10). He proved his eagerness in this regard when he reminded the elders in Asia, "In everything I showed you that by working hard in this manner *you must help the weak* and remember the words of the Lord Jesus, that He Himself said, 'It is more blessed to give than to receive'" (Acts 20:35, emphasis added).

The uprooting of worldwide poverty culminates in Revelation 21:24–26 when that majestic parade of saved nations that we have been referring to brings their restored national honor and glory to the New Jerusalem. This continuum from Jesus' hometown in Luke 4 to the New Jerusalem in Revelation 21 shows that the elimination of systemic poverty—which is the consequence of sin and is empowered by the Gates of Hades—was central to the message of both Jesus and the early Church.

Poverty Is More Than Material

When I was researching the issue of poverty for my book *Transformation*, every academic piece I read focused on material poverty, its causes and its possible cures. The futility of this approach is in evidence in Africa, where most nations receive substantial amounts of foreign aid. When foreign aid reaches 18 percent of a country's Gross National Product (GNP),[1] it goes into negative returns, and most African nations are past that marker already. So we end up with the irony that the continent that is the richest in natural resources is the poorest in material wealth because it is drowning in foreign aid.

I asked God to illuminate me through a scripturally based insight on poverty. He led me to a specific section in the Lord's Prayer: "Our Father . . . give us this day our daily bread," and showed me that poverty (as well as wealth) has four dimensions: *spiritual, relational, motivational* and *material*.

Those who don't know that God is their Father are *spiritually* poor.

Those who pray "give *me my* daily bread" are overlooking the fact that the first word in this prayer is not *my* but *our*. They are *relationally* poor.

Those who receive seeds and eat them without setting some aside for planting to help themselves out of poverty are *motivationally* poor.

And obviously, those who don't have enough are *materially* poor.

As I contemplated this, it greatly encouraged me because these four dimensions of poverty/wealth are also present in Jesus' maiden speech.

He announced good news to the poor (material), freedom to the down-trodden (motivational), liberty to the captives (relational) and sight to the blind (which included the spiritual).

I also found these four dimensions in prayer evangelism "a la Luke 10," when Jesus instructed His followers to bless (motivational), fellowship (relational), meet needs (material) and proclaim God's Kingdom (spiritual). So I was not surprised when I discovered them next in the agenda of the first-century Ekklesia. This is a very important point because once again, no other major religion has focused on eliminating systemic poverty, and much less in these four dimensions.

Victory over Poverty

We see victory over systemic poverty achieved in Acts 2:45, where members of the Ekklesia were sharing their wealth "with all, as anyone might have need." In the past, I had assumed that this reference spoke of wealth being distributed to its members during a closed meeting of the Ekklesia. But the following verse specifies that the Ekklesia met every day all over town, "breaking bread from house to house" (verse 46). Here we have a daily gathering centered on a meal that by custom was open to strangers. These definitely were not closed meetings of believers in one location, but public on-going gatherings all over the city that were open to nonbelievers. And this level of generosity granted the Ekklesia "favor with all the people" (verse 47).

> *The Ekklesia in Jerusalem was tackling systemic poverty not only among its members, but in the city as well.*

When we connect *all* and *anyone* in verse 45 to *all the people* two verses later, it becomes evident that the Ekklesia in Jerusalem was tackling systemic poverty not only among its members, but in the city as well. In this new social order, "the Lord was adding to their number day by day those who were being saved" (verse 47).

Being an evangelist, naturally I was captured by the reference that the Lord added daily *those* who were being saved. Notice that the word *those* is a plural pronoun. The lowest plural possible is two, which means that if God were to add that minimum every day, the Ekklesia in any given locality should grow by at least 730 new members every year. And we know from the figures mentioned in the book of Acts that the number of new additions in Jerusalem alone climbed into the thousands in a few weeks. Fascinating! There is a lesson here that the modern Church needs to learn.

What was the key for this extraordinary multiplication? Favors! The key to finding favor with people is to do favors for them, because doing favors generates favor. And to obtain favor with *all* the people, we must do favors for *all*.

No Needy Person among Them

We also see the four dimensions in the next snapshot of life in the Ekklesia:

> And the congregation of those who believed were of one heart [*relational*] and soul [*motivational*]; and not one of them claimed that anything belonging to him was his own, but all things were common property [*material*] to them. And with great power the apostles were giving testimony to the resurrection of the Lord Jesus [*spiritual*], and abundant grace was upon them all. For there was not a needy person among them, for all who were owners of land or houses would sell them and bring the proceeds of the sales.
>
> Acts 4:32–34

This passage describes the process that runs seamlessly through the rest of the New Testament, showing how the Ekklesia fulfilled Jesus' promise of good news to the poor in Luke 4:18. We see in Acts 4 that there was no needy person in their midst. Next, in Acts 6:1–7 we learn that there were no hungry people. In Acts 20:33–35 Paul explains that the way the Ekklesia took care of the needy and emulated Jesus by giving rather than taking was an integral component of what led everyone in Asia to hear the word of the Lord (see Acts 19:10–11).

All of this is fascinating because it shows a consistent commitment to the betterment of society. The Ekklesia did not, however, make eliminating systemic poverty the driver for its mission. Rather, it was the evidence that Jesus Christ was alive in their midst that in turn yielded extraordinary numbers of new converts. This is what Acts 4:33 reveals: "And with great power the apostles were giving testimony to the resurrection of the Lord Jesus, and abundant grace was upon them all."

> *The apostolic witness of the invisible resurrection of Jesus Christ was made credible by the visible transformation in the social arena.*

Notice that this verse is right in the middle of the passage I discussed above, which shows the Ekklesia dealing with the four dimensions of poverty. It intimates that when the apostles proclaimed that Jesus was alive, the response was sizable because abundant grace was poured out. In other words, large numbers of unbelievers came to the realization that Jesus was alive.

This is intriguing because Paul only reported around five hundred people seeing Jesus alive after He came out of the tomb (see 1 Corinthians 15:6). Why, then, did significant numbers believe that He was alive? Because the apostolic witness of the *invisible* resurrection of Jesus Christ was made credible by the *visible* radical transformation in the social arena.[2]

Consumers Turned Producers

The social entrepreneurship of the New Testament Ekklesia went far beyond redistributing material resources. It turned consumers into producers with unequaled effectiveness because of its power and authority in both the material and spiritual realms. We see a clear example of this in Ephesians 4:28: "He who steals must steal no longer; but rather he must labor, performing with his own hands what is good, so that he will have something to share with one who has need."

When we project on a graph what Paul was stating, it looks something like this:

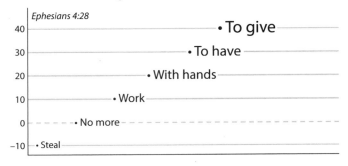

Turning Consumers into Producers

We see that the subject—a new believer who is still struggling with his old ways as a thief—registers in the negative, at -10, by stealing. When he stops stealing because he has entered the Kingdom of God, it places him at 0. At that moment, he is scoring at the same level as a thief locked up by law enforcement would score. But that is the point where the transforming power of the Gospel kicks in. It gives this new believer the spiritual motivation to move up to +10 by working. It also helps him aspire to self-sufficiency by learning a trade with his own hands, moving him up to +20, and it gives him the confidence to succeed, allowing him to score at +30. From there it elevates him to having a desire to be able to help others by sharing with them, a +40. In five moves, the Gospel has turned a consumer into a producer, a taker into a giver. No wonder the Bible states without ambiguity that there was no needy person in the Ekklesia.

This example addresses primarily the material dimension of poverty. Let's now take a look at the relational aspect of poverty more precisely, particularly as it relates to slavery. I have mentioned that the rich brought material and motivational wealth to the mix, whereas the poor contributed faith and relational assets.[3] Later on, Paul exhorted masters and slaves likewise to bridge with agape love the ugly divide imposed on them by society (see Ephesians 6:5–9).

In an era when the ruling classes looked down on labor, Jesus' disciples introduced the revolutionary concept that "the laborer is worthy of his wages" (1 Timothy 5:18). And Paul exhorted slaves who had to do the most demeaning jobs, "Whatever you do, do your work heartily, as for the Lord rather than for men" (Colossians 3:23).

This commitment to bridging the gap between masters and slaves permeated the lifestyle of the Ekklesia to the point that we find the epistle of Philemon was written specifically to reflect and emphasize its importance. Onesimus, a runaway slave whom Paul led to Christ in prison, and his wealthy master, Philemon, who was also Paul's spiritual son and who obviously was unhappy with the escapee, constitute a most illuminating case study on the radical social impact of Jesus and His teachings. The word pictures Paul uses in this epistle to build a case for reconciliation between the two are intended to demonstrate that the most cruel, despicable and revolting social sin, slavery, can be uprooted and eliminated by the power of love in action.

First, Paul presents himself as "also a prisoner [slave] of Christ Jesus" to highlight the redemptive dimension of having one's will subjected to someone else—in this case to the Lord. Next, he introduces Onesimus not as a slave, but as "my child Onesimus, whom I have begotten in my imprisonment." This slave is someone so desirable that Paul tells Philemon, his master, "I wished to keep [him] with me, so that on your behalf he might minister to me." But instead, Paul sends him back to Philemon as if "sending my very heart" (see verses 10–13). The apostle—a free man, and on top of that also a Roman citizen—identifies himself totally and unabashedly with this slave by equating Onesimus with his own heart.

Having personally modeled reconciliation between two opposite classes and social statuses, Paul next proposes something that no other belief system I am aware of has ever done. He asks Philemon to have Onesimus "back forever, no longer as a slave, but more than a slave, *a beloved brother* . . . both in the flesh and in the Lord (verses 15–16).

These examples reveal that the four-dimensional insight into poverty we have defined here holds the key for its elimination, the reason being that it shows how the traditionally poor, who are materially and motivationally deprived, are richer *spiritually* and *relationally* than the traditional rich, because the poor have more faith and friends than the rich do (see James 2:5). On the other hand, the rich are wealthier *materially* and *motivationally*. The brilliance of this discovery is that it shows how these two groups are strong and weak in complementary dimensions. As a result, both groups must interface and cooperate with each other to eliminate systemic poverty. This elevates the traditionally poor to a peerage as far as partnering with the traditionally rich to solve the problem of systemic poverty.

The key for eliminating poverty is to understand that the rich and the poor are strong and weak in complementary dimensions.

In this manner, the Ekklesia introduced a radical principle as a much better alternative to slavery. It was radical because it went head on against the status quo. It was better because it restored dignity to both the slave and the master. As Nelson Mandela articulated so powerfully in his autobiography *Long Walk to Freedom*, his captors were as much slaves as he was because everyone was enslaved to the system. One of his famous quotes captures it most eloquently: "No one is born hating another person because of the color of his skin, or his background, or his religion. People must learn to hate, and as they can learn to hate, they can be taught to love."[4]

The leaven introduced by Jesus' first-century Ekklesia into a society flattened by the evil of slavery caused society eventually to rise to heights of freedom and equality for all men. It was precisely the Ekklesia's focus on social justice that triggered and sustained social change in the Western world and inspired others educated in the West to declare, as Mahatma Gandhi did,

> When I despair, I remember that all through history the way of truth and love have always won. There have been tyrants, and murderers, and for a time they can seem invincible, but in the end they always fall. Think of it . . . always.[5]

The same dynamic was at work in the civil rights movement Martin Luther King Jr. led. In fact, the way King conducted himself and the civil rights movement was similar to the way Paul dealt with Philemon. First, he identified with the oppressed—the African Americans—as one of them. Next, he appealed to the oppressors, mostly the white men in charge of the system, as one with them—a fellow American. His extraordinary speech "I Have a Dream," delivered to the nation at the Lincoln Memorial, is nothing short of the Ekklesia in action. The backbone of his movement was made up of pastors and church members, and the message was nothing less than the pure Gospel. In fact, the vast majority of leaders who flanked him in that history-making assembly were not secular social activists, but pastors and elders in the Ekklesia.

The philosophy of victorious nonviolent protest that these two modern-day social revolutionaries—Nelson Mandela and Martin Luther King Jr.—led is rooted in the Christian ethics introduced by Jesus' Ekklesia.[6] It was also Jesus' teachings, modeled by His Ekklesia when the tide against it was at its highest in the first century, that introduced the ethics necessary for Abraham Lincoln to sign the Emancipation Proclamation in the United States and for William Wilberforce to lead the British Parliament to abolish the slave trade. It is the concept of a righteous God that gave birth to moral absolutes that allow for social justice to triumph over systemic evil and replace it with values and virtues.

The Restoration of Women

The Ekklesia's social agenda was not restricted to tackling systemic poverty and slavery, which would take a long process to eradicate globally. There was a third arena where it introduced faster social change: the social standing of women, which in New Testament times amounted to widespread female servitude. In fact, one of the main reasons Christianity spread so rapidly in the early years was because it restored honor and inner worth to half of the population—women.

The Ekklesia in the New Testament dignified women by teaching that in Christ "there is neither male nor female; for you are all one in

Christ Jesus" (Galatians 3:28). It acted without delay upon that radical and revolutionary principle by placing women in positions of honor and leadership. Priscilla was part of the apostolic team that founded the Ekklesia both in Corinth and in Ephesus (see Acts 18:2–3, 18–19, 26). Paul proudly identified two women as the headwaters of Timothy's faith: his mother and his grandmother. In a letter intended for wide circulation and public reading, Paul praised and identified another woman, Junia, as a fellow apostle (see Romans 16:1–16). It was Lydia's invitation to Paul that opened all of Galatia to the Gospel, and the apostle John wrote his second epistle to a "chosen lady" (2 John 1).

One of the main reasons Christianity spread so rapidly in the early years was because its message restored honor and inner worth to half of the population—women.

As a forerunner to what He expected His Ekklesia to model afterward regarding the trustworthiness of women, Jesus disclosed two of the most powerful truths first to women. He told Martha that He is the resurrection and the life, and He told the Samaritan woman that He is the living water (see John 4:10; 11:25–27).

Once Jesus began to itinerate, His carpentry shop was no longer able to support Him. At that juncture, the gospel record shows that a group of grateful women used their personal resources to support His ministry: "Mary who was called Magdalene, from whom seven demons had gone out, and Joanna the wife of Chuza, Herod's steward, and Susanna, and many others who were contributing to their support out of their private means" (Luke 8:2–3).

Jesus did not write a book or a manual for His followers so that they could learn His teachings. Instead, He modeled His teachings and imparted them to His disciples. His words were far more powerful than ink and paper; they are spirit and life (see John 6:63). In one case, even His silence was able to pierce men's hearts in defense of women. The scribes and Pharisees brought before Him a woman caught in adultery and demanded that He sanction her death, as prescribed by

150

the Law. At first, Jesus crouched down and wrote on the ground, while the religious leaders persisted in their demands for the use of lethal force (see John 8:3–6).

As severe as the woman's sin was, she should not have had to stand accused alone, since it takes two people to dance this particular tango. Jesus' silence was broadcasting a conviction of sin straight into the hearts of the accusers: *Where is the man? Why was he not also brought in? The Law specifies that both of them should be stoned.* But He chose not to demand that the male adulterer also be brought in. Neither did He tell the sanctimonious accusers that they were as guilty as the woman and man caught in adultery. He knew it because He was able to read men's hearts (see Matthew 9:4; Mark 2:8).

Why did Jesus hold His silence? Because He is a reconciler, not a divider. Dividing is what the devil does, and what the Gates of Hades institute by locking people behind the bars of their own shortcomings. Instead, Jesus came "to seek and to save that which was lost" (Luke 19:10). And what was lost is not in one piece or in one pile. It is broken and scattered all over the social landscape. Jesus does not pick the best-looking parts and reject the most damaged ones. He waits until He is able to embrace all the pieces, take them in His arms, place them close to His heart and then fix them.

Was Jesus' silent approach effective? Definitely! Those men, after seeing themselves reflected on the troubled face of the accused woman, must have realized how close they had come, at one time or another, to standing accused themselves. Jesus' silence forever stamped the ugliness of female *and male* adultery in their memory (see John 8:8–11).

Jesus had extraordinary empathy for women tainted by ill repute. His genealogy, listed in the first chapter of Matthew's gospel, covers 42 generations. Only the men's names are provided, except on five occasions when the wives' names are also listed: Tamar, Rahab, Ruth, Bathsheba and Mary. After becoming a widow, Tamar carried the children of her unaware father-in-law—after she was forced to trick him by posing as a prostitute. Rahab was a full-time harlot in Jericho. Ruth was a foreign widow treated as undesirable by the closest male relative of the family, who should have married her. Bathsheba was another man's faithful wife, until David forced her into adultery. Mary was the only virgin, but one who became pregnant outside of marriage (see Genesis 38; Ruth 4; Joshua 2; 6; 2 Samuel 11; Matthew 1:1–16). Jesus definitely knew the power of restoration that made those women icons of virtue, and He was determined to use the situation at hand with the adulterous woman to embed in His disciples' minds what later on would be a central element in the social agenda of His Ekklesia.

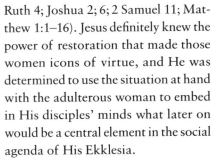

> *On the first day of the Ekklesia, female daughters and female slaves were presented on an equal footing.*

To that effect, after all her accusers had left, He said to the adulterous woman, "Go. From now on sin no more" (John 8:11). What a liberating message overflowing with hope! Rather than dwelling on the past, Jesus covered it with mercy and pointed the woman in the direction of restorative holiness. Sinning no more meant breaking up with her fellow adulterer and repairing her damaged marriage—a difficult, but necessary assignment that calls for gender reconciliation at the deepest level.

Consequently, when Peter preached the first sermon on Pentecost Day, he quoted God Himself, saying,

> And it shall be in the last days . . . that I will pour forth of My Spirit on all mankind [men and women]; *and your sons and your daughters* shall prophesy . . . even on My bondslaves, *both men and women,* I will in those days pour forth of My Spirit and they shall prophesy.
>
> Acts 2:17–18, emphasis added

On the first day of the Ekklesia, female daughters and female slaves were presented *on an equal footing* with sons and male slaves as God's mouthpieces.

This noble treatment of women went counter to the established culture. In fact, the Romans had such a low view of women that men commonly had so-called recreational sex with other men because women were perceived as inherently inferior. Jewish rabbis completely silenced women when they were inside the synagogue. Pagans used women as temple prostitutes. This degradation upstreams to the Fall in the Garden of Eden, where as the result of original sin, God pronounced sentence on Eve and her female descendants: "Your desire will be for your husband, and he will rule over you" (Genesis 3:16). This demotion was punishment for how she had instigated Adam to sin after she knew that what she had just done was wrong (see verse 6).

The way this judgment played out through human history resulted in men treating women as inferior. Even though the original sin happened only once, its consequences became embedded in womankind, something that has to do with the difference between sin and iniquity. I describe sin as an evil act itself and iniquity as its consequences—the deforming mark left on those involved in or touched by it.

Today God will not hold the sins of the parents over the children, because those sins have been forgiven through the atoning death of Jesus Christ. On the other hand, iniquities—the consequence of those sins—transcend generations, as in the examples of slavery and the treatment of women as inferior. Sin in itself is intangible, but its consequences, especially the social ones, are not. Because the *intangible* sins were washed away by Jesus' atoning death, the Ekklesia can and must reverse their tangible consequences, first among its members and eventually in society itself. This must be done through repentance, restitution and restoration, as we will see next.

Operating in the Opposite Spirit

Men in Jesus' Ekklesia are instructed to do the opposite of what Adam did after sin touched him through Eve. When God confronted him, Adam dishonored Eve as his wife, and in an act of supreme cowardice told God, "The woman whom You gave to be with me, she gave me from the tree, and I ate" (Genesis 3:12). In other words, Adam was saying, "*She* made me do it!"

But on this side of Calvary, where the original sin has already been atoned for, Paul commands husbands in the Ekklesia to do the exact opposite by standing unashamedly with their wives in public, by making provision for their godliness to be evident, and by teaching them in an intimate setting, the home (see 1 Timothy 2:8–13). In other words, Paul is saying, "Your wife is your God-given suitable help, your indispensable complement, so make her look better, feel better and understand better." This is the opposite of what Adam did in the Garden.[7]

Furthermore, in Ephesians 5 Paul instructs husbands to give themselves to their wives as Christ gave Himself to the Church, and to love them as much as they love their own bodies (see verses 21, 25, 28). These are absolutely radical and revolutionary concepts, and there are no gray areas in his instructions. Women are equal to men, and Christian husbands must model this at home as a point of inception for society to emulate it eventually. This passage complements 1 Timothy 2:8–13 and shows how men in the New Testament Ekklesia were taught to remove the social iniquity caused by Adam's response to Eve's transgression.

This restorative process went beyond the kitchen table and the bedroom. As full-fledged members of the Ekklesia, women in the New Testament were permitted and encouraged to participate in meetings, do public good works and receive teaching in the same manner and environment in which men had been taught in the Old Testament.

The social agenda of the Ekklesia was far more effective than the French and American revolutions combined, because it benefitted half of the world's population without resorting to war. Paul, writing to the Ekklesia in Asia pastored by his spiritual son Timothy, specified that women were no longer to be kept in ignorance, but should be instructed in the same manner that men had been through the centuries. Rather than merely a simple step in the right direction, this constituted a giant leap forward for women.

Women's Rights, According to the Bible

In such a context, Paul's argument that men and women are intrinsically linked—like head and body—is not a put-down toward women, but a significant step up. Again, this was another radical item on the Ekklesia's social agenda that later was thwarted by the introduction of the doctrine of female submission.

It is important to note that the word *submission* is never used in the section of Scripture from which, traditionally, much of the teaching on headship is derived. First Corinthians 7 is devoted to presenting women in equal partnership and status with men. Paul articulated what the Ekklesia believed and practiced by making the following points:

1. A man has a right to a wife as much as a wife has a right to a husband (see verse 2).
2. Both husbands and wives must fulfill their sexual obligation because their bodies belong to each other rather than to themselves (see verses 3–4).
3. If a husband and wife deprive themselves sexually, it should only be by mutual consent (see verse 5).

These are extraordinary statements issued at a time when women had no rights whatsoever, all of which upstream to Jesus' teachings in the gospels.

Divorce in biblical times always hurt the wife much more than the husband by turning her into a social pariah. The Pharisees raised the issue of divorce to test Jesus, asking, "Is it lawful for a man to divorce his wife for any reason at all?" (Matthew 19:3).

Jesus cut them off at the pass, so to speak, by reminding them that the issue involved both genders: "He who created them from the beginning made them male and female" (verse 4). Then He proceeded to describe an indissoluble union: "For this reason a man shall leave his father and mother and be joined to his wife, and the two shall become one flesh" (verse 5).

> *That men and women are intrinsically linked—like head and body—is not a put-down toward women, but a significant step up.*

To make sure that this new playing field would remain level from that point on, Jesus added an addendum to the Old Testament command, and in that way He provided further protection to women: "What therefore

God has joined together, let no man separate" (verse 6). He followed this immediately with a restriction on the issuing of certificates of divorce (see verse 9). By restoring women, the Ekklesia changed the world!

The Restoration of the Family

The family is the fourth aspect of society that the Ekklesia was instrumental in bringing restoration to, something that pagan religions definitely did not do. On the contrary, as I referred to earlier, pagan cultures undermined family values by their view of women.

To correct that, first the New Testament describes the Ekklesia as the Bride of Christ and climaxes with the wedding feast in the book of Revelation. And second, the teachings throughout the New Testament reveal an indivisible relationship between the family and the Ekklesia. The key to this foundational principle is found in the New Testament usage of the Greek word *oikos*,[8] a term that describes not only the dwelling place for the family,[9] but also the "household" of relationships and influence that the family has. Just as Jesus co-opted the secular word *ekklesia* and infused it with His DNA, so He also took the secular *oikos* and elevated it as the foundation of His Ekklesia.

Jesus' statement that salvation had come to Zaccheus's house was a reference to this man's *oikos* (see Luke 19:9). By it, He meant that Zaccheus, his family and his business had all experienced salvation. In Acts 2:2, it was also an *oikos* that the sound of a mighty wind filled, giving birth to the Ekklesia that from that point on grew from *oikos* to *oikos* (see Acts 2:46; 5:42).

The surprising move of the Holy Spirit that took the Ekklesia to the Gentiles happened in Cornelius' *oikos* (see Acts 10:2, 22; 11:14). The church in Philippi started in Lydia's *oikos* and grew further when the jailer and his *oikos* were saved (see Acts 16:14–15, 31–34). The Corinthian Ekklesia did not expand until it resettled in Titius Justus's *oikos*, and soon afterward Crispus and his *oikos* were saved (see Acts 18:8).

The Scriptures present the *oikos* as the foundation for the Ekklesia. That is why there is such an emphasis on key elements of the *oikos* in Ephesians, where terms derived from that word are mentioned 13 times and *oikos*-related terminology such as *father, mother, son, husband* and *wife* is found 64 times as Paul explains God's pattern for love, honor and respect in marriage and parenting. All this climaxes with the statement in Ephesians 2:19 that believers are members of "God's household [*oikeioi*]."

The Temple was known as the *oikos* of God (see Matthew 12:4; 21:13; Mark 2:26; 11:17). And on this side of Calvary, Paul weds the Ekklesia to the *oikos* when he says, "I write so that you will know how one ought to conduct himself in the household [*oikos*] of God, which is the church [*Ekklesia*] of the living God, the pillar and support of the truth" (1 Timothy 3:15).

Salvation is all about becoming part of God's family: "He predestined us to adoption as sons through Jesus Christ" (Ephesians 1:5). His family is the Ekklesia. A healthy congregation is composed of restored families where all these principles and components take place.

Nowadays, by dichotomizing the Ekklesia and family, we have boarded up the showcase where it is meant to be most prominently displayed, thus weakening the effectiveness of Christianity in the world. This is why as the biblical insights about the Ekklesia come into focus, every Christian home must become the point of inception for the Ekklesia. This is how it was in the beginning, when believers met "house to house." To that end, my wife, Ruth, shows how to turn the dining table into an altar and the home into an Ekklesia in her book, *Food, Family and Fun*.[10] But it must also go beyond the homes, institutions and organizations we are part of.

Our movement—Transform Our World—was catapulted to a higher level of effectiveness when we embraced the biblical principle of spiritual adoption, which enabled us to transition from being an organization to a family. It meant that our leaders stepped up to also become fathers and mothers to their followers in their respective spheres of influence in the same manner as Jesus, Paul and John described themselves in Hebrews 2:13; 1 Corinthians 4:14–15 and 1 John 2:1.

One pastor, after embracing this truth, repented to his congregation for not having operated in that role. He confessed that the pain ungrateful members had often inflicted on him led him to use the term *pastor*

157

as a shield. As he knelt down and asked for the privilege of being their spiritual father, the entire congregation came forward to be adopted. Among them was his elderly father. It was an awkward situation, but it was evident to him that God was leading this exercise. A few days later, this pastor's father shared how he had always struggled with addressing God as "Father" because of how undemonstrative and strict his own father had been, a trait that had also defiled him and that he had subsequently passed on to his pastor son. After witnessing in his son the attitude of a spiritual father, however, a generational stronghold was demolished and he became free to joyfully call God "Father" for the first time.

Similar examples occurred in the marketplace. A businessman was exposed to this teaching at one of our conferences. Just before traveling to attend the conference, he learned that his management team had lost a major order, and he scolded them rudely. At the conference, he realized that he was meant to be a father to them and not just a boss. Arriving home in the wee hours of the morning, he drove directly to the factory. He enthroned the presence of the Lord and accepted God's call to be a father to his employees and to turn his factory into an Ekklesia.

At the start of the next workday, he repented to the management team for his past harshness and told them about his encounter with God. He told them not to worry about the financial loss since God was in control. That left his employees pleasantly confused since in that culture, bosses never repented to employees. The next day, his general manager informed him that the client whose order was lost had submitted a much larger order!

I must admit that I was totally taken by surprise when I found myself acknowledged as a spiritual father. God used Bishop Vaughn McLaughlin from The Potter's House in Jacksonville, Florida, to articulate this truth to our movement as he shared his own journey through spiritual orphanhood. He closed his presentation with an invitation for everyone who considered me as his or her spiritual father to stand up.

I was totally caught off guard at the response. It was one of the most awkward, uncomfortable and overwhelming moments of my life as I found myself looking out on people whom I considered giants in the

Lord acknowledging Ruth and me as their spiritual parents, but I had no doubt that God was orchestrating this.[11] I prayed a prayer of adoption and then went straight to our room, where I fell on my knees, suddenly overwhelmed by a flood of weighty questions. Gently, God began to answer them. I want to highlight two of them.

What is my job as a spiritual father? I asked.

God specified to me, *Every time they see you, they must see Me, just as with Jesus.*

Jesus did not have biological children, but He declared, "He who has seen Me has seen the Father" (John 14:9). Later on, He is described as a father to His followers (see Hebrews 2:13).

Nothing drove me to my knees faster than that assignment. I also had another important question that I needed to ask the Lord: *How can I avoid the abuses of "spiritual fathering" that some proponents have made?*

God gave me two principles that, when used in tandem, resolve this dilemma. First, *the disciple is no greater than the master* (see John 15:20). This means that as a master builder, I must not dump a problem for which I don't have a solution on my "spiritual children." (If someone is given the authority to be a father, he is responsible for finding solutions to the problems affecting the family he heads.) Instead, I am to go to God for answers, and when I receive them, I must pass them on to my "children" for confirmation and implementation. Second, *the master must believe that his disciples will do greater works than he does* (see John 14:12). I must give them everything God has given to Ruth and me, so that when added to what God has deposited in them, they will outperform us. As long as those two principles were working in tandem, we would be safe from abuses.

Once those of us in our movement stepped into this realm of adopting and being adopted to form the *oikos* of God, it opened our eyes to the realities of Romans 8, where Paul enunciates in verse 15 that we "have not received a spirit of slavery leading to fear again," but that we "have received a spirit of adoption as sons by which we cry out, 'Abba! Father!'" We see the importance of this in verse 19: "For the anxious longing of the creation waits eagerly for the revealing of the *sons* of God" (emphasis added). This was the reason why "adopting" a city or a nation, as Poncho Murguía did, has become a hallmark in our Transform Our World family. Our cities and nations are no longer hopelessly orphaned places that we criticize; they are adopted *children* whom we bless and encourage, and for whom we seek the best.

We are still learning, but the lives of thousands have become meaningful and satisfying thanks to the discovery of the Ekklesia as God's *oikos* and the application of these principles, which have brought depth and breadth to the transformation movement beyond anything we had ever imagined.

Breaking the Cycle of Unrighteousness

In Solano County, California, we see a contemporary example of the transformational reversal of the iniquity embedded in poverty, gender inequality, modern-day urban slavery and family degradation. It came through the efforts of Michael Brown and his wife, Paulette, the founders of Michael's Transportation Services in Vallejo, whom we talked about in chapter 5. The Browns applied the full scope of the "Gospel of the Kingdom" within their own sphere of influence to address these issues.

The first thing they did in the process was to operate together as a couple, thus modeling gender reconciliation. Their commitment to each other played into how they treated their children, and also their employees and their company—in essence, their *oikos*. When an opportunity came to sell their company, instead of "selling up" to a multinational buyer for substantial personal gains, they chose to "sell down" by making 99 percent of their business shares available to their employees through what is known as an Employee Stock Ownership Plan (ESOP). An ESOP provides company workers with ownership in the company at no up-front cost to them, and ESOP shares are part of the employees' remuneration for work performed. This gives ownership to the employees, making them shareholders in the company. In this way, the haves and the have-nots become partners and share their spiritual, relational, motivational and material wealth.

Next, God led the Browns to tackle a systemic problem in the correctional institutions of their county, which fosters the equivalent of urban slavery. According to Solano County sheriff Thomas Ferrara, the recidivism rate (inmates going back to prison after serving their term) was close to 80 percent. That means that almost 8 out of 10 inmates would wind up back in jail to serve longer and harsher terms, which de facto was turning prisons into training camps for crime. This perpetuated a cycle of unrighteousness that was further fueled by the inmates' inability to find jobs whenever they were not incarcerated and to provide for themselves and their families. Using the graph I mentioned before, they were stuck in the negative all the time—at -10 when they were committing crimes, and then brought to 0 when they were incarcerated, with no hope of ever moving into the positive numbers. Furthermore, the resulting lack of peace and joy in them and in those around them was fodder for all kinds of disruption and violence in their families.

> *"They literally wrapped their arms around felons to help them be successful."*

The Browns, along with the Ekklesia in Vallejo, discerned that the most urgent needs of the formerly incarcerated were employable skills and training to successfully reenter society. They stepped up to make that social wrong right by using Michael's Transportation Services Training Academy to equip recently released inmates with employable skills.[12] According to Chris Hansen, Solano County chief probation officer, these were not easy trainees. Some had never worked, and they had very few skills and little communication ability. But Officer Hansen put his finger on why the program worked with these words: "[Transformation Vallejo] literally wrapped their arms around them to help them be successful."

The result? Solano County sheriff Thomas Ferrara gave this report: "One hundred percent placement for jobs is nothing less than amazing!"

Now, let's run this by the grid of what constitutes the Kingdom of God. A systemic wrong (unrighteousness) was made right (*righteousness*). Former inmates and their relatives found a *peaceful* harbor to repair to, and for the first time in their adult lives they felt *joy* that had a strong chance of being lasting because it was fueled by the *power* of God. Right there we have the four components that constitute the Kingdom of God, according to Paul: righteousness, peace, joy and divine power working in tandem to eliminate systemic social evils.

Ekklesia Canadian Style

In another example, the Canadian city of Brantford, Ontario, was slipping into despair and desolation because of addiction and poverty, until leaders equipped with the principles of transformation began ministering to its felt needs. They adopted in prayer and good deeds the downtown area, which was plagued with strip clubs, crack houses and all sorts of decadent activities.

This group, led by Pastor Brian Beattie, turned their original church site (for Freedom House) into housing for homeless and needy families. They began providing meals to address the relational needs of people on the streets—including Friday night street-side hamburger barbecues they called "Flipping Fridays." These were held from 10 p.m. to 2 a.m. to minister to the "partying" crowds when they left the clubs. The owner of one of the clubs was so touched that he offered to pay for the cost of the hamburgers. Pastor Brian, quick on the draw, accepted conditionally. He would take the money if the owner would let him and his associates clean the club after hours. Why? Because the Ekklesia wanted to pray for every chair and every table, rebuking the forces of evil and inviting the gracious presence of God to touch those who frequented the club for the wrong reasons.

The spiritual cleanup of the downtown area moved a local businessman to build Harmony Square right there, with nice office buildings and shops. The replacement of derelict buildings, many empty and abandoned, with beautiful offices, living spaces and a plaza where families could socialize definitely brought goodness (righteousness), peace and joy to everybody in town.

This commitment to the betterment of the city gave the emerging Ekklesia in Brantford increasing favor and standing with the government. When the city needed someone to organize the city's "Frosty

Fest" Winter Carnival, they asked the Ekklesia to do so. The Ekklesia had never done such a thing before, but these believers felt called to do it and it was a resounding success.

After analyzing the local culture, the Ekklesia also realized that a pervasive felt need in the city was kindness, so they created a superhero character called "Captain Kindness." The Captain has become famous around the city, hosting many major events and intentionally speaking hope, life and Kingdom values into the area's children through the "Superhero in Me" school curriculum that it gave birth to.[13] Soon the Captain and the kindness he was promoting had become so iconic that the city set itself on a journey embraced by the Canadian Parliament to become "the kindest city in Canada."

The favor these Ekklesia leaders gained is such that the city has commissioned a living Nativity scene each Christmas, which is put on by the Ekklesia. Public baptisms in the town square (named "Harmony Square") are a regular occurrence because the values of the Kingdom have proven to be good for the city. In fact, this is fast becoming part of the "new" culture, and shop owners gladly post advertisements for the public baptisms in their shop windows. On baptism day in the square, you can see a line of candidates carrying their baptismal application and being interviewed by members of the Ekklesia to make sure they are ready.

When I had the privilege of witnessing such public baptisms, I saw a young man dressed in business attire come down from his office, fill out the application, be interviewed, go under the water, come up dripping with joy and water, and after drying off, go back to work! On another occasion, the owner of the shop that prints the advertisement for the event was so touched by what he read in the submittal for printing that he brought his entire family to be baptized.

These testimonies exemplify the abilities that only the Ekklesia has. It can bridge the gender gap at home between spouses, between parents and children and between masters (owners) and slaves (employees) in the marketplace. It can also integrate seamlessly the four dimensions of wealth—spiritual, relational, motivational and material—to tackle poverty, in order to disciple a city, a region and eventually a nation. At the very heart of these things is a rediscovery of the social agenda the first-century Ekklesia had, so that it can be carried on. This is crucial because when we do that, we will gain favor with everybody—rich and poor—but most importantly, with people in authority who can open or close doors for the Gospel to flow freely, as we will see next.

A Steep Social Learning Curve

Bible-based, Spirit-led social action is absolutely necessary in this transformation process. Simply preaching without accompanying good works will not do it. Preaching will get people saved, but cities will not be transformed (much less nations), because the proclamation of the Gospel has to be validated by deeds that benefit society. This is a lesson that Paul had to learn, as we will see next. Looking at what he had to learn will keep us from the same pitfall and will accelerate the expansion of the Kingdom.

In his apostolic journey from Antioch to Ephesus, Paul learned progressively how Jesus' Ekklesia was to function in the marketplace to become an agent for social transformation (see Acts 13–19). At first, he did well as far as leading people to faith in Jesus and establishing them in local congregations, such as in Philippi, Colossus and Thessalonica, by doing what most pastors normally do; he preached weekly to God-fearing people in religious settings, with great success. Though he saw multitudes saved and many Ekklesias established, he did not see an entire region transformed until Acts 19, where "all who lived in Asia heard the word of the Lord, both Jews and Greeks" (verse 10). This report describes total saturation of a vast region with the word of God, without a single person left unexposed to the Gospel.

Simply preaching will not do it. . . . Cities will not be transformed (much less nations), because the proclamation of the Gospel has to be validated by deeds that benefit society.

Along the way, Paul learned a most valuable lesson that came as a result of two major setbacks and two stunning victories in the marketplace, which provide us key insights into how the Ekklesia must function in the social arena in order to disciple nations. His setbacks took place in Pisidian Antioch, a Roman colony, and in Thessalonica, another Roman colony and the capital of the Roman province of Macedonia (see Acts 13:44–50; 17:4–10). In each place, Paul and his team first enjoyed great favor as major revival impacted the region, for which the synagogue was the point of inception. But in both cases opposition arose from religious and city leaders, which ended with the apostles being forced to leave town, squelching the move of God.

The first major breakthrough took place in Corinth following the conversion of Crispus, a prominent leader in both the city and the synagogue. Crispus was saved, together with his entire household, which created a people movement into the Kingdom that was so enormous that Paul required divine reassurance as to its legitimacy, since it was happening not in or around the synagogue, but in the marketplace of a metropolis infamous for its lasciviousness (see Acts 18:8–9; 1 Corinthians 6:15–16). In Corinth, the negative reaction to Paul's success was similar to that which occurred in Pisidian Antioch and Thessalonica. The Jews "with one accord rose up against Paul and brought him before the judgment seat" (Acts 18:12). But this time the local authority, Proconsul Gallio, "drove them [Paul's adversaries] away from the judgment seat" (verse 16). Case dismissed! As a result, Paul was able to remain in the city, teaching and applying the Word of God in the marketplace with complete freedom.

Paul's second and more dramatic breakthrough took place in Ephesus—the most influential city in the Roman province of Asia. The move of God was so powerful there that it impacted the whole economic and spiritual structure of the city and spread to the entire province, so that "all who lived in Asia heard the word of the Lord, both Jews and Greeks," and "the word of the Lord was growing mightily and prevailing" (Acts 19:10, 20). True to form, "there occurred no small disturbance concerning the Way" (verse 23) as an out-of-control mob set out to do harm to Paul and his associates. But the Asiarchs,[14] high-ranking city officials whom Luke describes as Paul's friends, came to their defense (see verse 31).

Unlike Pisidian Antioch and Thessalonica, in Corinth and Ephesus the leaders and government officials sided with the local Ekklesia and became instrumental in giving its members favor and freedom because its ministry had changed the city. In the wake of that tipping point, the cult of a major pagan goddess in Ephesus was debunked, along with its influence on the economy. That became the detonator for the spread of the Gospel across the cities and regions around them, until everybody in the Roman province of Asia had heard the word of the Lord (see Acts 19:10).

Why the Defeats and Why the Victories?

Two important questions bear directly on the issue of the Ekklesia's need for social relevance: Why the defeats and why the victories? The answer to them is this: Paul's identity, and that of his associates in the cities where the defeats took place, was religious. He was a preacher identified with the local synagogue, an exclusivist religious body, whereas in Corinth and Ephesus he had moved his base of operations into the *marketplace*, which allowed him to become involved in the welfare of the city.

Obviously, no Roman officials would be inclined to give the slightest preferential treatment to a religious group that could upset the Pax Romana. So why would the Asiarchs befriend Paul and intervene on his behalf, particularly since his movement had a reputation of doing precisely that? In fact, their peers in Thessalonica had just run Paul and Silas out of town, shouting, "These men who have upset the world have come here also" (Acts 17:6).

I submit that it was because Paul and the Ekklesia he planted were assets to the city, and not just to Ekklesia members. The believers applied the principles Paul taught and practiced, working hard to help the weak and remembering the words Jesus Himself had said, "It is more blessed to give than to receive" (Acts 20:35). The Ekklesia was not an item on someone else's agenda; rather, it set the agenda in the city for both personal and social issues.

Yet Jesus' social agenda for His Ekklesia can easily be ignored or overlooked if we fail to grasp the fullness of His incarnation, as we will see in the next chapter.

13

A Fuller Understanding of the Incarnation

From Ethereal to Entrepreneurial

Jesus is definitely the most compassionate, selfless and accepting person to ever walk the earth. Why is it, then, that His name is one of the cuss words most frequently used in entertainment? And what must be done to remedy it?

In His own infallible words, Jesus said, "And I, if I am lifted up from the earth, will draw all men to Myself" (John 12:32). Why is it, then, that His name has become a swear word? And why is it that secular humanists—who will politely "put up" with a government official closing a speech with the habitual "God bless America"—will vociferously revolt if Jesus' name is substituted for God? Even with atheists, a deep-rooted anger springs to the surface when the subject of Jesus or God comes up, which is such an intellectual oxymoron—to get so emotionally worked up over someone they don't believe exists!

At the other end of the social spectrum, pagan theocratic religious/governmental rulers sanction and encourage cutting off the heads of innocent people and burning their homes and places of worship on account of these folks being called by Jesus' name. Why such a vicious reaction at the mention of someone who never hurt anyone, never owned slaves, never wielded a weapon, never discriminated on the basis of gender, race or age, and never incited anyone to violence, even when He was agonizing on the cross for no other crime than acknowledging that He was who He said He was—the Son of a loving God?

Ironically, from the very same cross Jesus provided what is needed to answer that question. Out of the torment of insults and mockery being hurled at Him by the people He had healed, He lifted His head toward the heavens and pleaded, "Father, forgive them; for they do not know what they are doing" (Luke 23:34).

The world hates Jesus because it does not know Him. The one they hate is a caricature—a misrepresentation of the real Jesus. He is not an enemy, but the best Friend they can ever have.

Will the Real Jesus Please Stand Up?

The main obstacle to discovering the real Jesus is not related to His character or the record of His actions while on earth. His resumé is unassailable. There is substantial agreement (even among those who do not believe in His divine nature or expiatory work) that He was an excellent person who genuinely cared about others. The problem lies in an erroneous perception that Jesus was a holier-than-thou hermit whose teachings were ethereal and whose actions made no contribution to society.

> *Jesus cataloged as evildoers people who claimed they had done what today are considered legitimate church and ministry activities.*

One of the most intriguing passages in the gospels, however, is the one dealing with the judgment of the nations, in Matthew 25:32: "All the nations will be gathered before Him; and He will separate them from one another, as the shepherd separates the sheep from the goats." At the end of human history, when the scorecard is disclosed, some will inherit the Kingdom, and others will not and will be remanded to eternal fire (see verses 34, 41).

We talked about this a little bit in chapter 5, but let me point out that the basis of admission was social work: feeding the hungry, clothing the naked, tending the sick and caring for those in prison. In other words, the standard was not what people professed (religion), but how they lived out what they believed (lifestyle) for the betterment of others. Jesus' judgment revealed His passionate interest in societal affairs.

Jesus, the Master Entrepreneur

What credentials did Jesus possess that put Him in a position to judge nations on the basis of their commitment to the down-and-out? What could He possibly know about social issues? Didn't He come from heaven, and wasn't He returning there?

I am convinced that in the same fashion that we fail to capture the full scope of the Atonement—that He redeemed not just people, but everything that was lost—we also fall short of grasping the full extent of His incarnation. As a result, we fail to represent Him properly. I submit that Jesus belongs more in the marketplace than in a monastery, because He was *fully* incarnated into the affairs of the world and its institutions.

The incarnation is a central doctrine that states that God assumed human nature and became a Man in the form of Jesus Christ (see John 1:14; Philippians 2:7–8; Colossians 2:9). It reveals His total identification with those whom He came to save. He became one of them, sharing their humanity. Hebrews 4:15 tells it plainly: "For we do not have a high priest who cannot sympathize with our weaknesses, but One who has been tempted in all things as we are, yet without sin."

The main message here is that because Jesus experienced what we face, He fully understands our struggles, and because He overcame them, He can show us how to do the same.

Even nowadays, we would more readily clothe Jesus as a teacher in rabbinical garb than as a businessman in a three-piece suit, engaged in everyday affairs in the marketplace, yet the latter is precisely the image presented in the gospels. Jesus spent the bulk of His life in the marketplace, beginning with His first minute of earthly life. He was born not in the Temple or in a synagogue, nor even in a home, but in a place of business, an inn (see Luke 2:7). His first visitors were shepherds—low-ranking workers (see verses 15–20).

Jesus lived most of His life in the marketplace. His neighbors in Nazareth, after hearing His eloquent pronouncement from the book of Isaiah, exclaimed, "Is not this the carpenter?" (Mark 6:3). They knew Him by His trade in the marketplace more than as a preacher. It was not unusual for His neighbors to see Jesus as a businessman, since many of them probably purchased products made by His hands. I suspect that they ate at tables made by Jesus and secured their homes with doors built in His shop. Their houses could have had beams cut and fit by the Savior. Even some of their oxen may have worn "Made-by-Jesus" yokes.

Even nowadays, we would more readily clothe Jesus as a teacher in rabbinical garb than as a businessman in a three-piece suit, engaged in everyday affairs in the marketplace.

Jesus did not do carpentry work as a hobby, but for a living. This required that He run His shop at a profit. His daily business routine involved calculating the cost of goods and labor, gauging the interplay between supply and demand, establishing competitive pricing to get a return on investment (ROI), and factoring in the costs of maintenance and equipment. Although it may be unusual for us to picture it, profitable labor was an integral part of Jesus' life. His instruction that "it is more blessed to give than to receive" (Acts 20:35) reveals that He had the means to acquire goods to be given away, since He practiced what He preached.

All of the above should be enough to squelch the notion of the ascetic Jesus whom many tend to picture. It is true that He spent long hours in prayer, but He usually did it at night (see Matthew 14:23; Luke 6:12). During the day, He interacted with all sorts of people in social settings not approved by the religious leaders. That gave Him a reputation as a friend of sinners: "The Son of Man came eating and drinking, and they say, 'Behold, a gluttonous man and a drunkard, a friend of tax collectors and sinners!'" (Matthew 11:19). The bulk of His teaching was done either around a table with food and drinks, or in the marketplace, and His conversation included the most diverse combination of business topics.

As I explain in my book *Anointed for Business*, Jesus' parables show that He was thoroughly familiar with the marketplace and its operation. His allegorical stories dealt with construction (see Matthew 7:24–27), wine making (see Luke 5:37–38), farming (see Mark 4:2–20), treasure hunting (see Matthew 13:44), ranching (see Matthew 18:12–14), management and labor (see Matthew 20:1–16), family-run businesses (see Matthew 21:28–31), hostile takeovers (see Luke 20:9–19), return on investments (ROI; see Matthew 25:14–30), futures markets (see Luke 12:16–21), crop yield (see Mark 13:27–32), management criteria (see Luke 12:35–48), research (see Luke 14:25–35), bankruptcy (see Luke 15:11–16), leverage (see Luke 16:1–13) and venture capital (see Luke 19:11–27). These are all subjects that ironically—and tragically, I would say—are not taught in seminary today.

Most of Jesus' miracles were what I call "Monday morning miracles," the miracles people need in the workplace, such as turning water into wine at a wedding feast to save the host from public embarrassment and his chief steward from severe punishment (see John 2:1–10). He also produced a tremendous return on a young boy's investment by turning a few fish and loaves into a meal for thousands of people (see Matthew 14:13–21). His instructions that led to two miraculous catches of fish, and then to Peter finding the money he needed to pay his taxes, are the modern equivalent of an insightful stockbroker's advice (see Luke 5:1–14; John 21:1–8; Matthew 17:24–27).

Jesus was someone who undoubtedly operated with great comfort and success in the marketplace. He recruited leaders from there—not from the Temple—to become His apostles. And He honored women in ways that the religious elite did not. When they scoffed at a woman of ill repute who was washing Jesus' feet, He honored her publicly and propelled her into a promising future by cutting off the shackles of the past (see Luke 7:37–50). And as we saw earlier, at a time when women were considered inferior to men, and marriage brought them into the husband's household in a subservient status, Jesus stated that a man shall leave his father and mother "and shall cleave to his wife" and the two shall become one flesh (Matthew 19:5 KJV). He vested women with equal status and stamped it with the divine seal of approval to make it inviolable: "What therefore God has joined together, let no man separate" (verse 6).

Jesus was ethnically Jewish, a people group that saw itself above other nations. But He experienced international exposure when He and His parents fled to Egypt to escape government-sponsored genocide. Jesus spent His formative years in a foreign land, where most likely He learned a foreign language and acquired a cosmopolitan worldview.

Going back to His maiden speech in Luke 4, we find Jesus introducing a revolutionary social agenda for solving problems on earth, with heaven as the source for the solution: "The Spirit of the Lord is upon Me, because He has anointed Me" (verse 18). He then proceeded to spell out the social dimension, which included bringing good news to the poor, releasing the captives, giving sight to the blind and setting free the oppressed (see the rest of verse 18).

In the same message, preached in a synagogue—a bastion of ethnocentrism since non-Jews were not admitted—Jesus reached across a huge social chasm to affirm two foreigners who found extraordinary favor with God, a Syrian general and a Canaanite widow (see Luke 4:25–27). So enraged was the congregation by what they saw as sympathy toward undesirable foreigners that they tried to kill Him. The gospel narrative that "passing through their midst, He went His way" reveals a gutsy Jesus who knew how to stare down a murderous crowd (see verses 28–30).

Jesus was also warm to contemporary foreigners like the Roman centurion He ministered to when He entered Capernaum. He publicly praised him, saying, "I have not found such great faith with anyone in Israel" (Matthew 8:10). On another occasion, He spent two days in a Samaritan town where He ministered first to a woman of ill repute and then to the entire citizenship (see John 4:4–42). None of the above would have happened if He'd had an ethnocentric mindset.

Jesus set in motion a process for the will of God to be done on earth, not in an ethereal sense, but in a practical sense in order to transform the fiber of society. His teaching and example on social justice became so ingrained in His disciples that, as I mentioned earlier, when they found themselves in charge of the Ekklesia right after Pentecost, no needy person could be found among those to whom they ministered, not even among the vulnerable widows of Gentiles who had converted to Judaism (see Acts 2:44–45; 4:32–35; 6:1–3).

This was an extraordinary outcome, to say the least. Here is a group of new believers numbering into the thousands who just had a most profound spiritual experience receiving eternal life in Christ and the infilling of the Holy Spirit, and what is on display for the world to see? A community that cared for the poor, for the widows and for the down-and-out in an atmosphere of miracles performed daily at Solomon's Portico, the place where Jews and Gentiles were able to stand together.

This care of the needy was not a one-time occurrence restricted to believers in Jerusalem. When a severe famine hit Judea, Gentile believers in Antioch followed suit by sending abundant relief to their Jewish brethren in Jerusalem by the hands of Paul and Barnabas (see Acts 11:29–30).

Jesus' Disciples Kept It Going

Jesus was the most selfless, extraordinary *and successful* social entrepreneur ever to walk on earth, because He tackled the most difficult social ills, replicating and multiplying Himself ad infinitum through His followers. In so doing, He introduced social ethics that, in the centuries to follow, would make the world a far better place. He taught the concepts, modeled them and instructed His disciples to carry them on.

The social conscience of His followers was central to their beliefs and praxis, as I noted before. Taking care of the needy was the only recommendation the more senior apostles James, Peter and John gave to Paul when they recognized him as a peer (see Galatians 2:10). But Jesus' disciples went beyond simply giving alms to the poor. His Ekklesia tackled systemic poverty, turning consumers into producers, as we saw in Ephesians 4:28.

This principle of caring for the needy was also embedded in the celebration of the Lord's Supper. Paul admonished the Corinthians to let those who had the least serve themselves first from the food on the Lord's table. So important was this that Paul warned that the consequences for not following suit were weakness, illness and premature death (see 1 Corinthians 11:18–34).

In an era when labor was looked down on by the ruling classes, Jesus' disciples popularized the concept that "the laborer is worthy of his wages" (1 Timothy 5:18). Paul exhorted slaves who had to do the most demeaning jobs to serve their masters with dignity by instructing them to elevate their service to the level of their real Master: "Whatever you do, do your work heartily, as for the Lord rather than for men" (Colossians 3:23). And as we already saw in Paul's treatment of Philemon, he tapped into the runaway slave Onesimus's spiritual resources that qualified him as a "son," not a slave, a "minister" of the highest caliber and a trustworthy emissary of Paul's own heart.

Reconciling Social Gaps

The stunning results of Jesus' all-encompassing radical social entrepreneurship are on display in Paul's epistle to the Ephesians. Paul lists as normative what were absolutely revolutionary concepts when he identified six social gaps that needed repair in order for the Ekklesia to have the authority to stand against the evil one. Although I touched on some of these in an earlier chapter, what took place here is so instructional and radical that it is worth revisiting. The Gospel of the Kingdom heals these gaps:

1. No racial schism: "For He Himself is our peace, who made both groups [Jews and Gentiles] into one and broke down the barrier of the dividing wall" (Ephesians 2:14).

2. No divisions among believers: ". . . and that you, being rooted and grounded in love, may be able to comprehend *with all the saints* what is the breadth and length and height and depth, and to know the love of Christ which surpasses knowledge, that you may be filled up to all the fullness of God" (Ephesians 3:17–19, emphasis added).

3. No disunity among the ministerial offices of apostles, prophets, evangelists, pastors and teachers, by exhorting them to be "diligent to preserve the unity of the Spirit in the bond of peace" (Ephesians 4:3).

4. Mutual love and honor between husband and wife, because husbands are commanded to love their wives as Jesus loves His Ekklesia, and wives to give honor to their husbands as to the Lord Himself (see Ephesians 5:22–30). It cannot get any higher than that!

5. Reciprocal respect between parents and children (see Ephesians 6:1–4).

6. Reconciliation between masters and slaves (see Ephesians 6:5–9).

Here we have six ugly and oozing social gaps involving parties that, in a world riddled with sin, are socially positioned to oppose and in some cases hate each other. What is the dynamic at work? It is evident that Jesus' mission and message are holistic—reconciling mankind to God, people to each other and people to their sphere of influence in the family and in the marketplace. It is equally evident from the same passage that the devil has the exact opposite agenda, which is why Paul instructs the Ekklesia to oppose him and his evil forces (see Ephesians 6:11–13).

God's Favorite Geometric Figure

What was the secret to bridging these gaps? Let me illustrate with what I like to think is God's favorite geometric shape—the cube—because the New Jerusalem is shaped like one, having identical height, width and depth (see Revelation 21:16). It is the same with the love of God, which is described in Ephesians as having infinite breadth, height, width and length—another cube (see Ephesians 3:17–19). Think of the dice we use in board games; each one has six different numbers printed on the sides. No matter how they land when they are rolled, however, any given number, like a 3, may be on the top, on the bottom, on the left or the right, the front or back. But that number will always be on the dice. It will always be included somewhere.

God's social order is like a cube, too—all-inclusive. But the devil serrates the cube diagonally to split it into two triangular prisms that can be manipulated to oppose each other. This is how we end up with labor versus management, black people versus white people, left versus right, and in the religious arena, Bible based versus Spirit led, charismatic versus conservative, traditional versus contemporary. In each one of these examples, both parties are part of the same social compact.[1] As such, they should work in harmony instead of in opposition since the latter results in the destruction of the common good.

In America, two major political parties alternate in running the country: Republicans and Democrats. Like the two triangular prisms, they are less than self-sufficient on their own because each one is a fragment of the whole. To make up for that shortage, each one has chosen or become captive to a base that is radically and irreversibly opposed to the other, thus preventing any attempt at reconciliation. The proponents of these extreme positions are a minority relative to the rest of the people in each party, but their stridency and entrenchment preclude cooperation, much less reconciliation.

The solution to the social gaps I have pointed out is for the Ekklesia to capture the middle ground in order to build bridges between society's factions, to rebuild the cube for a full-on, foolproof, undeniable display of righteousness, peace and joy for the entire nation.

Gaining Traction

In that light, it is most interesting to note that Jesus introduced *first* the Kingdom of God, and *then* the Ekklesia, even though they are both sides of the same coin (see Matthew 4:17; 16:18). This was necessary because the message of the Kingdom is expansive and encompassing, intended to touch society without preconditions, whereas the Ekklesia is meant to develop cohesiveness among those who embrace it for deeper traction in society.

By bringing two opposing parties into one, Christianity has an absolutely unique way of reconciling the six gaps Paul listed in his epistle to the Ephesians. Let's look at those gaps again, but this time let's see *how* Christianity bridges them by merging the two sides into one:

- We are a new nation in Christ that is *neither* Jewish nor Gentile, *but Christian* (see Ephesians 2:10–18).
- All the streams that constitute Christianity *fit together* to reflect the multidimensional love of God as the Ekklesia (see Ephesians 3:14–19).
- All the governmental offices in the Ekklesia are *part of one Body*, which is the Body of Christ (see Ephesians 4:1–13).
- Husbands and wives are to *cleave to each other* until the two become *one flesh* (see Ephesians 5:22–31).
- Parents and children must celebrate *their common Father* (God) to contribute mutual respect and honor *in building a common home* (see Ephesians 6:1–4);
- Masters (management) and slaves (labor) must respect and serve each other since they *both share a common Lord* (see Ephesians 6:5–9).

No other religion on earth (present or past) has come with a more constructive, life-giving ethic and its successful implementation, all of which is the fruit and the reflection of the *real* Jesus, first on His Ekklesia, and through it on the world. Paul again captures this eloquently in his letter to the Galatians:

> Now a mediator is not for one party only; whereas God is only one. . . . There is neither Jew nor Greek, there is neither slave nor free man, there is neither male nor female; *for you are all one in Christ Jesus*. And if you belong to Christ, then you are Abraham's descendants, heirs according to promise.
>
> Galatians 3:20, 28–29, emphasis added

Since these divisive gaps still exist in society, the insertion of the leaven of the Kingdom of God is the essential first step to lock and unlock (bind and release) the Gates of Hades using the keys of the Kingdom. When that takes place, captives can turn "from the dominion of Satan to God" and join the Ekklesia (Acts 26:18).

In Parañaque City in the Philippines, Vallejo in California, Brantford, Ontario, in Canada, and Ciudad Juárez in Mexico, apostolic leaders

(King Flores, Michael Brown, Brian Beattie and Poncho Murguía) took hold of what Peter was offered in Matthew 16:19—the keys of the Kingdom—and used them to overcome the Gates of Hades in their city. Out of that came new converts into the Ekklesia, showing once again that the Kingdom and the Ekklesia are two sides of the same coin. Where the Kingdom comes, the Ekklesia is established, and once the Ekklesia is planted, the Kingdom becomes evident.

Visitation versus Incarnation

Because Jesus was not just visiting the world but was incarnated into it, He consistently was able to affirm people who had no value in the opinion of their adversaries. Look how He opened the conversations with Zaccheus and the Samaritan woman—two social undesirables. He said to them, in effect, "You have something of value that I need." In the first case it was a bed and a roof. In the second, it was an implement with which to access the water in the well. His ultimate objective was not for them to supply *His* needs, but for Him to meet *theirs*. Yet the way He approached them, affirming their value, radically set Him apart from those who made a cult of despising and devaluing them. No wonder they responded so well!

The Kingdom and the Ekklesia are two sides of the same coin.

It hurts deeply when critics point out that the most racially segregated hour in the United States is Sunday morning. By rediscovering the Ekklesia not as a building where members meet once a week, but *primarily* as a multiracial people movement that operates 24/7 at all levels in the marketplace, we will burst through these walls of division and effect the transformation the world is longing for.

Jesus has given us the keys to open and shut the Gates of Hades so that He can come not only into human hearts but also into their businesses, schools, governments, cities and nations. When we talk about taking God's Kingdom into the marketplace, we are not dealing with a hostile audience, since "the whole creation groans and suffers the pains of childbirth together until now" (Romans 8:22). With anxious longing, creation "waits eagerly for the revealing of the sons of God" (verse 19).

The Ekklesia must never forsake the regular assembling of its members for the training and encouragement that the writer to the Hebrews speaks of (see Hebrews 10:25). But the Jesus that the Ekklesia learns about in such assembly and puts on display in the marketplace must be the *real* Jesus. And for this, it must love what God loves the most, as I will explain next.

14

A Fuller Understanding of What God Loves the Most

From "Out-reach" to "In-reach"

It may surprise you to hear that what God loves the most is not only the Ekklesia. And when we embrace everything that He loves, it radically changes for the better the way we see and do ministry as His Ekklesia. "Out-reach ministries" become "in-reach ministries" because the "congregation" just became citywide.

In addition to the Ekklesia, God also loves the world (see John 3:16; Psalm 2:8). The Ekklesia is the Body of Christ, of which Jesus is the head and for which He gave Himself (see Ephesians 5:25). But she is the fruit of God's primary love for the world. In fact, He loved the world when there was no Ekklesia around yet. The Ekklesia is His most precious gift to the world because it is His agent for reclaiming the world Jesus gave His life to redeem.

The Bible opens with the majestic portrayal of God creating the world and stating that it is "very good" as He contemplates what He has accomplished (see Genesis 1:31). Right after the devil deceived Adam and Eve, God made provision to restore what had been lost (see Genesis 3:15). The Fall did not diminish His love for the world.

The Bible closes with a magnificent report in Revelation 21 of renewed heavens and a renewed earth, where God's will is done as it is done in heaven. This amalgamation of a new heaven and a new earth constitutes a restored expression of what was lost in Genesis 3, with no death, no mourning, no crying and no pain (see Revelation 21:4). The nations that are bringing their honor and glory as a wedding present are existing nations that have been saved. This illustrates how much God loves the world in which we live today.

In between those two landmarks—God visiting His children in the Garden, and the new Jerusalem coming down to earth (where He will dwell forever with His children)—we see God depositing loving footprints into the world to restore what sin and Satan had defiled. In addition to the times when His power descended on burning altars or when He spoke through a burning bush, His presence eventually found residence first in the Ark of the Covenant, then in the more spacious Temple.

Everything in the Old Testament is a shadow of what was to be revealed in the New. This progressive revelation climaxed with the cross, where Jesus gave Himself in ransom for all, and in His majestic resurrection, exposing the devil as forever dispossessed of the keys of Hades and Death. God was deliberate when He said, "Ask of Me, and I will surely give the nations as Your inheritance, and the very ends of the earth as Your possession" (Psalm 2:8). Jesus passed on the same

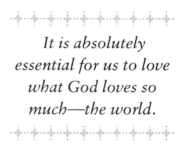

It is absolutely essential for us to love what God loves so much—the world.

request to His disciples when He told them to disciple nations. Surely God loved, loves and will forever love the world. This is why it is absolutely essential for us to love what God loves so much—the world.

Today, the world is overflowing with sin and corruption, and we do not feel inclined to invest ourselves in it. But the world is no different than the worst sinner, with perverted and evil desires, to whom we persistently present Christ. Why do we continue to do this when he or she repeatedly rejects the Gospel? Because we know that God loves people and that Jesus has paid the price for their redemption. We see them not as they are now, but as they will become once they come to Christ.

A biblical shift in paradigm is necessary for us to be able to look at the world in a loving way—to see it as already redeemed—the way Paul described how he saw people struggling with sin: "Therefore from now on we recognize no one according to the flesh" (2 Corinthians 5:16). What was Paul teaching the Corinthian believers, some of whom slept with temple prostitutes, one of whom was carrying on an affair with his stepmother, and still others who would get drunk at the Lord's table? It was this: "I choose to see you not the way you look now, but the way you are in Christ, fully forgiven and restored."

This is the path we need to follow with regard to the world. Paul could do it because the love emanating from the cross had overpowered him:

> For the love of Christ controls us, having concluded this, that one died for all, therefore all died; and He died for all, so that they who live might no longer live for themselves, but for Him who died and rose again on their behalf.
>
> 2 Corinthians 5:14–15

Look at how Paul shifts next from people to the world, to extend to it the same benefit:

> Now all these things are from God, who reconciled us to Himself through Christ and gave us the ministry of reconciliation, namely, that God was in Christ reconciling the world to Himself, not counting their trespasses against them, and He has committed to us the word of reconciliation.
>
> Therefore, we are ambassadors for Christ, as though God were making an appeal through us; we beg you on behalf of Christ, be reconciled to God.
>
> 2 Corinthians 5:18–20

We are very familiar with the verse previous to this passage: "Therefore if anyone is in Christ, he is a new creature; the old things passed away; behold, new things have come" (verse 17). These truths constitute a powerhouse of hope that dispenses a constant flow of mercy flooding us every time we find ourselves falling short. In times of need we confidently confess, "I am in Christ. I am a new creature; the old things have passed away. As such, I am forgiven. His blood atoned for all my sins, past, present and future."

We have no reservation whatsoever in applying that to ourselves, because we know that we are *in Christ*, but let's take a look at the next verse. Who else was in Christ? God Himself. And what was He doing? "Reconciling the world to Himself . . ." The same grace extended to us has also been extended to the world. And to that end, "He has committed to us the word of reconciliation," making us "ambassadors for Christ" (verses 19–20).

Imagine for a moment that you are the president of a nation and a new ambassador comes to present his or her credentials. By way of greeting, this person says, "I hate your country, and you are bound to be destroyed on account of your evil ways. I'd rather be back home than here, but I have no choice until I am transferred." Would you welcome anything he or she has to offer? Definitely not, because you are in the presence of a prosecutor more than an ambassador.

That is not the kind of ambassadors God means for us to be to the world. This is why Paul first exhorts the Corinthians to be reconciled to God *and to the world* in order "not to receive the grace of God in vain" (2 Corinthians 6:1). Paul urges them, in the same verse, to work together with God, who has reconciled Himself to the world.

> *If our favorite dish is barbecued lamb, God will not send us after a lost sheep.*

In other words, don't hold back God's grace from the world, because the world needs to hear precisely such Good News. If our favorite dish is barbecued lamb, God will not send us after a lost sheep, because when we find it, we will eat it! Jesus stated, "The good shepherd lays down His life for the sheep" (John 10:11).

In essence, we must become incarnated in the world the way Jesus was, to be its friend and attain the level of love Jesus described: "Greater love has no one than this, that one lay down his life for his friends" (John 15:13).

Binary Truths about Jesus

The way the Scriptures present Jesus reflects the love that a righteous God has for a sinful world. We find a prime example in John 1:14, "And the Word became flesh, and dwelt among us, and we saw His glory . . . full of grace and truth." John lists grace first, and then truth, to describe what sinners saw when they beheld Jesus. This sequence is very important. Not only are the words in the Bible inspired, but so is the order in which they are presented. I call such scriptural passages *binary truths*—scriptural truths presented in pairs that synergistically energize each other. Both components are essential, but there is an exponential power latent within each of them that is only released when apportioned in the correct sequence.

Think about Jesus being "full of grace and truth." If the pendulum swings excessively toward grace at the expense of truth, we end up with a "sugarcoated Jesus," the favorite of motivational preachers. They tell their audiences what will make them feel good, without including the responsibilities that the truth of who Jesus is demands: repentance, restitution and righteous living. And if the pendulum swings too far toward the truth side, we get a judgmental version of Jesus, whose immense gracious love and compassion are trodden under.

We also see the importance of honoring the word order in Romans 2:4 (NKJV), where Paul explains that it is "the goodness of God [that] leads you to repentance." Repentance is elicited by goodness. It is not God's wrath or anger, but His promise of grace to grant forgiveness that announces to the world, "Come! No sin can ever trump My grace!" Sinners flocked to Jesus, attracted by the grace He openly projected. His whole demeanor was engraved with "You are welcome," written in letters of grace. Once sinners came to Him, He taught them the divine truth—exacting and costly, but *always* palatable because of the context of grace in which it was presented.

184

When our hearts are not attuned to loving everything that God loves, our tendency is to lead with truth instead of grace, particularly when it comes to man's sinfulness. We find it all too easy to despise sinners because of their sins, instead of loving sinners *in spite of* their sins. Rather than seeing with the eyes of the Spirit the persons that God had in mind when He created them, we look through the eyes of the flesh and stiff-arm them. Instead of feeling acceptance, sinners sense rejection and turn a deaf ear to the "bad news" we preach. After all, no one wants to get an invitation to face a firing squad.

> *We find it all too easy to despise sinners along with their sin, instead of loving sinners in spite of their sin.*

This binary truth concept is also applicable when it comes to the interplay between power and wisdom, as Paul explained: "But we preach . . . Christ the power of God and the wisdom of God" (1 Corinthians 1:23–24). As I already mentioned in chapter 9, power comes first (to set people free from Satan's domain), followed by wisdom (to teach them how to stay away from it in order to develop into the likeness of Christ).

Not Just a Program

The modern-day Church does care for the world, and the evidence is in the myriad of its "outreach ministries," which do a lot of good for the community. Church people consistently can be found volunteering at hospitals, manning suicide hotlines, supporting local schools, building shelters, donating food and participating in a host of other activities by which the Church invests itself outside its four walls. These are called "outreach ministries." The preposition *out* indicates that we must come out of something to do these activities, and that "something" is the local Church.

But when the Church becomes the Ekklesia—*everything* inside the four walls expands for the better. The group that comes to the building for weekly services is no longer viewed as just sheep, but also as shepherds—ministers. The congregation no longer consists of only those who gather in the building, but also of the people in the city because now we see them as part of the flock, even though they are still lost.

The leaders become equippers for the saints to do the work of the ministry in their spheres of influence. And in that scenario, there would be no such thing as an *out*-reach anymore, but rather, everything would be an *in*-reach because Ekklesia members are invested all over the city.

My book *Anointed for Business*, and other books like it, have biblically validated Christians in the workplace as marketplace ministers. The calling of God on their lives is real because it derives from this same principle. When we love what God loves, then it makes sense that He would deploy qualified and skilled people into every aspect of the world to manifest His love.

Once this is understood, it bestows a clear sense of legitimacy on the believers who work in the marketplace once they are able to see with biblical certainty that what they do there ministry-wise is not a footnote or an appendix, but the very essence of what God called them to be.

Hong Kong: From Pulpit to Marketplace

Let's focus for a moment on one clear example of what I am talking about, in which we can see what pulpit and marketplace ministers are doing together under the banner of transformation in Hong Kong. These stories also serve to introduce something I want to bring up in the next chapter—the power of taking practical steps to exercise the spiritual authority the Lord has given us.

Pastor Wong Po Ling leads a transformational church that began the process of transformation in 2009, after she attended the global Transform Our World Conference in Hawaii. She immediately gathered her team of pastors and leaders, and they dedicated their district to the Lord. This was that *bapto* moment we talked about earlier that started a *baptizo* process.

Shortly thereafter, Pastor Wong and five school principals dedicated their schools to the Lord. She then began a process of discipling her church leaders, and eventually the whole church, in the operational

DNA of our movement: the five pivotal paradigms that I have referred to throughout this book, together with prayer evangelism. This resulted in her congregation realizing that they are ministers in the marketplace. Now the entire district, historically known as undesirable, has become the opposite because scores of believers take the power and presence of God into their spheres of influence. Transformation began to expand and become so evident that Pastor Wong was also invited to teach other pastors in the district these principles.

As a result, powerful transformational ministers are being equipped and released into the marketplace not only in Hong Kong, but also in other nations. These ministers are building transformation prototypes of excellence in schools, shops, medical clinics and other places. What used to be "out-reach" has now become an "in-reach."

The Kingdom of God in the Marketplace

Hong Kong is an entrepreneurial city. Creativity abounds in the marketplace, a most inspirational example of which is AMENPAPA, a clothing and accessory business that uses fashion as a canvas on which to share the Word of God.

Leo Chan, Geoff Poon and his wife, Salina (the latter two being a young couple in their thirties), started AMENPAPA together in 2010. They are connecting biblical truth with artistically designed fashion garments for young people in ingenious ways to entice them to consider righteous values. Every garment carries a Kingdom message, like the "I Choose Happy" line of clothing, or the Prodigal Son tote bags that carry a "LOVEKEEPSNORECORDOFWRONGS" motif. The sharp designs are appealing, the messages lift the spirit and many are turning to the Lord.

AMENPAPA is also successfully reaching out to the young through plays and themed events. The themes cause people to think about and confront eternal reality and truth. AMENPAPA is indeed a model of Ekklesia that uses the secular medium of fashion to convey messages with an eternal perspective, and it is impacting everyone who comes into contact with their business and fashion products.

Transformation is happening in insurance, in businesses, in the airline industry, in hospitals, in schools, in government and in the eighteen districts that make up Hong Kong as pastors mobilize marketplace people to become the Ekklesia that loves the world where it is planted.[1] We should never dichotomize between the world and the Ekklesia. The latter is God's vehicle to express His love for the world, for which the Ekklesia has been entrusted with extraordinary authority, as we will see in the next chapter.

But before you read on, pause and ask the Lord to impart to you His heart for the world. Remember that this is of vital importance because "without God we can't, but without us He won't."

15

A Fuller Understanding of Spiritual Authority

From Commiserating in Private to Legislating in Public

> Jesus invested His Ekklesia with the highest level of divine authority imaginable. The Ekklesia is to exercise that authority in ever-increasing concentric circles that begin with an initial and all-important point of inception.

Authority and power are two dynamics that we need to understand properly if we are to exercise them effectively. For instance, the power in a car is in the engine, but the authority that gives direction to that power resides in the steering wheel. As far as energy and noise, the engine has it, but the wheel *silently* determines where that power is directed.

There is no question that the devil still retains a measure of power in the world today (see 1 John 5:19). The Ekklesia, however, has been granted full *authority* over all the power of the evil one, since it has authority in heaven and on earth (see Matthew 28:18; Luke 10:19). Authority always trumps power. That is why the Scriptures describe Satan as having dominion (power), but never as being a king (authority), because he is not one. A kingdom is a legitimate institution, whereas a domain, or dominion, is something obtained and maintained by force.

Jesus, who is the King of kings, has invested His Ekklesia with the highest level of authority imaginable. And He defined the target of His authority very precisely for us: the Gates of Hades. Back in chapter 3, I devoted ample time and space to explaining what those Gates are and what they represent, but as I begin to bring this book to a close, I think it is necessary to show how we are to exercise that authority here on earth. I will do that by making two observations.

First, when the Ekklesia engages the Gates of Hades, we need to be aware that the authority to cast out demons is bestowed on individuals (see Mark 16:17), whereas the authority to confront principalities is something only the Ekklesia—the *corporate* expression of the Body of Christ, as opposed to an individual—is empowered to do. This can take place whether it be "a la the *conventus*"—two or three gathered in His name—or a larger group.

Ephesians 3:10 confirms this principle: ". . . so that the manifold wisdom of God might now be made known through the church [the Ekklesia] to the rulers and the authorities in the heavenly places." I make this observation because I have seen too many unnecessary casualties in spiritual warfare as a result of well-meaning, passionate, but biblically misinformed *solo* warriors.

Power Encounters from Day One

Let's next examine how the history of the early Church, as recorded in the book of Acts, reveals a pattern of ever-expanding, concentric circles of authority that begin with an initial point of inception. The first eight chapters of Acts show this pattern, and the first point of inception was on the Day of Pentecost. The Holy Spirit descended and brought the Kingdom of God to the city and to Jews from every nation gathered there. Evil power raised its head in the form of an accusation that the disciples were drunk, but Peter's authoritative rebuttal resulted in three thousand men being saved and baptized in one day—and the Ekklesia was born. It was a formidable beginning and provided a solid beachhead from which the Ekklesia could proceed against the Gates of Hades.

The next showdown came right away, when Jesus' Ekklesia had to take on the Sanhedrin—the functional equivalent of a Jewish ekklesia and the representation of the Gates of Hades inside the religious system. They tried to silence Peter and John, who had been teaching in what would soon become the classical Christian Ekklesia setting, the marketplace (see Acts 4:1–2; 5:12). They were questioned on the issue of whose authority they were operating under, turning the whole incident into a power encounter (see Acts 4:7). This was not unlike Satan's attack on Jesus' legitimacy when he audaciously prefaced his temptations with, "*If* you are the son of God . . ." In other words, he was assaulting Jesus' position of *authority* and taunting Him to come down to the level of merely demonstrating *power*.

Rather than turning tail, those rookie apostles highlighted Jesus' superior authority (see Acts 4:8–10), which trumped the Sanhedrin's: "Whether it is right in the sight of God to give heed to you rather than to God, you be the judge; for we cannot stop speaking about what we have seen and heard" (Acts 4:19–20).

This new level of authority, backed by signs and wonders, resulted in Jesus' Ekklesia taking over Jerusalem's social life just weeks after He was crucified as a criminal. As He had stated previously, the Gates of Hades could do nothing but crumble before the Ekklesia (assembly) of His people. Instead of running away from the powers at work in the city, these "sanctified renegades" engaged them head on. In so doing, they revealed why it was that Jesus chose the Ekklesia over the Temple or the synagogue: His agency would operate in the marketplace, the heart of every city and nation.

The subsequent cascade of breakthroughs quickly spread outward and reached the tipping point when Peter and John, after being released, "went to their own companions and reported all that the chief priests and the elders had said to them. And when they heard this, they lifted their voices to God with one accord" (Acts 4:23–24). Essentially, they constituted themselves into a legislative assembly to plead their case before the court of heaven:

And now, Lord, take note of their threats, and grant that Your bond-servants may speak Your word with all confidence, while You extend Your hand to heal, and signs and wonders take place through the name of Your holy servant Jesus.

Acts 4:29–30

Notice that the result was immediate, and it ushered in Kingdom-style economics:

And when they had prayed, the place where they had gathered together was shaken, and they were all filled with the Holy Spirit and began to speak the word of God with boldness.

And the congregation of those who believed were of one heart and soul; and not one of them claimed that anything belonging to him was his own, but all things were common property to them.

Acts 4:31–32

This resulted in greater authority both in the proclamation of the message and in the release of superabundant wealth to the Ekklesia:

And with great power the apostles were giving testimony to the resurrection of the Lord Jesus, and abundant grace was upon them all. For there was not a needy person among them, for all who were owners of land or houses would sell them and bring the proceeds of the sales and lay them at the apostles' feet, and they would be distributed to each as any had need.

Acts 4:33–35

The powers of darkness understood the force of this tsunami of blessing. And because they foresaw the ominous implications it would have for them, Satan intervened directly in the lives of a couple in the Ekklesia, Ananias and Sapphira, in an attempt to contaminate this spring of wealth. But Peter, discerning who it was behind it, called it out immediately: "Ananias, why has Satan filled your heart to lie to

> *The powers of darkness understood the force of this tsunami of blessing.*

the Holy Spirit?" (Acts 5:3). On behalf of the Ekklesia, Peter exercised its authority, and both Ananias and his wife dropped dead on the spot (see Acts 5:1–10).

City Streets Become Ekklesia Aisles

Victory in this power encounter resulted in greater authority for the apostles, and at their hands "many signs and wonders were taking place among the people" (Acts 5:12). This in turn led to the ongoing addition of multitudes of new converts: "And all the more believers in the Lord, multitudes of men and women, were constantly added to their number" (verse 14). That is what properly exercised authority does.

This phenomenon soon broke out of the Temple courts to impact the city, and in short succession the entire region:

> They even carried the sick out into the streets and laid them on cots and pallets, so that when Peter came by at least his shadow might fall on any one of them. Also the people from the cities in the vicinity of Jerusalem were coming together, bringing people who were sick or afflicted with unclean spirits, and they were all being healed.
>
> Acts 5:15–16

This set the stage for a second round of power-authority encounters between Jesus' Ekklesia and the Sanhedrin: "The high priest rose up, along with all his associates . . . and they were filled with jealousy. They laid hands on the apostles and put them in a public jail" (verses 17–18). A Higher Court immediately trumped their earthly power, however:

> During the night an angel of the Lord opened the gates of the prison, and taking them out he said, "Go, stand and speak to the people in the temple the whole message of this Life." Upon hearing this, they entered into the temple about daybreak and began to teach.
>
> Acts 5:19–21

The high priest and his cohorts were shocked when they heard that the prisoners were preaching to admiring multitudes, so they sent for them, but with visible trepidation: "Then the captain went along with the officers and proceeded to bring them back without violence (for they were afraid of the people, that they might be stoned)" (verse 26). This is what ultimate authority does; it supersedes power.

When they brought the apostles before the council, the high priest questioned them, saying, "We gave you strict orders not to continue teaching in this name, and yet, you have filled Jerusalem with your teaching and intend to bring this man's blood upon us" (verse 28).

The apostles gave a conclusive answer, in essence saying, "We have higher authority." Peter and the others replied, "We must obey God rather than men" (verse 29).

This did not sit well with the operators of the Gates of Hades: "When they heard this, they were cut to the quick and intended to kill them" (verse 33). At that point one council member, Gamaliel, convinced the council to desist by explaining that the whole polemic boiled down to the issue of authority:

A Pharisee named Gamaliel, a teacher of the Law, respected by all the people, stood up in the Council and gave orders to put the men outside for a short time. And he said to them, "Men of Israel, take care what you propose to do with these men. . . . In the present case, I say to you, stay away from these men and let them alone, for if this plan or action is of men, it will be overthrown; but if it is of God, you will not be able to overthrow them; or else you may even be found fighting against God."

Acts 5:34–35, 38–39

Gamaliel put his finger on the crux of the matter: "You may have power on earth to *try* to kill them if you so choose," he was telling them, "but you have no spiritual authority to overrule God." Nonetheless, the council could not resist firing a parting shot, so they "flogged them and ordered them not to speak in the name of Jesus, and then released them" (verse 40).

Rather than being discouraged by the punishment, the apostles stepped into their authority:

They went on their way from the presence of the Council, rejoicing that they had been considered worthy to suffer shame for His name. And every day, in the temple and from house to house, they kept right on teaching and preaching Jesus as the Christ.

Acts 5:41–42

God's Authority Turns Evil into Good

The devil tried again, this time with a batch of new recruits:

Some men from what was called the Synagogue of the Freedmen, including both Cyrenians and Alexandrians, and some from Cilicia and Asia, rose up and argued with Stephen. But they were unable to cope with the wisdom *and the Spirit with which he was speaking.*

Acts 6:9–10, emphasis added

So they dragged Stephen before the council, hoping that this rookie would not fare as well as Peter and John had fared. What happened next was a resounding victory for the Ekklesia as Stephen launched into a magnificent presentation of the authority of heaven (see Acts 6:15–7:51). He masterfully walked his listeners through the entire Old Testament, capping it conclusively with "'Heaven is My throne, and earth is the footstool of My feet. . . . Was it not My hand which made all these things?" (Acts 7:49–50). Then he boldly sentenced them: "You men who are stiff-necked and uncircumcised in heart and ears are always resisting the Holy Spirit; you are doing just as your fathers did" (verse 51).

When they began "gnashing their teeth at him" in what most likely was a massive demonic manifestation, Stephen boldly declared, "Behold, I see the heavens opened up and the Son of Man standing at the right hand of God" (verses 54, 56). In other words, "I am backed by the highest authority in the universe!"

Cognizant of the superior authority entrusted to him, in the midst of the hail of stones mortally pelting his body, Stephen exercised that authority with his last breath as he cried out, "Lord, do not hold this sin against them!" (verse 60). In so doing—and unbeknownst to those who had only the power to kill the body—he placed the keys of the Kingdom into the Gates of Hades and set in motion a process that soon would turn Saul, the relentless destroyer and persecutor, into Paul, the master builder of the Ekklesia. Such is our authority to bind and to release.

But for the moment, as part of the persecution that God would make use of to expand the Ekklesia into regions far beyond Jerusalem, "Saul began ravaging the church, entering house after house, and dragging off men and women, he would put them in prison. Therefore, those who had been scattered went about preaching the word" (Acts 8:3–4).

Unbeknownst to those who had only the power to kill the body, he placed the keys of the Kingdom into the Gates of Hades.

From there, the territorial expansion of the Ekklesia became exponential. The scattering resulted in Philip going down to Samaria, a region still untouched by the Ekklesia, to proclaim Christ to them:

> The crowds with one accord were giving attention to what was said by Philip, as they heard and saw the signs which he was performing. For in the case of many who had unclean spirits, they were coming out of them shouting with a loud voice; and many who had been paralyzed and lame were healed. So there was much rejoicing in that city.
>
> Acts 8:6–8

What began with the healing of a single paralytic at the entrance of the Temple spread unstoppably, first to the Temple courts, next to the entire city, and then to Samaria. The Sanhedrin lost every round because they were unable to match the Ekklesia's *authority*. Finally, they resorted to murderous persecution, but all it accomplished was to accelerate the deployment of transformation agents into society.

Infiltration Backfires on the Devil

It was at this juncture that the devil tried a new approach by proposing through one of his agents what on the surface looked like a good alliance:

Now there was a man named Simon, who formerly was practicing magic in the city and astonishing the people of Samaria, claiming to be someone great; and they all, from smallest to greatest, were giving attention to him, saying, "This man is what is called the Great Power of God."

Acts 8:9–10

When Peter and John came down and laid hands on the new converts, Simon saw the Holy Spirit come upon the converts as a result and offered to buy the anointing: "Give this authority to me as well, so that everyone on whom I lay my hands may receive the Holy Spirit" (verse 19). Instead the apostles exercised their God-given authority to deny his request and remand him to the court of heaven (see verses 20–23).

Apparently, all this loosed something in the heavenly realms, and the expansion went from the Temple courts all the way into the queen's courts. In the same chapter of Acts we see the conversion of the first government official, "an Ethiopian eunuch, a court official of Candace, queen of the Ethiopians, who was in charge of all her treasure" (verse 27). He came into contact with the authority of the Ekklesia in what could be considered the mother of all interceptions in the Kingdom Super Bowl football game.

This high-ranking official had gone to the Temple to worship, which gave the Sanhedrin the local advantage, so to speak. But on the way back home, he was reading the book of Isaiah in total perplexity. God deployed Philip to intercept him (see verse 26), and look what happened as a result:

Then Philip opened his mouth, and beginning from this Scripture he preached Jesus to him. As they went along the road they came to some water; and the eunuch said, "Look! Water! What prevents me from being baptized?" And Philip said, "If you believe with all your heart, you may." And he answered and said, "I believe that Jesus Christ is the Son of God." And he ordered the chariot to stop; and they both went down into the water, Philip as well as the eunuch, and he baptized him. . . . And the eunuch . . . went on his way rejoicing.

Acts 8:35–39

Historians tell us that this man, Simeon Bachos the Eunuch, was later "sent into the regions of Ethiopia, to preach what he had himself believed, that there was one God preached by the prophets . . . that the Son of this (God) had already made (His) appearance in human flesh,"[1] to the effect that the Gospel began to spread through a whole new continent.

The Point of Inception

As in the case of an amphibious landing, the point of inception is the key in the expansion of the Ekklesia. In Jerusalem, the disciples' first confrontation with the Sanhedrin was such a point of inception, because the Sanhedrin housed those who orchestrated Jesus' crucifixion in collusion with Judas, whose heart Satan himself had entered. No wonder this was fertile ground for the devil, because these folks were the ones reported as having "rejected God's purpose for themselves, not having been baptized by John [the Baptist]" (Luke 7:30).

We saw a point of inception in Ciudad Juárez, where, from a tent erected in the corner of a park, Poncho and the Ekklesia began a journey that took them through the transformation of a prison to the restoration of the city, which now is beginning to impact the nation.

After the Gates of Hades crumbled in Barbara Chan's courtroom under the weight of the Ekklesia's authority, more cases were being solved by mediation than in court.

We learned about a similar point of inception in the Philippines, where King Flores, after learning to take care of the "congregation" that stepped into his taxicab, kept walking in that authority until he saw his city officially dedicated to God.

There was also such an inception point in Vallejo, California, where Michael Brown aligned himself and his company with God's authority by making God the Chairman of the Board, the Lord Jesus the CEO, and the Holy Spirit the legal counsel of his company. From that beachhead of authority, the Ekklesia has been instrumental in bringing a city out of bankruptcy into solvency and taking on the county's bastions of systemic poverty.

In Hong Kong, there was a point of inception when Barbara Chan began walking in the authority of the Ekklesia as a judge. After the Gates of Hades crumbled in her courtroom under the weight of that authority, more cases were being solved by mediation than in court. Later on, she exercised that authority with other members of the Ekklesia at Victoria Peak, overlooking Hong Kong, to proclaim the spiritual adoption of the city. Today, the Transform Our World Network–Hong Kong movement involves thousands who are influencing the city's districts and beyond.

The point of inception is always key—no matter how small it might be—because it shatters darkness. *Darkness* and *hopelessness* are terms that have no plural form, whereas *light* and *hope* do. Once you punch a hole in the darkness, light floods in. The following three stories graphically illustrate this point.

"My School Is My City"

Daniel Chinen's transformation journey was set in motion during a Harvest Evangelism transformation mission trip to Argentina in 2002. Daniel says,

> When [I heard] my school was my city, the energy inside of me felt like fire. God began to give me His heart and vision. A fire and passion burned inside of me to see revival come to Hawaii, starting with my school . . . not to simply start a Christian club on campus but to reach the whole campus and eventually all of Hawaii!

That personal *bapto* infused Daniel with an awareness of authority he had not felt before. He began to walk in it with other Christian students and with his father, Pastor Cal Chinen, and along with the network of pastors his father led, they launched a prayer movement that initially focused on Daniel's school campus. They first repented to the principal for not being the role models that Christians should be. The principal forgave them. They then asked permission to pray for every student, teacher, staff member and administrator.

Struck by their sincerity, the principal said, "Yes, but let me give you guidelines so that we don't violate issues of separation of church and state."

After that was taken care of, Daniel and his group engaged students, parents and partnering congregations, and soon they were praying for every person on campus. By the end of the first year, it became evident that the climate was changing. Fights on campus had diminished, three major drug dealers were apprehended, which reduced drug violations on campus significantly, and grade point averages started inching upward.

The following year, the expansion continued. Soon other pastors and their churches were joining together to pray for their communities and high schools. The circle of influence was growing ever wider, into new schools, pushing back the darkness. By the fall of 2006, every public (and nearly every private) high school campus was being prayed for. That December, the Ekklesia of the islands led 72 simultaneous prayer gatherings on public school and university campuses across the state. The then–lieutenant governor, Duke Aiona, accepted the invitation to attend the prayer gathering and led a powerful prayer based on the Lord's Prayer:

Right now, whether we feel it or not, whether we know it or not, whether our circumstances show it or not, we declare by faith in our Lord Jesus Christ that He is the Light of the World.

And we invite You, Lord, to be the light of our school, to be the light of our town, to be the light of our island, to be the light of our state, to be the light of all of Hawaii.

And we declare that our school will become God's school, our town will become God's town, our city will become God's city, our island will become God's island, and our state will become God's state.

Lord Jesus Christ, as it is in heaven, so also in our school, in our town, in our island, and in our state: Let Your Kingdom come! Let Your will be done! Amen.

Daniel commented, "When Duke Aiona pronounced his *Amen*, it thundered across Hawaii as people shouted *Amen!* at all of those venues." And as Daniel put it, "Spontaneous joy and praise broke out. It was as if something broke in the heavens over Hawaii. Believers rejoiced, clapped their hands and shouted. We had come together and invited God's Kingdom and His will to fall upon our land."

It is clearly evident how those first droplets of authority that Daniel Chinen and his fellow Ekklesia members exercised at the point of inception rippled outward to touch all the school campuses, and they kept rippling. That act of obedience became the catalyst for the formation of the Transform Our World–Hawaii movement that has seen towns like Nanakuli experience transformation. The state's prison system also changed, and the state is making restitution to native Hawaiians for lands usurped in the past. In the process, the Ekklesia is earning favor with unsaved people.

> *"Spontaneous joy and praise broke out. It was as if something broke in the heavens over Hawaii."*

And it keeps going. As I was writing this chapter, Pastor Cal Chinen wrote about Michele Okimura, a fellow pastor who developed a ministry for young people in the area of sexual healing. While the ministry had been germinating for years, it was not until Michele tapped into the corporate authority given to the Ekklesia for transformation that explosive growth took place.[2] Her point of inception was her own "Jerusalem" in Hawaii. In the past months she has been invited to Singapore to minister healing and restoration to youth, and then to the Philippines by the churches and schools of Baguio City, Benguet Province and Manila to do the same. She recently wrote from Southern California, "Please pray! God keeps accelerating everything beyond my comfort level, but I know it is Him." That is the path of God's authority.

Will the Real Supreme Court Please Rule?

In the early 1990s, Dr. Clifford Daugherty and his school board were struggling to keep Valley Christian Schools in San José, California, afloat, subsisting on rented public school campus facilities and carrying a deficit in the hundreds of thousands of dollars. But exposure to the principles of transformation that had changed Resistencia, Argentina, baptized him with hope and put him in touch with a new authority. Upon returning home from our conference, he decided to move on what he had learned, first by gathering with intercessors, and then by engaging the student body in prayer evangelism to change the spiritual climate on campus.

Shortly after that initial point of inception was established, the powers of darkness began to recede. The financial deficit was taken care of. The suppressed hope for a new campus took on new life. Today, Valley Christian Schools is housed on a $150 million campus and is considered the top-rated school in the nation. Its accelerated programs in science and math are allowing students to launch their own satellite from the International Space Station.

It was then that Dr. Daugherty experienced a new illumination: *To whom much is given, much will be required. What can we do for public education?*

Inspiration came to establish a Junior University and Lighthouse Initiative that involves sending Valley Christian student mentors every week to a local public school to assist underprivileged students with skill development, tutoring and extracurricular activities. The results were outstanding. Hellyer Elementary School principal Jerry Merza reported that in the fifth year of the program, "we catapulted ourselves to above [the state-mandated score of] 800, which was a huge accomplishment." Hellyer went from being one of the lowest-performing schools in the county to being among the top five in two counties in their socioeconomic bracket.[3]

That the mentoring program provided influence at the relational and motivational levels was tremendous, but what about at the spiritual level? Dr. Daugherty confessed, "It was my opinion, like many Christians, that there wasn't much hope for our public schools because we didn't feel that [because of church and state regulations] we could have much of an influence."

That mindset derived from the U.S. Supreme Court rulings of 1962–63 to prohibit prayer in the schools, and by default, anything that had to do with religion. Dr. Daugherty recounts, "When I lodged my complaint [to the Lord], I sensed an immediate reply. 'So you think the highest law in the land is the United States Supreme Court?'"

Dr. Daugherty admitted his faithlessness and immediately felt the Holy Spirit speaking to him again: "Why don't you put the rulings of . . . 1962 and 1963 . . . on appeal to the Supreme Court Judge of the Heavens and Earth? I'll take the case."[4]

The heavens opened as Dr. Daugherty shifted from a natural power perspective to a supernatural authority mindset. God began to peel away in his mind the many misconceptions about how those rulings could impede what God wanted to do in public education, and He poured in new concepts and ideas. Among these was a music program based on the words of the Declaration of Independence that would develop a common virtues-oriented relationship with the public schools: "We hold these truths to be self-evident, that all men are created equal, that they are endowed by their Creator with certain unalienable Rights, that among these are Life, Liberty and the Pursuit of Happiness."

"So you think the highest law in the land is the United States Supreme Court?"

Those words suddenly sounded very similar to "righteousness, peace and joy" to Dr. Daugherty—the very components of the Kingdom of God. Valley Christian Schools was off and running, and the doors of influence and favor continued to increase. Today, the school is a functional Ekklesia, even though the word is not used. It exerts a rapidly growing outward ripple of authority that is ministering to the felt needs of multiple public schools, even to the point of sharing the resources of its Applied Math, Science, and Engineering Institute to help other schools put science projects in space, something they otherwise would not be able to do. The initial breakthrough at Hellyer Elementary led the superintendent and the Franklin McKinley School District to become a member of the Quest Institute for Quality Education, opening the door for even more goodness, peace and joy. As a result, the new mentoring programs have led to the establishment of Kids Clubs on those campuses, and over six hundred students have come into the Kingdom of God in the first year alone.

Barrio Las Flores: Standing in the Gap

In 2011, Barrio Las Flores in Rosario, Argentina, was overrun by battling drug cartels. Then Gregorio Avalos ran for president of the neighborhood association for Barrio Las Flores—and won by four votes. Gregorio is a taxi driver who experienced a power encounter with the Lord as a member of the transformation church pastored by our colleagues Aldo and Roxi Martín. Believing God could and would rescue his barrio, he began speaking peace over every house, literally walking out Luke 10:5–9 in prayer evangelism.

It "just so happened" that Michael Brown and Tony Mitchell from Transformation Vallejo were in Argentina, equipping regional leaders in transformation. When they heard about Gregorio's incipient beginning at the barrio, they asked him, "How can we help?"

Gregorio suggested providing supplies to paint the run-down community center. The Ekklesia in Vallejo, through Michael and Tony, provided the resources, and with every stroke of the paintbrush a blessing was deposited on what until recently had been the embodiment of the Gates of Hades.

As these droplets of authority began to fall, Gregorio was emboldened to ask God to send people with barrio-sized solutions. The sign would be that they would ask, "How can I help you, Gregorio?"

First came the mayor of Rosario, then the governor of the province, and finally the national security chief, all posing the same question: "What can I do for you?" The latter deployed troops to demolish the drug bunkers. The other two brought renovation. Today, Barrio Las Flores has paved streets, a sewer system, streetlights and a new school. The new regional hospital (the largest in the province) is being built there, as well as Rosario's brand-new train station.

That Jesus had come to the neighborhood was never more in evidence than when, within a few months and for the first time in memory, over ten thousand people in Barrio Las Flores felt safe enough to leave their homes to publicly gather for the proclamation of the Gospel by renowned Argentine evangelist Carlos Annacondia, with thousands making decisions for Christ. And that authority of heaven is now moving beyond the boundaries of the barrio as the growing Ekklesia of Rosario ministers to both the mayor and the governor regularly.

How the spiritual authority entrusted to the Ekklesia trumps the power of godless secular government became patently evident recently. Rosario is situated in the province of Santa Fe, Argentina. This particular province is the only one governed by socialists, who take pride in their agnosticism or atheism and in espousing a humanistic social agenda. As such, they are the least likely to be open to spiritual things, much less to the Church.

First came the mayor of Rosario, then the governor of the province, and finally the national security chief, all posing the same question: "What can I do for you?"

Nevertheless, Aldo and Roxi Martín adopted the governor spiritually and began to practice prayer evangelism, blessing him in their prayers and fellowshiping with him "a la Luke 10." They were also able to minister to his felt needs, leading him to experience goodness, peace and joy—in essence, the Kingdom of God.

As a result, the socialist government the governor leads convened a meeting with pastors at Aldo's place and asked them to mentor fifty thousand youngsters who have gotten in trouble with the law. These are folks who neither work nor study and have already done time in the juvenile hall or prison. In essence, they are a social ticking bomb.

The government specifically asked that every participating church building be turned into a training center three days a week where these kids could learn life and work skills. The government would pay for the construction of workshops—carpentry, plumbing, computer labs, etc.—on church property and would provide financial support for the students and full salary for two church leaders to serve as mentors for every fifteen youths. And if this is not already supremely extraordinary, this socialist government asked that 33 percent of the training time be devoted to Bible classes. Basically, the government asked the Ekklesia to disciple the province. This is indeed an extraordinary miracle!

All these stories portray a powerful demonstration of the impact the ever-expanding concentric circles of authority have on both the spiritual and natural realms. In order to keep that expansion properly focused and uncompromisingly aligned, we need a better understanding of the operational methodology that Jesus designed for His Ekklesia. That operational methodology is what we will look at next.

16

A Fuller Understanding of the Ekklesia's Operational Methodology

From the Swamp to the River

There is life in a swamp, but one has to go there to find it. A river is different because it carries life beyond its source. The Ekklesia is called to take life to the world. That is why it must flow like a river. And to break out of the swamp, it must find the banks God has for it. What are those banks?

I hope by now you are saying, "Okay, I get it! I am discovering the Ekklesia, God's instrument to change the world, and I am a vital part of His plan." And next, you will find yourself facing the daunting question, "But where do I begin?"

The short answer is, "Right where you are, but with the right paradigms!"

That is the way it was with Wanlapa, an ice-cream vendor on the streets of Phuket, Thailand. She took the words of her pastor seriously when he told his fledgling congregation, "We are called to disciple this nation—each one of us . . . and the way to do it is by taking the Kingdom of God to our spheres of influence."

What Wanlapa started doing from her ice-cream cart has led thousands to salvation. Her story, which I will share in more detail later, is a powerful example (among many) of how the small congregation she is part of has brought thousands to salvation in three provinces in Thailand.

Before I relate more of Wanlapa's story, however, let's first set the framework for how we can begin to apply all the transformation principles we have discussed so far. In reality, transformation is happening millions of times every day, everywhere in the world. Myriads of people come to the Lord, lives are changed, churches are planted, worship conferences enthrall believers, youth camps enrich campers, and anointed Bible teaching brings direction to millions every day on every continent. All of that is transformational. So why is it that we are not seeing cities and nations transformed? Because more often than not, that kind of change is happening in the context of a swamp or a lake, which means that unless people go to it, they will not benefit from it.

Transformation is like a river. The swamp contains life, but the river carries life.

Transformation is like a river. The swamp contains life, but the river *carries* life. The swamp, while nourished by the rain, has no inner movement and is susceptible to stagnation. The river never stagnates. The swamp will take us nowhere. The river's flow will carry us to new horizons with every bend.

Turning a Swamp into a River

What can turn a swamp into a river? The addition of banks! And when the swamp is connected to a constant water source, first it turns into a stream, then into a creek and finally into a river. Essentially, that is the story of the Transform Our World Network. In chapter 2, I shared the major milestones we have seen through many years of ministry, and I likened the process to the dawn of a new day that grows brighter and brighter with each hour. But I could just as easily have chosen this riverbank metaphor to express the process. We found the riverbanks that turned a ministry swamp that pooled around a prayer chapel in Argentina into a life-giving river taking transformational life to the farthest reaches of our world.

The two banks that have been guiding us have proven themselves transcultural, transgenerational and transdenominational. They are not a project; they are principles that lay a foundation for every project. They do not constitute a program, but a lifestyle. They are available and applicable to all, regardless of age, social level, race, color or gender.[1]

The first of the two banks is what I have been calling the five pivotal paradigms for transformation. They define the *what*, the *why*, the *how*, the *where* and the *what for*. They are absolutely indispensable when it comes to keeping us focused on the end result. Anything short of that focus will derail the process or cause it to stagnate.

The second bank is what I have been calling prayer evangelism. It embodies the precise instructions Jesus gave a group of followers He was sending on a mission that turned out to be the major game changer in the gospels. I explained this in detail in chapter 4, where I showed how prayer evangelism conveyed the Gospel of the Kingdom, something that resulted in everyone "forcing their way" into the Kingdom (see Luke 16:16).

To be vulnerably candid, I wish I could say that I know there are many ways to do city or nation transformation and they all work, or that it does not matter how you do it because in the end everything will turn out fine. But the evidence does not support that. I don't mean to imply that this is the only way to do transformation, but rather that this is *the only one I know of that works consistently.* To paraphrase John, "that which I have seen, touched, heard and experienced, that is what I testify about" (see 1 John 1:1). In such a context, what I can convey to you with certitude is that where we find lasting, sustainable and scalable transformation happening, we consistently find it within these two "banks."

Ruth and I are part of a multicultural, multilingual, interdenominational, multinational company of men and women irretrievably invested in seeing the world transformed. This is our passion and where we put all our time, energy and resources. And from our vantage point, without the five pivotal paradigms and prayer evangelism *applied in concert as a lifestyle,* transformation either does not happen, or if it happens it does not last, or if it lasts it does not reach beyond its point of inception. I bless every other transformation initiative, and I humbly and respectfully offer the banks of this river as a proven framework ample enough for all to work together in, since it will take the whole Ekklesia to present the whole Gospel to the whole world.

Here are the two comments I hear most frequently about the transformation process entrusted to us: "You gave me the language for what I was already trying to do, but could not explain." And, "You have concrete examples—verifiable prototypes. It's not just a theory or a good idea."

While the examples in this book are proofs of a transformational concept that at the moment seems unique or rare, it is our objective that it will not remain so. Rather, it will become the "new normal" as the Church begins operating more and more as the Ekklesia. With that objective in mind, let's take a closer summarizing look at the banks of this river.

Bank 1: The Five Pivotal Paradigms

I have touched on the five paradigms elsewhere and listed them in chapter 2, but they are so pivotal in the transformation process that I want to focus on them here in greater detail.

1. The Great Commission is about discipling nations and not just individuals. "Go therefore and [as you go] make disciples of all the nations" (Matthew 28:19).

This first paradigm defines the *what*. We have been developing this theme throughout the book, so I won't dwell on it except to underline that seeing nations discipled is the God-ordained finish line, and when this is defined properly, everything else begins to make sense.

When it finally dawns on us how grand the magnitude and the implications are for what God has called us to do, we will never be able just to settle for a bigger church, a bigger business or a bigger charity. All of that will become subservient to this much higher calling.

God has entrusted to us the message and the authority to bring goodness, peace and joy to nations so that they will be part of the majestic parade described in Revelation 21:24, and we must find ourselves crying out like Paul, "Woe is me if I do not preach the gospel" (1 Corinthians 9:16).

2. The Atonement secured redemption not only for individuals, but also for the marketplace, which is the heart of the nation. "For the Son of Man has come to seek and to save that which was lost" (Luke 19:10).

This paradigm defines the *why*. The world has already been redeemed by Jesus, and this is why now we, as His Ekklesia, must reclaim it. This is the full scope of the redemptive work of Christ and the authority entrusted to us as God's agents for transformation.

To keep you from realizing that Jesus redeemed everything that was lost, the devil will try to deceive you into believing that Jesus died only for some things. God will settle for nothing less than nations because that is what Jesus redeemed (see Psalm 2:8; Revelation 21:24–26).

3. Labor is worship, and since all believers are ministers, they are to turn their jobs into places of worship to God and ministry to others. "Whatever you do, do your work heartily, as for the Lord rather than for men" (Colossians 3:23).

Now that we have identified the *what* and the *why*, this paradigm shows the *how*. Nations will be transformed by believers properly trained by their leaders to do the work of the ministry in the marketplace day in and day out as members of Jesus' Ekklesia. Imagine for a moment the catalytic impact of this. If, in your city, there are ten thousand believers, but none of them have embraced this paradigm yet, this means that they go to work with the "worship" switch in the OFF position. They wait for a break to turn it ON, pop in their earbuds, listen to the music and for the next twenty minutes or so worship God until the break is over . . . and then they go back to work.

> *To keep you from realizing that Jesus died for everything that was lost, the devil will try to deceive you into believing that Jesus died only for some things.*

Now picture those thousands of believers embracing this paradigm and going not just to work but to minister because they now see labor as worship. Whatever work they do, they now do it as an act of worship to God. A waitress will bring food to the table "for the glory of God." A taxi driver will do the same in driving his vehicle. A lawyer will file a brief in the power of the Spirit. Now observe the same city from the heavenlies, and you will see thousands of acts of worship taking place all over every hour of the day. As a result, the spiritual climate will improve, first in the lives of those who are worshiping at work, and then through them in their spheres of influence.

I have found that this is the paradigm people find easiest to grasp and run with. This is the one pastors preach the most. But it is key to attach it to the other four paradigms. Unless they make that connection and live it out, they will become more fulfilled at work and will be part of a more fruitful church while still falling short of being the Ekklesia, because they will not be committed to its ultimate destination—discipling the nations.

4. Jesus is the One who builds His Church, not us. Our assignment is to use the keys of the Kingdom to lock and unlock the Gates of Hades in order for Him to build His Church where those Gates stand. "I will build My church, and the gates of Hades shall not prevail against it" (Matthew 16:18 NKJV).

This fourth paradigm defines the *where*. Jesus made it crystal clear: "*I* will build *My* church." You and I are not doing the building. And the Gates of Hades will not prevail against it. What are we expected to do? Pick up the keys of the Kingdom, which used to be the keys of Hades and Death, and unlock those gates so that the Ekklesia's building material—saved sinners—will become available.

Here is one example of using the keys of the Kingdom to bind evil and release goodness. After we built the prayer chapel in Argentina mentioned in chapter 2, we made a sobering discovery. The reason for such spiritual darkness enveloping so many unevangelized towns was that a major warlock had his national headquarters in a nearby town. He was so famous that I was told even presidents came to him, incognito of course, for "ministry." Before his death, he appointed twelve apostles and cast a spell on a well where "holy" water was drawn to accompany their incantations.

The presence of this powerful and well-organized witchcraft center had defiled the entire region and was the reason for such spiritual bleakness. I tell the full story in my book *That None Should Perish* (Chosen, 1995),[2] but when we learned basic spiritual warfare, I led a team of pastors and intercessors to serve an eviction notice on the principalities and powers behind this elaborate evil scheme.

Since then, all the children of the warlock have become Christians. One of his grandsons is a missionary. The building where his headquarters was now houses a church, and his lead apostle today is its leading deacon. And on top of that, there are 20 churches in the town, and every one of the 109 towns in the region has been evangelized. We simply used the keys, and Jesus built His Ekklesia!

5. The elimination of systemic poverty in its four dimensions—spiritual, relational, motivational and material—is the premier tangible social indicator of transformation. "The Spirit of the Lord is on me, because he has anointed me to proclaim good news to the poor" (Luke 4:18 NIV), and "The Son of God appeared for this purpose, to destroy the works of the devil" (1 John 3:8).

This paradigm defines the *what for*. The focus here is on changing the systems that keep people in poverty (we discussed this in detail in chapter 12). This is the paradigm that opens doors with government officials because they see that we have something valuable to offer.

Bank 2: Prayer Evangelism

Those five pivotal paradigms make up one bank of the river. The way to live them out is through a *prayer evangelism* lifestyle. Discipling a nation begins with changing the spiritual climate at a point of inception and then progressively continuing to change it. Is this possible? Yes!

It is possible because we already know from experience that the spiritual climate inside a home, in a church building, or at a stadium during an evangelistic crusade can be changed. The concept of changing the spiritual climate is not foreign to us, but we usually have a problem believing that the same change can happen all over our city. Yet we are promised this in 1 Timothy 2:1–8, where we learn that if we pray for everybody, everywhere, we will be able to "lead a tranquil and quiet life in all godliness and dignity" (verse 2). For godliness to increase in a city, ungodliness must decrease, and this requires a change in the city's spiritual climate.

For far too long, we have left control of the spiritual climate in cities and nations in the hands of the devil. This is evident when we look around at the mire of sin, the criminal activity and the crushing weight of hopelessness in our cities. Every week thousands get married hoping for a bright future, and every week a similar number watch their marriages disintegrate. Satan is busy keeping things either too hot or too cold, and in so doing, he forces the Church to go on the defensive, either putting destructive fires out or trying to keep its own people from freezing. That is not what the Ekklesia is designed to do.

For far too long, we have left control of the spiritual climate in the hands of the devil.

Early in Jesus' ministry, the spiritual climate in Galilee and Judea was so unfavorable that at one point Jesus sounded as though He were tempted to quit, saying to His disciples, "You unbelieving and perverted generation, how long shall I be with you and put up with you?" (Luke 9:41). By the next chapter, however, He felt entirely differently: "He rejoiced greatly in the Holy Spirit," and He praised God for what His disciples had done (Luke 10:21). Something had taken place that caused Satan to lose his grip on those whom he was oppressing. That "something" is the second bank of the river: prayer evangelism.

Prayer Evangelism According to Jesus

It happened in Luke 10. Jesus had sent seventy of His disciples out two by two to proclaim the coming of the Kingdom in every city He planned to visit. The passage relates, "The seventy returned with joy, saying, 'Lord, even the demons are subject to us in Your name'" (verse 17).

Jesus explained the reason behind this extraordinary turn of events: "I was watching Satan fall from heaven like lightning" (verse 18). In other words, Satan himself suffered a *major* defeat.

Now that we know *when* the climate changed, let's see *how* it changed. What was it that produced this dramatic turnaround? This is the only occasion where Jesus spells out an evangelistic method. Here He calls for four things to be done in a sequential manner for the benefit of the lost. The first step opens the door to the second, the second step to the third and the third step to the fourth, since the four steps are interconnected. To be effective, we must implement these steps in the order Jesus specified. We will soon see why this is so, but here is the core of His instructions:

> Whatever house you enter, first say, "Peace be to this house." . . . Stay in that house, eating and drinking what they give you. . . . Whatever city you enter and they receive you, eat what is set before you; and heal those in it who are sick, and say to them, "The kingdom of God has come near to you."
>
> Luke 10:5–9

Here are the steps in list form:

1. Bless: Speak peace to them (verse 5).
2. Fellowship: Eat with them (verse 7).
3. Minister: Take care of their needs (verse 9).
4. Proclaim: The Kingdom of God has come (verse 9).

Let me unpack these steps to show more clearly why they have such a powerful effect. In essence, Jesus is calling us to become shepherds to the people in our circle of influence. They may not know yet that we are their pastor, but we should know they are our sheep, and we begin the process by blessing them.

1. Bless, don't blast.

"Whatever house you enter, first say, 'Peace be to this house'" (Luke 10:5).

This speaking peace involves not just words, but an intentional impartation. It is transferring something to an intended recipient. We know this is the case because Jesus specifies that if the peace is not received, it will *return* to us, which implies that if we can tell when it bounces back, the recipient should certainly feel it when we send it.

The words that we speak should impart "spirit and life." They cannot be casual or flippant. They are intended to touch the recipient. Here are three important reasons for speaking peace:

Reason #1: We need to declare peace because we may have been at war with the lost. Too often, "Repent or Burn" is the banner under which we approach the unsaved in our circle of influence. Unfortunately, we have a tendency to dislike sinners, and this soon becomes obvious to them.

> *I became aware of my own belligerence toward the lost when, instead of claiming the promises of God for my neighbors, I told God about everything that was wrong with them.*

I became aware of this the first time I tried to implement the Luke 10 strategy in our neighborhood. Instead of claiming the promises of God for my neighbors, I told God about everything that was wrong with them. I pointed out in disgust the morally loose, unwed mother who was such a bad example to our daughters. I demanded that He do something about the couple who kept us awake at night with their fighting. I complained about the depressed neighbor whose front yard was a disgrace and a bane to real estate values on our block. And, of course, I did not forget about the teenager on drugs. I made it perfectly clear to the Lord that I wanted Him to deploy an angel with a flaming sword to keep that young man away from our daughters.

All of a sudden, I sensed God saying, *Ed, I am so glad you haven't witnessed to any of them yet.*

Surprised, I asked, *Lord, why is that?*

His reply was sobering: *Because I don't want your neighbors to know that you and I are related! I constantly extend grace to them. I love them. But you don't. You resent them. Rather than being an advocate for them, you are a witness for the prosecution . . . if not the prosecutor himself. Ed, unless you love them, I cannot trust you with their lives.*

Right there on a sidewalk I cried out to God to make my heart more like His. Preaching the truth without love is like giving someone a kiss when you have bad breath. No matter how good the kiss, no one will come back for a second one. This is what happens when, in anger or disgust, we tell the lost how terrible and depraved they are. Even though it all may be true, our negative approach blocks and distorts the central message of the Bible—that God sent His Son not to condemn the world, but to save it (see John 3:17).

Reason #2: Blessing the lost will keep us from cursing them. We do not realize how often we curse others. When we say, "The lady across the street is a drunkard; she's going to die of cirrhosis of the liver," we are cursing her unaware. When we point to rowdy teenagers and complain, "They are nuisances who drink and drive and experiment with drugs, and soon they are going to kill themselves," we are also cursing them. But when we pronounce blessings on our neighbors, it edifies our city: "By the blessing of the upright a city is exalted" (Proverbs 11:11).

Reason #3: When we speak peace, we neutralize the demons assigned to blind the lost to the light of the Gospel. The Bible explains clearly why people have not yet come to the Lord: "The god of this world [the devil] has blinded the minds of the unbelieving so that they might not see the light of the gospel" (2 Corinthians 4:4). This means that the devil is *actively* blinding them, and since he is not omnipresent, we must conclude that he is using his demons to do it, as implied in Matthew 13:19.

When we bless people in our circle of influence, sooner or later those who used to avoid us will begin to seek us out, opening the door to fellowship—step 2 in the process. They will do it because they will feel the blessings we are speaking over them. They may put it like this: "When I see you walking by, I get a positive vibration." That is New

Age lingo for peace, but what they mean is that in our presence, they feel a tangible peace.

2. Engage in two-way fellowship.

"Stay in that house, eating and drinking what they give you" (Luke 10:7).

Once you have made initial contact, fellowship is the next step, not proclamation. You may wonder, *What value is there in fellowship with the lost unless I first share the Gospel with them?* Fellowship provides an opportunity to show unconditional acceptance by welcoming people the way they are instead of the way we want them to be.

In fact, Jesus' instruction here is that we let the lost host us. Why? When we allow unbelievers to do something for us, we affirm their value and dignity as God's creation. In Jesus' day, the custom was to offer food and lodging to visitors, even to strangers. Today, playing football or organizing a multifamily garage sale with the lost allows us to speak blessings at close range. It most likely can set in motion a process to be hosted for a meal, too, as they sense how much we appreciate their fellowship.

Jesus always treated sinners with respect. The worse the sinners, the greater the respect with which He treated them. Remember how Jesus began His dialogue with Zaccheus and the Samaritan woman by asking each of them to do Him a favor. Of Zaccheus He asked a bed, and of the Samaritan woman He asked a drink of water.

3. Minister to their felt needs.

"Heal those in it who are sick" (Luke 10:9).

Fellowship eventually leads to step 3—an opportunity to meet people's felt needs. This will only happen after they trust us enough to disclose them. Once we establish such trust, they may share that their marriage is rotting inside. They may tell us about their fear of losing their job, or they may seek our help with an addiction they cannot overcome. They will begin to share heart-to-heart because they sense that we have an answer and that we care for them.

It is at this precise moment when we can say to them, "I've been praying for you, and I would be glad to pray about this, too."

Amazingly, most people will say yes! When we start praying *for* them, soon we will be praying *with* them.

Now you may be thinking, *Shouldn't we lead them to Christ first?* Not necessarily. What the lost are sharing at this time is what *they* feel is most important to them. Granted, their most important need is salvation, but they don't know that yet. Praying for their felt needs will open the door for that.

What if I pray and nothing happens? you may wonder. *I don't want God's reputation damaged.* What if you don't pray? Nothing will happen! Prayer is the most tangible trace of eternity in the human heart; even atheists have prayed in moments of desperation. When you let the lost know that you are praying prayers of faith[3] for *their felt needs*, you touch them at the heart level.

This is why we must be filled with the Holy Spirit at all times to be able to pray prayers of faith. Divinely answered prayers constitute the tipping point in prayer evangelism. Jesus assured us, "He who believes in Me, the works that I do, he will do also; and greater works than these he will do." Then He proceeded to give us a blank check, as it were, to bless sinners, because He said, "Whatever you ask in My name, that will I do. . . . If you ask Me anything in My name, I will do it" (John 14:12–14).

4. Finally, let the lost know that the Kingdom has come near them, and invite them to come into it.

"Say to them, 'The kingdom of God has come near to you'" (Luke 10:9).

Once you have taken the first three steps—blessing the lost, fellowshiping with them, and taking care of their felt needs, *something* is bound to happen. You have imparted to them peace that upstreams to God, which is what unbelievers lack the most. You have provided them with the most caring and healthy fellowship they have ever enjoyed. And you have offered prayers for needs that they have not been able to meet on their own. After you have taken those three steps, don't be surprised if they say something like, "I feel something! I don't know what's happening to me right now." Or, "Tell me, who is this God who loves me even though I don't know Him?"

Prayer evangelism is very much like driving through the desert in an air-conditioned truck stocked with cold drinks, and then spotting a weary hiker.

The lost will feel safe approaching you because of the gradual improvement in the spiritual climate as you moved from step 1 to step 4. At that point, you can explain, "It's the Kingdom of God that has just come near to you. Would you like to come into it?" Then gently lead them to Christ.

Rather than trying to coerce or convince the lost into the Kingdom, we are taking the Kingdom to them. Prayer evangelism is very much like driving through the desert in an air-conditioned truck stocked with cold drinks, and then spotting a weary hiker. You don't need to beg him to come on board; all you need to do is pull over near him or her and open the door.

How Satan Falls

The fall of Satan in Luke 10 was precipitated by Jesus sending the seventy "to every city and place where He Himself was going to come" (Luke 10:1). We saw how entrenched evil fell in San Nicolás, Argentina, during a weeklong prayer evangelism thrust, as reported in my book *Prayer Evangelism*.[4] On Sunday, we taught the participating congregations about prayer evangelism, and members were invited to tune in to a one-hour live radio program each day for the next three days. On Monday night, we gathered with a group of pastors at a local radio station for the broadcast, and we guided believers to dedicate themselves as shepherds over their homes, their schools and their workplaces. On Tuesday, we led them to invite the Lord to show them anything that was wrong or unholy, and we directed them to get rid of those items by throwing them in a bin set up in the room. On Wednesday we had them prayer walk their neighborhoods, with a portable radio receiver in hand, and speak peace over every home, school and place of business. As every sidewalk was prayer walked, a canopy of prayer went up over the city.

The local believers accepted the mandate on Monday to pastor their sphere of influence. On Tuesday they sanctified themselves and their environs. Doing that put them in a powerful position by Wednesday to speak blessings over everybody and everything that had been cursed by the devil in their city. Because blessings break curses, this citywide exercise caused the devil to fall and his demons to submit. When the commanding general surrenders, his soldiers follow suit immediately: "Lord, even the demons are subject to us in Your name" (Luke 10:17).

When we did this citywide blessing on Wednesday, I sensed that something powerful had taken place, but I did not understand the extent to which it had happened. It was like a slight shift in the wind, small but noticeable, that precedes greater changes in the weather. This became evident on Saturday, when every home was visited and prayer was made available at a "prayer fair." An extraordinary number of unsaved people came to the fair, which confirmed the change in the city's spiritual climate. Another confirmation was the way in which the power of God flowed so freely at the various prayer stations, and a greater confirmation was the many people who came to the Lord.

The God of *Peace* Crushed Satan

I asked the Lord why the spiritual change had felt so easy, and He directed me to Romans 16:20: "The God of *peace* will soon crush Satan *under your feet*" (emphasis added). This verse opened my eyes to a monumental mistake we had been making in spiritual warfare: *We had rated war higher than peace.* It is not the God of war, but the God of *peace* who crushes Satan, and He does it under *our* feet—hence the need for us to walk in peace.

Jesus has defeated the devil already, and as we walk in peace God crushes Satan's head under our feet. We see this truth as central to Paul's instructions in Ephesians 6 about how to put on the armor of God. The third piece of armor is key to the subject at hand: "having shod your

[our] feet with the preparation of the gospel of peace" (verse 15). For the sake of easier visualization, I will describe this as "putting on the sandals of the gospel of peace." We never put shoes on when we are going to bed; we put them on when we are about to walk. The instruction to put on this piece of armor therefore implies that we are to walk—and not just walk, but walk in peace.

We had been making a monumental mistake in spiritual warfare: We had rated war higher than peace.

This is exactly what happened on Wednesday evening as we prayer walked the entire city of San Nicolás in peace. It is also what took place in Resistencia when "Houses of Light" were established all over the city. It is the backbone for what has been happening in prisons like Olmos and El CERESO, in cities like Vallejo, California, in states like Hawaii, and in nations like the Philippines and Mexico. As an amazing example of the process, let's now return to the story we started with in this chapter, that of Wanlapa in Phuket, Thailand, and her ice-cream cart.

The Kingdom on an Ice-Cream Cart

I have already shared some of the breakthroughs that happened in Phuket, Thailand, especially the story involving Pastor Brian Burton and the provincial mayor. Now I want to tell you "the story behind the story" about Wanlapa. When Pastor Brian first met her, she was a spirit medium dying of stage 4 cancer. After he prayed for her, she was instantly healed. Brian also detected a latent gift for business in her and bought her a three-wheeled motorcycle equipped with an attached ice-cream box.

For about ten years after that, Wanlapa had been telling people about God's healing miracle in her life, but she had not been able to lead anyone to Christ—that is, until she began to practice the principles that constitute the banks of the river we are talking about. She learned about them as a result of her pastor attending one of our conferences in Argentina. At the time, Brian and his wife, Margaret, had served as British missionaries in Thailand for sixteen years. Their sacrificial hard service had produced a congregation of just 43 members. But they took heart that, as small as their congregation was by Western standards, it was among the top five evangelical congregations in that region of Thailand—a sobering reflection of how miniscule the Gospel presence has been in that nation.

The day after the conference, Brian asked me, "How can I go about transformation with a small group of believers in a country that is 96 percent Buddhist and almost 4 percent Muslim?"

I instructed him that as soon as he returned to Thailand, he should begin to train his people in the principles found in two of my books, *Prayer Evangelism*

"How can I go about transformation with a small group of believers in a country that is 96 percent Buddhist and almost 4 percent Muslim?"

and *Transformation*, since they describe the two banks of the river. I also told him to use my book *Anointed for Business* to help church members envision how they could take the power and presence of God into their workplace.

Brian took me at my word and began teaching his people. After the first sessions, sixteen people left, unhappy with the new direction. But Brian persisted. Among those who remained was Wanlapa, and the teaching transformed her life *and her lifestyle*. Now she no longer saw herself as an ice-cream vendor, but as someone "anointed for business," who instead of going to work, went to worship God with her labor.

Wanlapa then dedicated her ice-cream cart to the Lord and even anointed it as a "chariot of fire." The ice-cream cones became "arrows in the hands of a mighty warrior." She laid hands on the cartons of ice cream, asking God that when her clients tasted it, they would also taste the goodness of the Lord. And she began to silently speak peace over them to upgrade the business transaction to a budding relationship, all in line with what she understood from the four steps for prayer evangelism.

The results were amazing. Her patrons thought that she had changed brands because the ice cream tasted so much better, when actually what happened was that she had turned her ice-cream cart into a "mobile Ark of the Covenant" to carry God's presence all over the city. It began to change the spiritual climate. As people shared their felt needs, Wanlapa offered prayers of faith. God answered them, and within a year the church Brian and his wife pastored grew to over seven hundred members, due in part to Wanlapa's boldness in applying prayer evangelism.

As exciting and encouraging as this was, Wanlapa was not satisfied. She had also caught on to the first paradigm, that we are to disciple nations and not just individuals. To that effect, she made a point to drive by the office of the provincial mayor to offer a prayer for him. Unable to make direct contact, she would "lob" a blessing over the wall, declaring, "He does not know I am his pastor, but I surely know he is my sheep!" She blessed him doubly because those who opposed him politically were accusing him of corruption. This did not intimidate Wanlapa since she had also learned from her pastor that a blessing, once imparted, breaks curses.

Sure enough, one day she met the man himself, and she did not miss the opening in the spirit realm to invite him to church. This was a long shot because she was a simple citizen inviting one of the most prominent government officials in the region to attend an evangelical service in a Christian church pastored by a British missionary. Yet the anointing breaks the yoke, as it certainly did in his case, since the following Sunday the provincial mayor showed up in church!

Wanlapa had not told her pastor about this, and just as Brian had begun to preach on the fifth paradigm (the elimination of systemic poverty through the uprooting of corruption), in walked the one whom many considered the most prominent representative of a corrupt system.

Brian asked the Lord, *Why has he come?*

God told him, *Because you asked Me for sinners, and I sent you the best one I have!*

Yes, Lord, cried Brian, *but I am about to preach against corruption! What's the problem with doing that, Brian?* God asked.

Well, replied Brian, *this man can revoke my visa.*

224

I can revoke your next breath, replied the Lord, with evident irony. *Take your pick, Brian.*

Under "divine duress," Brian proceeded to preach, fearing the provincial mayor would not like the message. Indeed, this important man gave every sign that he did not. His face got longer and longer with each point Brian made, and he left without saying a word.

Brian warned his wife, "Honey, we'd better begin packing, because he's going to call me to let us know he is canceling our visas."

Sure enough, the following week the provincial mayor asked for a meeting over lunch. Brian, trying to find some silver lining in an ominous cloud, told Margaret, "Well, it looks as if he'll feed me before kicking us out."

The two men met at a very nice restaurant. After the opening pleasantries, the provincial mayor got down to business. "Sunday I was at your church," he said.

"Yes, I noticed," intoned Brian.

"I heard you preach against corruption."

Uh-oh, thought Brian, *here it comes!* As the man continued, Brian tried to project an assurance that he did not have.

"I did not like it at all!" thundered the provincial mayor.

Brian was holding his breath, waiting for the second blow to hit him, when he heard what became music to his already troubled ears.

"Because last Thursday," continued the provincial mayor, "I accepted a $1 million bribe to sign the permits to build a new hospital. As I listened to you, I realized that I have not taken money from the ones offering the bribe, but from the poor in Phuket, who will receive inferior services because of my actions. I became so convicted that I left immediately to return the money."

When the provincial mayor tried to return the money, the man behind the bribe thought the mayor was carrying out a government sting operation, so he admitted right away that he had kept half a million dollars for himself. This money he readily put on the table, with the intention of returning it. Each man was perplexed that the other did not want the returned bribe money. They proceeded to meet with an administrator involved in the project to give him the money, but he also refused it. "I can't take it," he told them. "We don't have an account in our ledger for 'Returned Bribes'!"

The discussion that ensued between the provincial mayor and Brian at that point would have been comical if it had not been triggered by malicious actions. At that very moment, the provincial mayor produced a brown paper bag from under his chair. The bag literally contained 1.5 million dollars in Thai currency. He put it on the table in front of Brian—the bag that no one wanted!

With eyes that betrayed his fear of rejection, this Buddhist provincial mayor asked Brian, "Do you think Jesus can forgive me?"

Brian obviously was delighted, but he was also blown away by this impossible breakthrough (humanly speaking). It was as if he had gone fishing and before he threw the line into the water, the largest fish in the sea jumped into the boat, kissed him on both cheeks and asked for directions into the frying pan.

"We don't have an account in our ledger for 'Returned Bribes'!"

After Brian led the man to the Lord, the provincial mayor told him to take the money and use it as he wished. Brian refused and pushed the bag back, which quickly turned into a semblance of a championship Ping-Pong match between the two as the bag went back and forth across the table—except that the "ball" they were using was a bag full of money.

Brian finally scored the tie breaker by masterfully applying paradigm numbers 2, 3, 4 and 5 in rapid succession. He first asked the provincial mayor to invite Jesus into the government so that his household would be saved, as had happened before in the Bible (see Acts 16:30–31). Then, with the keys of the Kingdom, Brian directed the man to set up a fund to distribute the money to the poor who had been so severely impacted by the devastating tsunami that had hit Thailand (including Phuket) on December 26, 2004. It had wreaked havoc that, in addition to causing massive losses of life and property, disrupted the infrastructure, which was taking years to repair. By this time things were much better, but the poor in the community were at the bottom of the pile, awaiting their turn.

The provincial mayor then crowned this by appointing Brian as his "advisor of righteousness," helping him think about "what would Jesus do" in the mayor's position. Brian was to review every document that would cross the provincial mayor's desk to make sure that it complied with the mayor's newfound ethics.

The results were even more astonishing than anyone imagined. First, more bribes were returned, until the fund had netted seven million dollars. Three years later, the federal government recognized this provincial mayor as number one in the nation because of the way his administration had cleaned up corruption and attended to the felt needs of the people, particularly the poor.

This is a modern-day version of Zaccheus's story, is it not? Yet it did not stop there. Once transformation begins to happen inside the two banks of the river I described above, the water level rises, the current accelerates and it takes life farther and farther—in this case, from the provincial mayor's office to the police department. The new relationship with the provincial mayor opened the door for Wanlapa to visit the chief of police in Phuket. She started to pray blessings over the department. The police were poorly paid for the work they were expected to do, and one method they had of raising funds was through setting up roadblocks to check that riders had the necessary documentation to be on the road. This created much tension between the police and the people. Something needed to change.

Ekklesia Karaoke-Style

Brian decided to go all out for prayer evangelism in his new capacity as advisor of righteousness. He, Margaret and the growing Ekklesia invited the police chief to dinner in a top-notch restaurant. The chief was double-booked, but the deputy chief of police accepted the invitation and brought his wife. At first, he was as nervous as a cat in a room full of rocking chairs because the people looked and acted unusually nice to him, and Brian introduced him as *our* deputy chief of police. No one had ever done that. They always kept their distance by calling him chief, but never *our* chief. On top of that, the man and his wife were guests of a *church group*. No doubt they wondered what that was going to mean.

But Brian had wisely planned a nonreligious program, and the evening progressed as they enjoyed the food and took turns singing karaoke, the deputy chief included. That was the equivalent of taking everybody through the first two steps of prayer evangelism: bless them and fellowship with them.

Toward the end of the evening, Brian decided to go for the third step and asked the deputy chief if he had any needs that they could pray for. By then the atmosphere was very warm, and this senior police officer no longer felt threatened, on account of the first two steps. But he was not ready for prayer and told them he did not believe in it. Brian put him at ease by clarifying that he himself did not need to pray, but rather, Brian, his wife and their people would pray since they believed in it.

Not totally sold yet, the deputy chief countered, "But I don't believe in miracles, much less in Jesus. I am a Buddhist."

Brian then made him an offer that was impossible to refuse: "It does not matter, because we believe in miracles in the name of Jesus, and that's all that matters at this time."

Within a week, the deputy chief called Brian to say, "Your Jesus works really fast!"

The deputy chief acquiesced (more than agreed) and shared that the main problem was that the federal government in Bangkok did not have the funds to authorize money for more police officers. Yet having more was absolutely necessary because the population, plus the number of tourists, had increased 500 percent, while the police force remained the same.

Brian and Margaret proceeded to lead the Ekklesia to pray a prayer of blessing and a request for a miracle. The evening ended on a high note, and everybody went home happy.

Within a week, the deputy chief called Brian to say, "Your Jesus works really fast!" He then went on to explain excitedly that he had just hung up with the federal commissioner in Bangkok. The commissioner had authorized not seventy or seven hundred, but seven thousand new officers!

Blindsided into a Transformational Solution

The following Sunday the deputy chief of police turned up at the morning service and sat in the front row, near the provincial mayor. That Sunday turned out to be extraordinary. The pastor of Brian's Burmese congregation asked if one of his new members could share a testimony. Brian agreed, even though he did not know the details.

With the provincial mayor and the deputy chief seated in the front row, this man shared how he was driving his motorcycle without a license because, "Praise God, I am an illegal immigrant." Then he came across a police checkpoint. At that moment, he related, he asked Jesus if He who had opened the eyes of the blind so many times could now blind the police since he was heading for church. And with overflowing joy, the man shouted, "And Jesus did it. I drove through!"

Brian experienced a replay of what he had experienced when he had seen the provincial mayor walk in after he had begun to preach against corruption. With the deputy chief listening to the man's story, Brian felt like praying for the Rapture to take place immediately. He was going to apologize to both officials, but the Lord stopped him: *Don't do that. These folks are victims of unscrupulous businessmen who bring them illegally into the country for greedy projects, and then they dump them. This is not a setback but a setup.*

Following the service, Brian walked up to the two officials to try to put some perspective on what had taken place. But the provincial mayor surprised him by asking for his help to get the illegal Burmese properly documented. He went on to explain that he was aware that most of them were victims and in the past he had tried to help them, but every time he set up a post to help them regularize their situation, no one came. Since it was the government doing it, they must have felt like chickens being invited to a banquet organized by foxes. He then proceeded to ask if Brian and the Burmese pastor and his associates would take charge to man a processing center funded by the government.

And did they ever take charge! Every workday at the processing center began with prayer and praise. Immigration interviews were conducted "prayer evangelism" style. Myriads of illegal Burmese received help, and scores received the Lord on the spot. Why? Why not! The Lord's Ekklesia, faithful to its divine DNA, co-opted an ekklesia that represented the Gates of Hades. Using the keys of the Kingdom, His Ekklesia proceeded to set the captives free.

The main point we should not miss in this story is that this continually expanding river of righteousness touching businesses, government and education was set in motion by a very humble, obedient ice-cream street vendor when she began to minister within the banks of the river we have talked about. Since then, Wanlapa has led thousands of people to Christ, including entire villages. This is why I am so passionate about the effectiveness and efficiency of these two banks. Prayer evangelism is the lifestyle by which we live out the five pivotal paradigms for transformation.

"Observe All That I Commanded"

As I searched the Scriptures for a reason why these principles work so unusually well, it dawned on me that both prayer evangelism and the five paradigms come straight out of the teachings of Jesus. Why is this important? Because Jesus was very specific—and to a point even restrictive—when He instructed us to disciple people and nations by "teaching them to observe all that *I commanded you*" (Matthew 28:20, emphasis added).

He did not say, "Teach nations what I will teach Paul, Peter, John and James, who in turn will teach it to you." Instead, Jesus said, "Teach them what *I* have taught and show them how to observe it."

Of course, we must not dichotomize between Jesus' teaching in the gospels and the apostolic teachings that make up the rest of the New Testament. They both represent the canon of God's Word, which the Holy Spirit inspired to guide us. But we need to understand how they should interface, and particularly in what order.[5]

It is a common axiom in theological institutions that we should never build church (Ekklesia) doctrine from the historical books of the New Testament (the gospels and the book of Acts). Rather, "real" church doctrine should be derived from the epistles. This assumption is appealing because the apostles wrote mostly to Ekklesias (churches) and members of Ekklesias, making it too easy for us today, with our "building" mindset, to apply such teachings to life and activities inside the four walls of our churches.

But that does not line up entirely with Jesus' instructions. The gospels carry the very words of Jesus, and the book of Acts presents the proof for His teaching. Keep in mind that the Ekklesia in Acts did not have anything except the words of Jesus. The root problem is that when we do not align properly the historical experiences of the apostles

> *We must not dichotomize between Jesus' teaching in the gospels and the apostolic teachings that make up the rest of the New Testament.*

as reported in Acts with the doctrinal books that they wrote, we end up with an incorrect, or at least a limited, application of the doctrine they taught.

Furthermore, the fact that Jesus mentioned the Ekklesia only three times, as I explained earlier, but talked about the Kingdom over one hundred times, has led many to the erroneous conclusion that His teachings have to do with the Kingdom that is still to come and not with the Church (Ekklesia).

I submit that Jesus' teachings constitute the foundation, the apostles provide the walls that rest on this foundation, and the book of Acts provides the blueprint for certification.

That is why, as the two banks of the river, prayer evangelism and the five pivotal paradigms work so well. They fluidly connect right doctrine with right application in the right place and sequence.[6]

Limiting ourselves to using apostolic doctrine without first instructing believers how to observe Jesus' teachings has proven good for planting and growing a traditional church, but it falls short of the objectives Jesus has for His Ekklesia. The transformation of cities *and nations* is no longer a distant hope. Rather, it is a fast-approaching reality, as confirmed by the inspiring prototypes that are emerging within the "banks of the river." All of that can be yours once you grasp and activate these "Jesus principles." His Ekklesia is designed to bring His presence and His power to bear as an expression of the Kingdom of God, first in our immediate sphere of influence, and eventually in our cities and our nations when we flow in a river of transformation guided by these biblical banks. Are you ready to go? Keep reading!

17

The Way Forward

From Doing Church to Being the Ekklesia

How do we transition from the Church to the Ekklesia? It is a challenge because what we have in the Church today is good, but in order to become the Ekklesia, we have to make room for the "much more" of God. In this chapter I will present the pathway to that transition.

Now that you are raring to go, it is essential to take stock of what you need and where to find it. In the previous chapter, I covered in-depth the topics of prayer evangelism and the five pivotal paradigms. In my experience and that of those with whom I minister, these two sets of principles have effectively proven to be the two banks of the river whose waters will carry you to see your city—and even your nation—transformed. In addition, we have posted on the Transform Our World website all the components of what we call a "transformation continuum" designed to take you from A to Z. This continuum embodies over five decades of ministry experience, garnished with inspiring examples and replicable prototypes. We believe this is the toolbox you need to do the job of getting transformation under way wherever you are.[1]

The big question right now is, where do you begin? Hopefully, I have been able to answer a big portion of that question by sharing about the empowering principles we have discovered and by providing you with inspiring examples that can get you on the road to rediscovering the Ekklesia. Now allow me to put at your disposal some practical insights that will help you be effective and contagious in applying what you have been reading here.

The 5-15-80 Percent Principle

First of all, remind yourself that not everyone has read this book. On top of that, the paradigms of transformation may be new to them. And most importantly, not everybody will respond to this information in the same way.

In the early days of our ministry, we customarily challenged the entire audience or congregation to go for it, and usually everybody did, especially if the pastors and leaders led the way. The biblical principles involved in the transformation process are so inspiring that it is nearly impossible not to respond affirmatively to such challenge. Unfortunately, within two years we found that the original participation had dwindled considerably, which made the original launch look like a failure. That is when we discovered the 5-15-80 percent principle, which outlines the different ways people respond to challenges. This provided us with the ability to map out the most effective way to present and teach transformation principles.

What we learned is that 5 percent of the people are *visionaries*. As soon as these visionaries hear the transformation principles, they are immediately on board, because by faith they have already seen the process taking place. These people are the *immediate adopters*.

The next 15 percent are *implementers*, meaning that when they hear the visionaries describe the transformation principles, they are ready to make it happen. These are the *early adopters*.

The remaining 80 percent are *maintainers*. As such, they are the *late adopters*, because they need to see transformation happening in order to embrace it. This is not meant as a put-down, because God made them that way. They are the ones who, by taking care of what is already in place, keep the wheels of ministry turning day in and day out. You can easily identify this group when you are presenting something radically new, because they will ask, "But if we do that, who will take care of . . . [this or that]?" As maintainers, they are the first responders when something breaks down. They are very responsible about their God-given role in maintaining what is already in place. We would be lost without them.

The first step in launching a transformation process is to connect with the 5 percent who are the visionaries. Then with them, discover the 15 percent who are the implementers, so that the two groups can begin to build together. To find the 5 percent and the 15 percent, implement what I have been calling the banks of the river. Do prayer evangelism every day. Think about discipling nations constantly "as you go on your way." That exercise will do two things: It will attract others who are like-minded to you, and it will make you more aware of those around you who have the same mindset.

This process holds two important keys for success. First, it enables you to walk out the expanding circles of authority that we discussed in chapter 15, moving from victory to greater victory. Second, teaming up with your 5 percent and 15 percent associates allows you to put something *visible* in place so that those in the 80 percent category can gravitate toward it.

Few can believe without seeing—this is why Jesus called them "blessed." But the majority of people need to see in order to believe. That is not a sin; it is a biblical fact. We can see this in Thomas when he cautioned his fellow apostles, "Unless I see . . . I will not believe" (John 20:25). On his next visit, Jesus said to him, "Because you have seen Me, have you believed? Blessed are they who did not see, and yet believed" (verse 29).

Jesus did not accuse Thomas of lacking faith. He just acknowledged two categories: those who believe without seeing, and those who need to see in order to believe. Jesus had His own 5-15-80 group. I classify Peter in the 5 percent, as a visionary, since time after time he broke new ground, such as when he declared that Jesus was the Son of God before anyone else did. Peter was the only one who dared to walk on water, while everybody else was immobilized by fear. He also proclaimed without any hesitation that he would never deny the Lord, and later on, in the Garden of Gethsemane, he added, "Even though all may fall away, yet I will not" (Mark 14:29; see also Matthew 26:35).

James and John, with the addition of Peter, constituted the equivalent of the 15 percent, because Jesus would call them apart from the others: "And He allowed no one to accompany Him, except Peter and James and John the brother of James" (Mark 5:37). These are the three He took with Him to the Mount of Transfiguration; they are also the ones He shared His distress with in the Garden. He placed them closer to Him than the others as He faced the cup He did not want to drink (see Mark 9:2; 14:33–34). Jesus took these three aside to explain things that, later on, they most likely explained to the rest.

As you begin to implement transformation principles, follow the 5-15-80 percent principle. Don't stop what you are already doing with and for the 80 percent, the maintainers, or you may lose them. Just do the "new" with the 5-15 percent group, because they will not mind adding to their current workload. And once the other 80 percent see transformation taking place, they will begin to swing your way.

This is why we lead with prototypes and not just principles or ideas. The strength of our movement is that we do both; we teach principles, *and* we implement them so that people can see and believe them. We search the Scriptures and listen to the Holy Spirit to hear what He is saying to the Ekklesia, we articulate it, we validate it biblically and then we implement it for the benefit of all.

The Old and the New

New concepts like the ones being discussed in this book are bound to challenge existing perceptions. In light of that, it is key to process them constructively so that we apply them without damaging or dishonoring what is already in place.

In this book, I have built on the premise that we must find what we have been missing in the modern expression of the Church in order to add it to what is already in place and make it complete. To do this effectively, we find specific guidance from Jesus in Matthew 9:16: "No one puts a patch of unshrunk cloth on an old garment; for the patch pulls away from the garment, and a worse tear results."

The implication is that both pieces of garment have intrinsic value, but the new must age before it can be of any good to the old. It is an issue of time. Jesus' subsequent statement regarding old and new wine further explains this: "Nor do people put new wine into old wineskins; otherwise the wineskins burst, and the wine pours out and the wineskins are ruined; but they put new wine into fresh wineskins, and both are preserved" (verse 17).

In both the examples of the garments and the wine, Jesus' intent is to show the importance of both the old and the new, hence the reference to *both* wines needing to be preserved. People who equate a new illumination with the new wine and declare that it is better than the old do not seem to know enough about the intrinsic value of old wine. Aged wine is the more preferred one, which is what makes its wineskin so valuable. That is why, according to Luke's account, Jesus adds, "And no one, after drinking old wine wishes for new; for he says, 'The old is good enough'" (Luke 5:39).

To better understand two important principles in this passage, let me equate wine with divine revelation and wineskin with human doctrine used to express it. First, once the old wine is consumed, the old wineskin automatically loses its value. Second, there is an innate preference for old wine that keeps the consumer from welcoming the new until the old has run out.

This is why it is so important to work first with the 5 percenters and 15 percenters, because they are the visionaries and implementers who, while not despising the old wine, are eager and thirsty for the new. This process will give the 80 percenters—the maintainers who definitely prefer the old wine—time to observe and embrace the new.

We have seen this play out through history with those who launched ministries with challenging new paradigms, such as William Booth and The Salvation Army, the Wesley brothers and the Methodist denomination, and later on the Pentecostal and charismatic movements. All of them introduced new concepts that eventually came to be accepted, but it took more than one generation. I think that in many instances, the delay had to do with presenting the new paradigms as mandatory for those who were not ready or not open to it because they were still drinking the old wine and the new had not passed the test of time. Bishop Vaughn McLaughlin put it succinctly: "The new is only weird until it works." Like every accomplished vintner, we, too, must continuously "risk forward" from the vintage past.

In this book I have diligently, to the best of my ability, worked to honor and affirm the old wine while extolling the virtues of the new wine, because there is no need for this to be a contentious issue. To that effect, I see these observations related to the 5-15-80 percent principle as a most practical resolution.

Cohesiveness versus Inclusiveness

The tension between cohesiveness and inclusiveness also presents a challenge. The application of the 5-15-80 percent principle can help resolve that tension. When a powerful new principle is discovered, the natural response is to go as wide as possible to get others involved. But this is not the most effective way to go about it. Let's look at this projected on a graph (see next page).

A core group that is totally cohesive will at first score 100 percent on the vertical axis, but the farther it moves toward inclusiveness, the less cohesive it will become. This is because as you approach less cohesive prospects, you will be asked, or be tempted, to make compromises that will *diffuse your focus on the strategic objectives* in order to secure people's participation.

It also happens with evangelistic crusades. There is always a core group on board when the idea is first launched. But when it is pitched to others, many of them are thinking, *What is the minimum commitment I need to make to get the maximum return without risking what I have?* And in the end, evangelistic crusades that should be an integral part of the normal lifestyle of the Church are limited to just a few days.

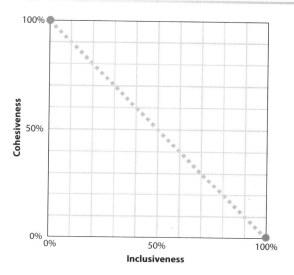

Unity versus Purpose

We have had the privilege of pioneering unity among pastors. We did it in Resistencia when unity was unpopular, since those were the days when denominational and doctrinal walls were very high and thick. The city was described as a place where "pastors loved to hate each other." We continued to pioneer unity every place we went during the next decade or so. But *unity* cannot be the driver; rather, *purpose* must be the driver because unity is a means to a higher end, which is transforming the city and the nation.

When my friend Dr. Joe Aldrich (now with the Lord), president of my alma mater, Multnomah Biblical Seminary in Portland, Oregon, launched Pastors' Prayer Summits, a refreshing breath of divine air blew over the Church, first in the United States, and then in other nations. The formula was simple: Pastors agreed to go on a three-day retreat to pray, with no preset program. Joe Aldrich established the "no agenda" requirement because, at first, many in the Portland area where he prototyped this were suspicious as to his intentions since he was an inspiring and successful leader with an enormous platform. So he made it a point of order not to set an agenda, which was the right move at the time.

239

But later on, "no agenda" became the agenda that ended up killing those gatherings, because, if after three or four years of spending time in God's presence with the leaders in the region, we still did not know what God wanted us to do as a Church, then what was the purpose of it? Was God speaking at those gatherings? Of course He was, but were we listening? Possibly not with the intention of acting on what He was saying, because we had agreed to the "no agenda" rule. We still believe in the need for total unity mentioned in Psalm 133, and we practice it, but rather than going wide with it, we concentrate on achieving it within a core group, from where it should expand to others according to the 5-15-80 percent principle. Otherwise, to satisfy the least committed participants, you have to lower the bar accordingly.

This is why in building a prototype, we first look for a Lydia-type leader in a transformation process. Lydia was the businesswoman who, after hearing Paul, invited him and his companions to her place, where her *entire* household was baptized (see Acts 16:13–15.) That high level of purpose became the point of inception from where the marketplace in Philippi experienced the power of God. The city jailer and his household were saved, and the first Ekklesia in what today is modern-day Europe was planted. It is not hard to see the higher value of purpose in the 5-15-80 dynamic in play here, as well as in our prototypes in Ciudad Juárez, Parañaque, the Philippines, Vallejo and many other places.

Competence versus Commitment

It would be ideal that the core group, the vortex of cohesiveness, be made up of the most competent people. Since we don't live in an ideal world, however, that is seldom the case. Instead, we have consistently seen competent leaders attract very committed people who at first are not necessarily the most competent ones.

You should not be discouraged, much less be paralyzed, by this. In fact, there is biblical precedent for it. David's mighty men were not members of the nobility. On the contrary, they were the ones who had gotten in trouble with the king and the law. But they were totally committed to David, and they became the ones who carried him to the throne.

The good news is that you can always teach competence to committed people. Look at how this plays out in the graph below:

We can be distracted, and even derailed, by constantly looking for someone "better"—more competent—than we are to do what needs to be done. Don't get pregnant with transformation and then go looking for an adoption agency. It is okay to be overwhelmed. It is okay to ask, as Mary did, "How can this be, since I am a virgin?" (Luke 1:34). But like Mary, you must also accept in faith the answer: "The Holy Spirit will come upon you, and the power of the Most High will overshadow you. . . . For nothing will be impossible with God" (Luke 1:35, 37). That is all you need to hear and accept, that the Holy Spirit will do it in you and through you. Once you accept this humanly speaking impossible task, the Holy Spirit baptism becomes an *absolute* necessity.

Tradition versus Vision

It is of pivotal importance that as we sail into unfamiliar waters in the quest to rediscover the Ekklesia, we become aware that tradition can be the ballast that gives us stability or the anchor that immobilizes us.

241

This type of immobilization is what happened to the Ekklesia in Jerusalem when tradition arrested the phenomenal initial growth recorded in the first ten chapters of the book of Acts. Let me explain. Tradition is important since it is the transmission of past customs or beliefs from one generation to the next. Vision is the ability to think about or plan the future with imagination. Those two, if not properly synchronized, can collide with each other. To avoid that, let's learn from five dynamics at work in the path from birth to death in every movement, including the Church: *dissatisfaction, convergence, expansion, institutionalization*, and either *death* or a *new dissatisfaction/ relaunch*.

New churches are often planted out of a healthy *dissatisfaction* connected to a feeling that "there has to be something more." This dissatisfaction leads to a *convergence* with others who are feeling the same way, and everybody begins working hard to produce *expansion*. Such expansion creates the need for more organization—policies and procedures, staff, buildings, boards, etc., which in turn ushers in *institutionalization*, and at that moment the operational focus shifts. Administrators who "protect and steward what has been accomplished" become more welcomed than visionaries who are always pursuing next horizons. Dichotomizing those two important roles is the slip that leads to *death*, since the impetus that gave birth to the expansion becomes lost in the demands required to maintain what institutionalization has created.

Death can be avoided, however, by reinserting the dissatisfaction phase halfway through the institutionalization phase. That produces a

Tradition versus Vision

1. Dissatisfaction

Relaunch

2. Convergence

3. Expansion

4. Institutionalization

New Dissatisfaction

5. Death

relaunch of the cycle, and as long as that relaunching keeps happening, the movement will not die. This lesson has tremendous value to us in transitioning to the Ekklesia.

The rediscovery of the Ekklesia as God's instrument to transform the world is what this book aspires to help accomplish. But for us to succeed, let me illustrate the value *and the perils* of tradition with two biblical examples. One is the Church in Jerusalem, and why it lost its role as the vortex for the global expansion of Jesus' Ekklesia and ended up relegated to the Jewish world. The other is the apostle Paul, who became the most successful leader of the global expansion after he turned his Jewish roots into a propeller rather than an anchor.

The Perils of Tradition

In Acts 8:1 we read, "And on that day a great persecution began against the church in Jerusalem, and they were all scattered throughout the regions of Judea and Samaria, *except the apostles*" (emphasis added). Why were the apostles, the leaders of the Ekklesia in Jerusalem, permitted to stay, while their followers had to flee for their lives? It does not make sense because the persecution was against the movement they led. And why did Antioch, a merchant city, become the point from where Christianity eventually reached the ends of the earth, instead of Jerusalem, as originally outlined by Jesus in Acts 1:8?

The statement that the apostles were not impacted by the persecution hints at the reason for this. I wish to offer this hypothesis: The apostles were able to stay because they justified the coexistence between the Old and the New Covenants—a tragic accommodation. They did this by maintaining Old Covenant practices as "necessary" in the New Covenant. This unhealthy addition came into evidence when Peter, while visiting Antioch, felt intimidated by a recently arrived group from Jerusalem whom Paul describes as "the party of the circumcision" (Galatians 2:12; see also verses 13–21). Apparently, this was a very influential group who reported directly to James, the acknowledged leader in Jerusalem. As a result of this group's influence, the Jewish believers in Antioch, including Barnabas, became confused, and Paul called the visitors hypocrites. He put his finger on this unhealthy adherence to tradition when he confronted Peter and warned the Galatians about having been bewitched, apparently by emissaries from Jerusalem (see Galatians 2:11–13; 3:1–4). I submit to you that tradition in Jerusalem trumped the vision Jesus spelled out in Acts 1:8. How did that come about?

During the Ekklesia's infancy in Jerusalem, the Temple and the priestly order were still in operation, something that did not come to an end until AD 70. This presented the Ekklesia leadership with a monumental challenge by pitting Jewish ethnocentrism, rooted in the Old Covenant, against the New Covenant—the devastating consequences of which the epistle to the Hebrews describes when it issues a compelling warning against the former order (see Hebrews 8:13; 9:15; 10:23–31).

In a nation that made the Temple and its rituals the very heartbeat of its existence, it is not hard to imagine these inexperienced elders of the recently established Ekklesia being intimidated. With the Temple's long shadow still looming in the background, they certainly were challenged by "a great many" of the priests becoming obedient to the Christian faith, while still being dependent on their Temple stipend for their daily substance (Acts 6:7).

How were these priests to support themselves if they left their ministry in the Temple? I submit that this was a key factor in the decision not to break completely with the Old Covenant. Succumbing to these theological and social pressures is, in my opinion, what prevented them from taking the Gospel of the New Covenant beyond Samaria; that is, to culturally non-Jewish peoples. As a result, the privilege to take the Gospel "to the ends of the earth" fell on Antioch. What had begun so well ended up so poorly because tradition trumped the vision that Jesus had outlined for them in Acts 1:8. Their ethnocentrism blinded them at the worst possible moment.

This is what often happens in Church circles between the old and new generations when they clash over the new way versus the old way. There is a hope for us, however, because Paul fared quite differently.

244

Tradition as "Paul's" Propeller

Paul's initial ministry focus was on the synagogues, where he saw many people come to Christ (see Acts 13–17). Basically, he and his associates were preaching once a week to God-fearing people in religious settings. But while doing this, Paul did not see a city, much less a region, transformed. That did not happen until he moved his base of operations from the synagogue to the marketplace, first in Corinth, and then definitively in Ephesus.

For this shift to happen, Saul—a Jewish rabbi, a Hebrew of Hebrews and by tradition a Pharisee, as he described himself in Philippians 3:5— had to go through a significant metamorphosis. This led him to a public shift toward the Roman culture, marked by a name change.[2]

Let me elaborate. When Saul and Barnabas left Antioch on their first missionary trip, Paul's name is recorded as Saul, as it had been in the preceding chapters of the book of Acts (see Acts 13:1–2). Barnabas was the leader, as implied by the order in which their names are reported. Something changed in Cyprus, however, where now Saul is listed for the first time with a Roman name. Such a name change marked a shift away from his Jewish roots and toward the Hellenistic culture.

Saul, as he was known then, was also a Roman citizen well known around his native Tarsus, making it safe for him to travel in an adjacent region. But a trip to Cyprus, in the middle of the Mediterranean Sea, definitely would have been risky because he did not have a Roman name. In a day where there were no passports, his Roman citizenship would only be considered valid if fellow citizens in the cities that he visited welcomed him as one of them. Otherwise, he could easily have been sold into slavery.

Barnabas was originally from Cyprus, where at the time of their missionary trip Sergius Paulus was an influential Roman citizen who was serving as consul. His family, the Paulii family, was very prominent in the Roman Senate. After Saul ministered to him, Sergius Paulus bestowed on him his family name, Paul*us*, which was a well-known name in Asia Minor.[3] (Notice that the root for his new name is the consul's family name: Paul-Paulii.) Paul became the team leader from that moment on, as indicated by his name preceding Barnabas in the narrative from then on. It is also important to highlight that Paul planted Ekklesias primarily in Roman colonies: Corinth, Ephesus, Philippi, Galatia, Pisidia, Thessalonica and so on.

This change in Paul's public identity was the result of his choice to openly embrace the Gentile world over his traditional ethnicity, in order to reach it without any ethnocentric blockage. Nevertheless, he was always able to draw from the divine deposits of his rich cultural and religious heritage as a baseline from which to take the Gospel to cultures shaped by other religions. Unlike the leaders in Jerusalem, he succeeded at it. In this journey to rediscover the Ekklesia, this is an essential lesson we must learn. And when we do, like Paul, we will find immense and unexpected favor with unsaved leaders in cultures other than our own.

This is why tradition must become a propeller, and not an anchor, in order to enable us to transition successfully from the old to the new. With that clearly in mind, let's now venture to contemplate the fact that God's eyes may be upon you in a special way, that you may have been divinely favored with a transformation assignment.

God Has Favorites

It is incorrect to state that God has no favorites. Of course, He has no favorites when it comes to our salvation. We all stand in identical need of His grace and forgiveness. Whether we have sinned a lot or a little, we all need forgiveness. We should never discriminate against those who sin differently than we do. It is not the kind of sin, but sin itself that makes us all equal. And we have all sinned and fallen short of the glory of God. There are no favorites at the foot of the cross.

But God does have favorites when it comes to ministry assignments. He chose Jacob over Esau. He chose David over Saul. And He chose Mary, whom the angel addressed as the favored one. Choosing is a divine prerogative. Jesus said that many are called, but few are chosen (see Matthew 22:14). He chose His apostles, and Matthias over Justus in the Upper Room (see Acts 1:2, 24–26). Jesus said, "You did not choose me but I chose you" (John 15:16).

The devil will point out that you are not the best candidate for this divine assignment, and he may be right! There are likely many—perhaps thousands out there—who are better qualified for the task at hand, and who have more resources and better training. But the criterion is not whether we are the best, but whether we are the anointed ones, the chosen ones, as the direct result of God's sovereign choice to bestow unmerited grace on us. This is a divine prerogative. As an African American colleague told me once, "God is God and He has an attitude about it!"

Realizing that you have been chosen by grace will keep you humble on the one hand, since grace leaves no room for pride. But on the other hand, it will keep you secure, because grace can never be renounced since it constitutes unmerited favor. So when God puts the spotlight on you, remain humble like a lamb, but roar like a lion when necessary. It is not enough just to believe in your heart what is right; you must confess it with your mouth in order for salvation to materialize (see Romans 10:10). Like Jesus, speak with authority so that others will recognize that you have been with Him.

Who Is on the Rolls?

The parable in Luke 14:31–32 tells of a king who wisely assesses how strong his army is before declaring war. As we come to the end of this book and you face a call to action, a similar assessment is worthy of consideration. Why? Because we are the Ekklesia destined to confront the Gates of Hades, both on earth as well as in the heavenly regions. For that, we must be aware of how many soldiers are in the army we are part of, how they are deployed and, specifically, where the battlefield is.

Let's first address a question related to church membership, because it bears directly on how large the army we serve in is. Whose church is it we are members of, and who is on the rolls? We often hear assertions like, "This is my church" or "I belong to Pastor So-and-so's church." Such statements are contradictory to the nature and structure of the Ekklesia. The Church presented in the New Testament *belongs to the Lord and to no one else.*

Nonetheless, when asked a question about how many members their church has, most people will report the number of *attending* members in *their* congregation. If they are asked how large the Church is in their city, they will compute the membership of all the congregations in town. If this is scaled to the district, the province or the nation, the numbers will go up accordingly. Eventually, when church membership rosters in every nation on earth are added up, that figure would be considered to represent the global membership of the Church.

But get ready for a most pleasant and empowering surprise. The Scriptures compute a much larger number as *active* members of the Ekklesia. This is how the writer of Hebrews puts it: "But you have come . . . to the general assembly and church [Ekklesia] of the firstborn who are enrolled in heaven . . . and to the spirits of the righteous made perfect" (Hebrews 12:22–23). In other words, the writer is indicating that the membership rolls in heaven take into account every person who has believed in Jesus, *whether still on earth or in heaven already*.

This is a crucial point because we tend to believe that the devil and his demons will keep control of the spirit world until the end of time. But the picture of the Ekklesia painted in the epistle to the Hebrews is one of a growing Body gradually occupying more space in the heavenly realms due to the constant addition of new members—from Pentecost to our present day. This means that the devil's theater of operation is becoming progressively smaller. In fact, nowhere in the Scriptures is there a reference to Satan's followers (whether demons or unrepentant sinners or both) constituting a growing and proactive group of supporters in the heavenly places. But the book of Hebrews tells us of such a group in the Kingdom of God—the great cloud of witnesses.

Jesus' Ekklesia is continuously growing, whereas the devil's ranks are not.

If this were not as sobering a thought for Satan as it should be an encouraging thought for us, consider that this cloud of witnesses may not be a metaphor after all, but a statement of fact. I say this because these are *active* members of the Ekklesia who have already run their assigned legs in this relay race, and they now constitute God's cheerleading team: "Therefore, since we have so great a cloud of witnesses surrounding us, let us also lay aside every encumbrance and the sin which so easily entangles us, and let us run with endurance the race that is set before us" (Hebrews 12:1). We can assert that those in this cloud of Ekklesia members are actively engaged since they are *witnesses*. To qualify as such, witnesses must be able to see or hear something and testify about it.

Let me state it again: The strategic significance of this is that it debunks the misbelief that the devil and his demons possess unalterable control in the heavenly places, as well as in the natural world, until the end of time (see Ephesians 6:12). This is not the case at all. In fact, Jesus' Ekklesia is continuously growing, whereas the devil's ranks are not. Not only are his ranks being outnumbered, but also, as we stated earlier, according to the Scriptures they have been defeated twice already, and the third and final defeat is coming.

Satan was first cast out of God's presence by the Lord Himself (see Isaiah 14:12). He was subsequently beaten by Michael and the angels under Michael's command in the heavenlies, from where he and his hosts of demons were thrown down to earth to be defeated one more time by the saints (see Revelation 12:7–11).

This is the fight that is still going on, but we are assured of victory because Jesus stated unequivocally that the Gates of Hades will not prevail against the Ekklesia (see Matthew 16:18). And to prove it, we have the final score posted in Revelation 21:24–26 in the form of saved nations—nations that inhabit *the earth*. Yes, the next *and final* stop for the devil and his demons, and a permanent one, is the lake of fire (see Revelation 20:10).

My fellow Kingdom soldier, we are part of a larger, stronger and mightier army. Let us engage the enemy. Victory is assured, unless we allow tradition to derail the vision!

From the Ordinary to the Extraordinary

I wish to revisit what I stated at the beginning of this book: The issue is not so much what we may be doing wrong, but what else we need to do. To that effect, I submit to you a list of transition points drawn from the teachings in this book. We must consider each of them to get from doing what is good to stepping up to a more excellent way.

Now that we have addressed, I hope conclusively, the questions I raised in the introduction—questions that gave birth to this book—we must begin to transition in these ways:

From personal salvation to household salvation

The engine for this transition is the realization that "it is not about you," but about others—specifically about everybody in your sphere of influence, including your family, neighbors, co-workers and others. Now that you have believed in the Lord Jesus, settle for nothing less than your entire household being saved (see Acts 16:31). Besides, the brighter the light shines at home base, the farther you will be able to venture outside.

When my parents, my sister Maria Rosa and I became believers, we fully embraced that promise. Today, all our relatives are believers, and hardly anyone in our neighborhood has died without accepting Christ. The latter was ensured by the fact that my mom was the practical nurse whom everybody came to for injections at a time when doctors made house calls and most terminally ill patients convalesced or died at home. She definitely had a captive audience, and when needed, she firmly but gently "forced them to enter" the Kingdom before they stepped into eternity.

From doing church once a week to being the Ekklesia 24/7

All the wonderful, life-changing things that happen inside the church building should be happening all over the city—and in greater measure and frequency. Before, we could not do it because we were dependent on the building. But once we understand that the Ekklesia is a movement of transformational people who constitute a flotilla of mobile Arks of the Covenant all over the marketplace, it is easy to do Ekklesia 24/7 "as we go." Keep in mind that as few as two or three can form the Kingdom equivalent of the Roman *conventus*, and whatever they bind or release shall be bound in the heavenly realm, where the Gates of Hades are still entrenched.

From pastoring believers to shepherding the city

As you begin to shepherd or disciple in the marketplace, remember that even though those in your sphere of influence may not be aware that they are your sheep, you, like Wanlapa, know that you are their shepherd. It is the shepherd who looks after the lost sheep, not the other way around. Prayer evangelism is the operational "rod" in the hand of that shepherd: to bless, fellowship, minister and then proclaim. As my close associate Dave Thompson likes to say, "Speak peace and follow the trail that will open before you, because now you know there *is* a trail!" It has never been easier to pastor a city.

If you are a pastor with one hundred people under your care, lead by example and envision them to become shepherds to one hundred lost sheep each. Each person adopting in prayer five houses to the right, five to the left and ten across the street will reach that total easily. By just doing this, you will expand your own sphere of influence from one hundred to ten thousand!

If you are a marketplace minister, invite Jesus to come into your workplace, whether you are in leadership there or not. In Revelation 3:20, Jesus was speaking of coming inside a *place*, not a human heart, when He said, "Behold, I stand at the door and knock; if anyone hears My voice and opens the door, I will come in to him and will dine with him, and he with Me." In fact, the word used in verse 14 of that same chapter to describe the "Church in Laodicea"—as well as the word used for the six other churches Jesus addressed in the book of Revelation—is *Ekklesia*.

Jesus is asking to come into your sphere of influence. He will do it once you open the door, as the verse we just looked at teaches. Like the owner of the motel chain in the Philippines, you, too, should invite Jesus to come in. Then do everything He tells you. Like the businesswoman in China who set up a Jesus chair in her factory, expect to be surprised!

Don't be afraid of rejection, because "the creation waits in *eager expectation* for the children of God to be revealed" (Romans 8:19 NIV, emphasis added). Just make sure that you proclaim the Kingdom of God and not the Law and the Prophets. Don't hold back from being bold about it. It is the devil who is afraid because he knows that "greater is He who is in you than he who is in the world" (1 John 4:4). When you read the context of that verse, you will see it is referring to the over-coming spirit of the antichrist present in the same world you inhabit. Be encouraged!

From preaching with words to proclaiming with deeds

The Gospel of the Kingdom is not proclaimed just with words, but also with deeds designed to bring about justice, peace and joy. The Savior who saved you is also the Savior of the entire world. Beyond being a Savior, He is the King, because "The kingdom of the world has become the kingdom of our Lord and of His Christ" (Revelation 11:15). You must now walk under that royal authority, and your proclamation as His herald must be with demonstration of the Spirit and of power. He is in you, with you and for you, eager to confirm the word (proclamation) by signs as He did in the case of the apostles when they first went out (see Mark 16:20). But for Him to do it, you have to proclaim it first. Be bold, because God is willing and able to perform extraordinary miracles through your hands, as He did with Paul. Those miracles were extraordinary because they happened in the marketplace. They were an integral and most catalytic expression of "the Gospel of the Kingdom." Paul did not just have a Kingdom company, but a Kingdom lifestyle. Everything he did, he did to the glory of God. He was so overflowing with the Holy Spirit that everything that touched him in the workplace became a vehicle for transformation. Like Paul, don't be satisfied with having a Kingdom company; instead, develop a Kingdom *lifestyle*!

From saving souls to discipling nations

Leading others to Christ has eternal rewards for the recipient and for you. He who saves souls is wise (see Proverbs 11:30). That is very important, but it remains part of the even more important ultimate objective: discipling nations.

The spiritual empowerment required to believe God for nations comes from a clearer and compelling vision of the cross and the resulting understanding of the totality of what took place there. At the cross, Jesus paid the price for everything that was lost, but He also categorically defeated the devil and made a public spectacle of him and his principalities and powers. Our Savior rendered him powerless. God knows it. Jesus knows it. The devil knows it. And now that you know it, act on it! *Bapto* your sphere of influence by claiming it for God, and then establish God's authority in a point of inception from where, like leaven injected into dough, it will progressively expand until it reaches the nation.

Don't despise small beginnings. The devil will point to the smallness of what you are doing now, but you should focus on the *beginning* part. He who began the good work in you (and through you) will finish it. Poncho began in a tent, King Flores in a taxi, Michael Brown at a seminar, and Gregorio in a run-down community center. And they all saw a transformation process launched in their city that is now beginning to disciple their nations.

From contemplating God to partnering with God

Remember, Jesus did not give you a commission, but rather a partnership. He, the source of *all authority in heaven and on earth*, has promised to walk alongside you *all the way to the end*.

It is biblically proven that we play a vital role in God's redemptive work, and to do that, we must move from contemplation of what God is doing to partnership with Him. In the same way, Jesus declared even as a young lad, "I must be about My Father's business" (Luke 2:49 NKJV). Like Him, we must be about our Father's business.

We are needed *and wanted* by God. This is where the "third" command I highlighted before becomes essential: We must love ourselves, because we can only love others to the degree that we love ourselves. And we can love ourselves because God loves us.

Granted, it is overwhelming to think that God would want and expect our cooperation, but it is something we must accept by faith. Faith does not mean that we cannot ask questions or express perplexity. Even the disciples doubted, but they did it in Jesus' presence and He dispelled all their doubts, as He will dispel yours. Say the two most catalytic words anyone can say to Him, "Yes, Lord!"

From water baptism to Holy Spirit baptism

Without the baptism of the Holy Spirit, we can do nothing transformational, either at the personal or the Ekklesia level.

On the Day of Pentecost, the Spirit fell first on the 120 who had been waiting in the Upper Room. From there it fell on the people watching this phenomenon in the marketplace. All of this resulted in three thousand men—heads of household—believing and being baptized right away, both in water and in the Holy Spirit (see Acts 2:37–39).

Those two baptisms working in tandem eliminate the possibility of having believers who are *convinced*, but not yet fully *converted*. Experiencing the initial *bapto* power encounter will soften the skin of their soul so that the subsequent exposure to God's Word will readily transform them into the likeness of Christ.

In the same fashion that an army facing a formidable enemy cannot afford to do it with ill-trained soldiers, Ekklesia members need to be thoroughly familiar with and fully equipped by the Holy Spirit, the ultimate source of power, to handle the weapons of our warfare. For this, the ongoing baptism of the Holy Spirit and the Spirit-led study of and dependence on the Word of God are *absolutely indispensable*.

This outpouring of the Holy Spirit was not a one-time experience in the book of Acts: "And when they had prayed, the place where they had gathered together was shaken, and *they were all filled with the Holy Spirit* and began to speak the word of God with boldness" (Acts 4:31, emphasis added). Notice that *all* were filled with the Holy Spirit. This included those who had received the Spirit on the Day of Pentecost. This is why we are admonished to be *continually* filled with the Spirit (see Ephesians 5:18).

The baptism in the Holy Spirit is the indispensable source of power for the Ekklesia to disciple individuals and cities and nations. It is the Holy Spirit who will remind us of everything that Jesus taught (His words), and the Spirit is the one who will confirm with signs and wonders that word when we preach it. I cannot stress enough how pivotal it is for the entire Body of Christ to rediscover the fullness of the Holy Spirit baptism, because Jesus is the head of one Body, not two. We are instructed to maintain the unity of the Spirit in the bond of peace in order not to be doctrinally bipolar anymore. Such unity already exists in Christ, the head of the Ekklesia (see Ephesians 4:3). It does not have to be created. All we need to do is discover and maintain it. The Holy Spirit desires you fervently and is eagerly interceding for you (see James 4:5; Romans 8:26–27). Let Him baptize you with fire now!

From going to church to being the Ekklesia

We already know what the Church is like today, but what would the Ekklesia look like, once rediscovered? Let me share candidly what I see happening when I peek over the horizon, as I have been privileged to do so many times before. As a growing number of pulpit and marketplace ministers take the power and presence of the Lord to the public square, we will eventually experience an "Acts 18" phenomenon. What I mean by this is that the conversion of a modern-day Crispus will set in motion an extraordinary chain reaction of individual and household salvations.

If such a phenomenal breakthrough in Corinth took place because Paul and a few associates moved their base of operations from the synagogue to the marketplace, just imagine how much greater the next breakthrough will be now that multitudes are emulating them after realizing that they have been anointed for business! Wanlapa the ice-cream vendor alone was instrumental in leading thousands to Christ. Look at the impact already of people like Barbara Chan, Aldo Martín, Gregorio Avalos, Michael Brown, King Flores, Francis Oda, Cliff Daugherty and Poncho Murguía. They constitute a small cloud, but one that announces the coming of a divine flood that will climax with the parade of saved nations we see in Revelation 21.

In my quiet time before God, I have sensed that this breakthrough definitely is coming, and it will result in millions saved in a matter of days. It is just a sensation, not a prophetic word, but one that I sincerely believe originates with the Holy Spirit. Just for the sake of a holy argument, imagine if someone like Donald Trump or Bill and Hillary

Clinton were to have a Zaccheus-type experience. When they publicly acknowledge their new faith in Christ, dedicate their households (the Trump empire and the Clinton Foundation) to God and make provision to correct past wrongs generously, millions could come to Christ. And if the Ekklesia is already in place, these millions could and should be baptized both in water and in the Holy Spirit, *in the marketplace*, as was the pattern in the book of Acts.

This is not entirely implausible, because it happened, albeit embryonically, before, but we were not prepared to bring it to its fullness. When Mel Gibson produced the movie *The Passion of the Christ*, the pure Gospel was presented in theaters all over the world and incredible numbers of people in the audience were in tears and under conviction when the lights were turned back on. But instead of leading them to Christ and baptizing them right on the spot, we timidly invited them to church and lost most of them "in transit." Worse yet, without the presence and covering of the Ekklesia, Mel Gibson was soon neutralized by the enemy.

The entire creation is eagerly awaiting the manifestation of God's children. God is our Father, we are His children, and the world is waiting for us to "come out of the closet."

To see in greater detail how this might happen, we need to study the examples in the book of Acts. Paul's initial ministry focus was the synagogues. Some rejected the message, and some became "Christian synagogues." By this I mean that they kept the old rituals and ceremonies while adding the revelation that Jesus is the Messiah. But Paul did not see a city, much less a region, transformed until he moved his base of operations to the marketplace, first in Corinth and then definitively in Ephesus, where he planted Ekklesias.

The converts in these Ekklesias, unlike those in the synagogues before, were mostly Gentiles. In fact, Luke, Paul's close associate, dedicated the book of Acts to a Roman noble, Theophilus. When we read Paul's salutations in his epistles, there are very few Jewish names; *they are mostly Greek*. Why?

Because Paul's most receptive audience was made up of "God-fearing Gentiles." These folks hung around the synagogue because they admired and desired Jewish ethics, but they were unable to enjoy them unless they converted to Judaism. To do this, they had to renounce the Gentile culture, be circumcised, adopt the customs of the Jews and observe the Jewish festivals. But when Paul moved out of the synagogue, these converts flocked en masse to the newly planted Ekklesias without any of those cultural restraints.

Today, there are millions of "God-fearing Gentiles" outside the four walls of our churches who admire our Christian ethics, our lifestyle and our teachings. The evidence is in the large number of unbelievers who send their children to Christian schools. But they are not willing to join "our church" because we represent a subculture that will uproot them from the place where they are already planted in the marketplace. And our requirements for membership are not helping either, because they are functionally similar to those of the synagogue: a new members' class, tithing, home group participation and involvement in church activities that compete with their responsibilities in the marketplace.

But worse yet, by relegating them to the back pews "until they mature" (i.e., learn to talk "Christianese"), we squander—or drive away—top-level leaders. Paul led them to Christ *in the marketplace*, showed them how to lead their households to faith, and constituted them in Ekklesias *in the marketplace*. He tapped into the already existing pool of leaders *in the marketplace* to establish the Ekklesia where they lived and worked—and he let them contextualize the truth and power of the Gospel in their own sphere of influence.

To see what we have never seen, we (the Ekklesia) must do what we have never done, or else we will continue to see the old (church), no matter how much we dress it up as new.

A Fork in the Road

Today's churches, generally speaking, more closely resemble the synagogue than the Ekklesia. That is not a put-down. It is a respectful observation intended to elicit a reality check. And there is a fork in the road ahead for them where they must make a definitive choice. Some of today's "church synagogues" will not be open to Ekklesia insights and will remain the twenty-first century equivalent of first-century "Christian synagogues" like the ones Paul ministered in before Acts 18. Others will make the transition to become an Ekklesia, especially those whose pastors are bivocational and, as a result, already have an active marketplace focus.

But I believe the greatest expansion—and more than an expansion, it will be an explosion—will come through the reoccurrence of the Acts 18 phenomenon I mentioned before. Millions will come to Christ rapidly, will be baptized both in water and in the Holy Spirit right at the moment of conversion, and will become part of a New Testament–like Ekklesia.

All of this will be plausible because by then, there will be multitudes of pulpit and marketplace ministers operating in the marketplace, either as an embryonic expression of the Ekklesia or as the *conventus*.

God's Blueprint for You

I don't know about you, but "as for me and my house"—my family and Transform Our World/Harvest Evangelism—I want to be on the cutting edge of what I believe will be the setup for the end time revival. To be in that position, we need to accept that God has chosen us to partner with Him. And for that, He has given us a measure of faith to which we need to add corresponding works (because faith without works is dead).

Let me explain. The most fascinating and intriguing point in this partnership with God is that "without God we can't, but without us He won't." This entails both a privilege and a responsibility, for which we are to give an account: "For we must all appear before the judgment seat of Christ, so that each one may be recompensed for his deeds in the body, according to what he has done, whether good or bad" (2 Corinthians 5:10).

Picture now the moment that you stand on the threshold that separates your earthly life from eternity. It is just a few seconds before you will step into eternity and the record of everything you have done while on this planet will be closed and examined. What will that record say?

Happily, God has already provided a blueprint for you: "For we [you] are His workmanship, created in Christ Jesus for good works, which

God prepared beforehand so that we [you] would walk in them" (Ephesians 2:10). God wants you to succeed, and for that He has made ample provision.

This is a three-part *God*, one-part *you* recipe. He created you, He saved you and He has a plan for your life. His three parts are already in place. Now you have to begin to walk in His plan. That plan consists of good works He has prepared beforehand, which, like a series of motion-activated lights along a path, do not come on until you take the first step. At that moment the first light comes on, and as you progress, the following ones light up in succession. All you have to do is begin to walk and keep on walking.

God has a hope and a future for you. He has more faith in you than any faith you can ever have in Him. But faith without works is dead. The principles and the testimonies you have read about in this book have already imparted faith to you. The next step is for you to add your works to that faith.

"Cashing in" Your Measure of Faith

Paul exhorts us to renew our minds so we can experience the will of God for our lives, which he describes as "good and acceptable and perfect" (Romans 12:2). After that, he adds, "For through the grace given to me I say to everyone among you not to think more highly of himself than he ought to think; but to think so as to have sound judgment, as God has allotted to each *a measure of faith*" (verse 3, emphasis added).

The first key is this: You are not to think too highly of yourself, but you are not to think too lowly either. How do you achieve that equilibrium? You do it through the measure of faith that God has given you already as a gift from Him. It is important that you use it, and for that, you need to activate it by adding works to it. If God is calling you to begin your transformation journey by dedicating your desk, or your kitchen, or your toolbox as a point of inception for Him to dwell in, do it!

Once you have added works, God will replace the prior measure of faith with a larger one, which in turn will require a corresponding greater level of works on your part. I am not talking about salvation through works but about moving up to greater measures of faith as a result of applying the faith that you have been entrusted with. By cashing your measure of faith in for a larger measure when you do the work for which that measure of faith was given, you are placing yourself inside a faith-work-growth continuum. Remember what I shared in chapter 2 about the light of dawn growing brighter and brighter until the day becomes perfect? That was—and still is—our journey.

When my doctors told me in 1980 that I only had two years to live, I did not have faith for much, except to stay alive one more day. My level of weakness and pain was such that to overcome the temptation to give up and let myself die, every night I placed photos of my wife and our four daughters next to my bed. I looked at those pictures until I gained the strength to fight for another night of life. As I obeyed Him, my faith grew every day, until the time came when God could entrust me with a measure large enough to believe Him for my healing.

As I continued to "spend" the increasing measures of faith with corresponding greater works, God took me farther, wider and higher than I ever could have imagined. As a result, today I know that as long as I continue to respond with corresponding works to the expanding measure of faith I am given, I will be able, by God's grace, to move from victory to victory, and I will end strong.

I believe that the reason why pastors and ministry leaders too often burn out and quit in discouragement is because at some point they stop cashing in their faith with works for which the faith was given. When they first began the race, they had very little to risk. But as their ministry grew, the temptation simply to maintain the "much" that was now there placed them in a destructive pincer between greater faith and lesser works.

This happens because the most recent greater measure of faith God gave them requires corresponding greater works in order to take them to the next level. But their refusal to assume a corresponding risk makes the pressure unbearable and leads to burnout. They know deep down what should be done—the same obedience as when they had nothing, or very little, and they trusted God for everything. But the temptation to become a manager or caretaker instead of continuing to be a pioneer becomes crushing without the release of obedient works. They settle for the status quo, allowing tradition to trump vision, and their vision is compromised and eventually lost.

It has happened before, but it should not happen to us. The concentric circles of growth that took the Ekklesia in Jerusalem from the Temple courts to the courts of the Ethiopian queen were eventually arrested by the negative dynamics I am describing. It took a persecution to get the Gospel past Samaria and Jerusalem, and the torch was not carried by the apostles, but by newcomers. And Jerusalem, the city that was offered the privilege in Acts 1:8 of being the vortex from where the Gospel would reach the ends of the earth, was replaced by Antioch, a merchant city.

To avoid this pitfall, let the Lord take you back to the day when, under the power of the Holy Spirit, you said *yes* to His call. You had nothing to offer but yourself, yet God took you and He gave you fruit. But there is *much more* fruit ahead, and access to it requires you to cash in your current measure of faith. God can turn on a dime, but you have to give Him the dime.

Yes, God has a hope and a future for you, but it is not just about you; it is about the world—the peoples and the nations that Jesus redeemed. What He has prepared for you is beyond anything you can think or imagine. But you have to commit unconditionally first, as Mary did. She was a young teenager when the angel announced to her that she had been chosen to carry God's Son in her womb. I am absolutely sure that she never thought or imagined anything remotely close to that. Obviously, she was perplexed, so she asked, "How can this be, since I am a virgin?" (Luke 1:34). The answer she got was, "*The Holy Spirit will come upon you*, and the power of the Most High *will overshadow you*" (verse 35, emphasis added). All she needed to hear was that the Holy Spirit would come upon her for her to respond, "Behold, the bondslave of the Lord; may it be done to me according to *your* word" (verse 38, emphasis added). And the rest is history . . . which changed history for the last two thousand years!

Dream with Me

With those thoughts in mind, now go back to the threshold I described a moment ago. What would you like to find when you step into eternity, besides the Lord Himself?

Allow me to challenge you to envision a company of men and women, young and old, who will cheerfully welcome you, full of gratitude because the works you added to the faith God entrusted you with helped bring them into God's Kingdom.

Dream with me about your nation. Picture its flag, waving in the wind of the Spirit and carried by its president or prime minister, bowing before God Almighty, with you having had a part, no matter how small, in bringing it about through your obedience to His call.

> *Dream with me about your own nation. Picture its flag, waving in the wind of the Spirit and carried by its president or prime minister, bowing before God Almighty.*

In every journey—no matter how long—the most important step is the first one because it represents a commitment to its final destination. Let's take bold steps into this journey by becoming an inspiring voice for the future rather than just an echo of the past.

As you envision that threshold one more time, let the Holy Spirit baptize you afresh and anew with power *and with fire*. And then, lift up your eyes, your heart and your arms to God, and let the two most powerful words in His Kingdom spring from your lips: "Yes, Lord!"

Go for it! You will never be the same. And better yet, the world, beginning with your sphere of influence, will never be the same. There are multitudes and nations waiting to be discipled.

Yes, go for it, because in Jesus' Ekklesia, the best is always ahead!

Notes

Chapter 1: Church: A Radical Proposition

1. The Romans conquered the Greeks, but Greek culture conquered the Romans, making the Roman Empire Hellenistic.

2. For more information on this, see Young-Ho Park's *Paul's Ekklesia as a Civic Assembly: Understanding the People of God in Their Politico-Social World* (Mohr Siebeck, 2015).

3. *Blue Letter Bible* Lexicon: Strong's G1577, s.v. "*ekklēsia*," https://www.blueletterbible .org/lang/lexicon/lexicon.cfm?strongs=g1577.

Chapter 2: Transformation Is a Journey

1. For a report on how the 109 towns were evangelized, see the documentary DVD *The Transformation Journey of Ed and Ruth Silvoso*, available at https://transformourworld .org/transformationondemand/product/the-transformation-journey-of-ed-and-ruth-silvoso/.

2. To read more of this story, see page 48 of my book *That None Should Perish: How to Reach Entire Cities for Christ Through Prayer Evangelism* (Chosen, 1995).

3. *That None Should Perish: How to Reach Entire Cities for Christ Through Prayer Evangelism* (Chosen, 1995) was first published in 1994.

4. *Prayer Evangelism: How to Change the Spiritual Climate over Your Home, Neighborhood and City* (Chosen, 2000).

5. *Women—God's Secret Weapon: God's Inspiring Message to Women of Power, Purpose and Destiny* (Chosen, 2010) was first published in 2001.

6. *Anointed for Business: How to Use Your Influence in the Marketplace to Change the World* (Chosen, 2009) was first published in 2002.

7. See http://thegoodlifehawaii.com/feed-sheep-joyce-kawakami/.

8. *Transformation: Change the Marketplace and You Change the World* (Chosen, 2011) was first published in 2007.

9. Though the title is provincial mayor, functionally it is equivalent to provincial governor.

Chapter 3: A Fuller Understanding of the Gates of Hades

1. Dick Bernal, senior pastor at Jubilee Christian Center in San José, California, pointed this historical insight out to me. See also http://www.padfield.com/acrobat/history/Caesarea _Philippi.pdf.

2. For more on this, see page 105 in chapter 3 of my book *That None Should Perish* (Chosen, 1995).

3. King James (1566–1625) reigned as King James VI of Scotland from 1567–1625 and King James I of England and Ireland from 1603–1625. See https://www.britannica.com /biography/James-I-king-of-England-and-Scotland.

4. *Episcopal* is an ecclesiastical term denoting church government by or related to a bishop or bishops. See http://www.thefreedictionary.com/episcopal.

5. Jack P. Lewis, *The English Bible from KJV to NIV: A History and Evaluation* (Grand Rapids, Mich.: Baker, 1984).

6. For more on Constantine, see https://www.christianhistoryinstitute.org/study/module /constantine/.

7. See more on this in Warren Carroll's *The Building of Christendom* (Christendom Press, 1987).

8. James Bryce, 1st Viscount Bryce, *The Holy Roman Empire*, 3rd ed., rev. (London: Macmillan and Co., 1864), 62–64.

9. *The Catholic Encyclopedia: New Advent*, s.v. "St. Francis of Assisi," http://www .newadvent.org/cathen/06221a.htm.

10. For more on this, see https://www.britannica.com/topic/Christianity.

11. As the early Church father Tertullian said in *Apologeticus*, his defense of Christianity.

12. How the Ekklesia is to exercise this authority is the subject of chapter 15, "A Fuller Understanding of Spiritual Authority."

Chapter 5: A Fuller Understanding of Proclamation

1. For more on this city's transformation, see the Transform Our World DVD *Transformation in Vallejo*, https://transformourworld.org/transformationondemand/product /transformation-in-vallejo/. See also the *Transformation in the Silicon Valley* DVD, from which Pastor Summers's quote is taken: https://transformourworld.org/transformationondemand /product/transformation-in-silicon-valley/.

2. See more on this in the *Transformation in Vallejo* video as well.

3. For more information on this coalition, you can visit them online at http://www .transformationvallejo.org/index.html.

4. You can find more on *Adopt Your Street* at http://adopt.transformourworld.org/en /adopt-your-street/create.

5. Os Hillman, "Reclaiming the 7 Mountains of Culture, Part 1," 7culturalmountains.org, http://www.7culturalmountains.org/apps/articles/default.asp?articleid=41492&columnid=.

Chapter 6: A Fuller Understanding of the Cross

1. According to online sources, Guatemala is ranked the fourth poorest country in the Caribbean and Central America. DCAF-ISSAT's article "Guatemala Country Profile: Executive Summary" listed Guatemala as the fourth least secure nation as of 2015 (Haiti is now the fourth most secure nation). See http://issat.dcaf.ch/Learn/Resource-Library/Country-Profiles /Guatemala-Country-Profile. Sources also list Guatemala among the bottom five nations

of the Caribbean and Latin American nations when it comes to security and governmental transparency. See also http://www.aneki.com/poorest_caribbean.html?number=all.

2. For more detail, see *Bible Hub*'s text analysis of Luke 19:10 at http://biblehub.com/text/luke/19-10.htm. In particular, see the Nestle GNT 1904 entry. Its literal translation reads, "Came indeed the Son of Man to seek and save that having been lost."

3. The Reina Valera Spanish Translation of the Bible (the most widely used version in Spanish) renders Revelation 21:24, "And the nations that have been saved will walk by its light . . ." I vividly remember how the reference to saved nations grabbed my imagination in the beginning of my walk with God. I like to think that my passion to disciple nations was seeded by that insertion. Even if it does not reflect exactly the letter of the original text, it definitely reflects its spirit.

Chapter 7: A Fuller Understanding of the Great Commission

1. Table entries are taken from the *Bible Hub* text analysis of Matthew 28:19, found at http://biblehub.com/text/matthew/28-19.htm.

2. I describe this paradigm more fully on page 97 of my book *Transformation: Change the Marketplace and You Change the World* (Chosen, 2010).

3. See Barnes' Notes on Romans 8:22 at http://biblehub.com/commentaries/barnes/romans/8.htm.

Chapter 8: A Fuller Understanding of Cooperation with God

1. Rev. Beverly Jaime, an associate pastor at Cathedral of Faith in San José, California, coined this expression.

2. See http://paranaque.gov.ph. You can also acquire the documentary DVDs *Transformation in Parañaque City and the Philippines* and *Transformation in Parañaque City Part 2* at https://transformourworld.org/transformationondemand/store/dvds/.

3. CERESO is an acrostic that stands for *Centro de Readaptación Social* in Spanish (Center for Social Rehabilitation). See the DVD *Transformation in El CERESO Prison, Mexico*, https://transformourworld.org/transformationondemand/product/transformation-in-el-cereso-prison-mexico/.

4. The documentary DVD *Transformation in the Marketplace with Ed Silvoso* is available that tells the story of Olmos Prison's transformation under the leadership of Juan Zuccarelli, and the birthing of the first "Christian" prison under the leadership of his disciple Daniel Tejeda. See ttps://transformourworld.org/transformationondemand/product/transformation-in-the-marketplace/.

5. The documentary DVD *Transformation in Ciudad Juárez Part 3* is available at https://transformourworld.org/transformationondemand/product/transformation-in-ciudad-juarez-mexico-part-3/.

6. For more on this, visit http://www.larodadora.org/.

7. Damien Cave, "Ciudad Juárez, a Border City Known for Killing, Gets Back to Living," *The New York Times* online, December 14, 2013, http://www.nytimes.com/2013/12/15/world/americas/a-border-city-known-for-killing-gets-back-to-living.html?_r=0.

8. Sam Quinones, "Once the World's Most Dangerous City, Juárez Returns to Life," *National Geographic*, June 2016 issue, and online article at http://www.nationalgeographic.com/magazine/2016/06/juarez-mexico-border-city-drug-cartels-murder-revival/.

9. See http://gadling.com/2012/01/06/worlds-worst-places-top-10-places-you-do-not-want-to-visit-in/ and http://www.cnn.com/2015/04/21/americas/mexico-ciudad-juarez-tourism/.

10. Clifford G. Howell in *The Advance Guard of Missions* (Pacific Press, 1912), as quoted in "William Carey: Pioneer Baptist Missionary to India," WholesomeWords.org, http://www.wholesomewords.org/missions/bcarey10.html.

Chapter 9: A Fuller Understanding of New Testament Baptisms

1. Matthew 11:13 states, "For all the prophets and the Law prophesied until John." See also John Piper's message on the Old versus New Covenants, "Jesus: Mediator of a Better Covenant, Part 1," http://www.desiringgod.org/messages/jesus-mediator-of-a-better-covenant-part-1.

Chapter 10: A New Understanding of Baptizing Nations

1. *Blue Letter Bible* Lexicon: Strong's G907, s.v. "*baptizō*," https://www.blueletterbible.org/lang/lexicon/lexicon.cfm?t=kjv&strongs=g907.

2. *Blue Letter Bible* Lexicon: Strong's G911, s.v. "*baptō*," https://www.blueletterbible.org/lang/lexicon/lexicon.cfm?t=kjv&strongs=g911.

3. *Bible Study Tools* New Testament Greek Lexicon, s.v. "*Baptizo*," http://www.biblestudytools.com/lexicons/greek/nas/baptizo/html.

4. W. E. Vine, *W. E. Vine's New Testament Word Pictures: Matthew to Acts* (Nashville: Thomas Nelson, 2015), 764.

Chapter 11: A Fuller Understanding of *How* to Baptize a Nation

1. *English Oxford Living Dictionaries*, s.v. "training," https://en.oxforddictionaries.com/definition/training.

2. *English Oxford Living Dictionaries*, s.v. "culture," https://en.oxforddictionaries.com/definition/culture.

3. The documentary DVD *Transformation in Ciudad Juárez Part 3* covers much of this. You can find it at https://transformourworld.org/transformationondemand/product/transformation-in-ciudad-juarez-mexico-part-3/.

Chapter 12: A Fuller Understanding of the Ekklesia's Social Agenda

1. The GNP or Gross National Product is the market value of all the products and services produced in one year by labor and property supplied by the citizens of a country.

2. For a fuller treatment of this subject, see chapters 10–17 in my book *Transformation: Change the Marketplace and You Change the World* (Chosen, 2010).

3. For more on this, see page 115 onward in my book *Transformation*.

4. Nelson Mandela, *Long Walk to Freedom* (Randburg, South Africa: Macdonald Purnell, 1994), Kindle edition, 622.

5. "Top Five Mahatma Gandhi Quotes," The Borgen Project blog page, August 2, 2013, http://borgenproject.org/top-five-mahatma-gandhi-quotes/.

6. Let's keep in mind that the backbone for both William Wilberforce and Martin Luther King Jr. was the Church acting as the Ekklesia—a legislative assembly standing for righteousness, peace and joy that contributed prayers, people, articulation of righteousness, resources and living examples. And in the case of Ghandi, it was the Christian ethic in the British culture, as defective as the latter might be, that brought the British to dialogue and accept rather than to annihilate (as has happened, and continues to happen, in cultures with no Christian ethic in its fiber).

7. My book *Women: God's Secret Weapon* (Chosen, 2010) is totally devoted to this subject.

8. I want to credit Pastor Cal Chinen, CEO of Transformation Hawaii, for his valuable insights on this subject of family transformation.

9. *Bible Hub* Concordance: Strong's 3624, s.v. "*oikos*," http://biblehub.com/greek/3624.htm.

10. To preview Ruth's book through a visual tour, or to purchase *Food, Family and Fun: A Glimpse into Our Family's Table, Traditions and Travels*, go to https://transformourworld .org/transformationondemand/product/food-family-fun/.

11. You can watch this moment online at https://transformourworld.org/2016/09/28 /spirit-of-adoption/, beginning at about 00:42:50 to get the full impact.

12. For more on this story, see the documentary DVD *Transformation in Vallejo, CA*, available at https://transformourworld.org/transformationondemand/product/transform ation-in-vallejo/.

13. For more on this story, see our documentary DVD entitled *Transformation in Brant-ford, Canada* at https://transformourworld.org/transformationondemand/product/trans formation-in-brantford-canada/.

14. According to *Fausset's Bible Dictionary* online, Asiarchs were officers whom cities in that part of Asia chose, of which Ephesus was the metropolis. "Each city chose one deputy, and out of the whole number ten were chosen, over whom one presided, selected by the Roman proconsul." For more on this, see http://www.bible-history.com/faussets/A/Asiarchs/.

Chapter 13: A Fuller Understanding of the Incarnation

1. A social compact is "an agreement, entered into by individuals, that results in the formation of the state or of organized society, the prime motive being the desire for protec-tion, which entails the surrender of some or all personal liberties." *Collins English Diction-ary*, s.v. "social contract or social compact," http://www.collinsdictionary.com/dictionary /english/social-contract.

Chapter 14: A Fuller Understanding of What God Loves the Most

1. This is documented in the documentary DVD *Transformation in Hong Kong*. You can find it at https://transformourworld.org/transformationondemand/product/transformation -in-Hong-Kong/.

Chapter 15: A Fuller Understanding of Spiritual Authority

1. *Wikipedia*, s.v. "Ethiopian Eunuch," last modified October 1, 2016, https://en.wikipedia .org/wiki/Ethiopian_eunuch.

2. Cal Chinen leads a weekly pastors' meeting that is the functional equivalent of the Ekklesia in Hawaii since, in addition to prayer and fellowship, they devote time to legislate in the heavenlies for the Kingdom of God to expand in the islands.

3. Dr. Clifford E. Daugherty, *The Quest Continues: Light, Life and Learning* (Quest for Excellence Media, 2015), 64.

4. Ibid., 69.

Chapter 16: A Fuller Understanding of the Ekklesia's Operational Methodology

1. I treat this topic in greater detail in my books *Prayer Evangelism* (Chosen, 2000) and *Transformation* (Chosen, 2010), and I recommend that you go to those for the bigger picture. Here I am providing the condensed version to show you how to turn a ministry swamp into a transformation river.

2. You can also see more on this story in the DVD documentary *The Transformation Journey of Ed and Ruth Silvoso*, https://transformourworld.org/transformationondemand /product/the-transformation-journey-of-ed-and-ruth-silvoso/.

3. I make a distinction between *prayer* and *prayer of faith*. The former is an open-ended desire for improvement that we include in our thoughts and prayers. The latter hangs on to the promises of God and claims them, fully persuaded that God is listening. This is what James refers to in James 5:15–20.

4. The booklet *My City . . . God's City* that Dave Thompson and I coauthored is also a helpful resource. It is available at https://transformourworld.org/transformationondemand /product/my-city-gods-city/.

5. It was a "divine coincidence" that while I was studying this subject, God led me to meet Steve Scott, who has done the best job I am aware of highlighting the central and foundational role of Jesus' teachings. He and his team have developed valuable teaching materials that are available on their website, www.knowinghim.org.

6. The Bible references used for both prayer evangelism and the five pivotal paradigms come from the gospels. The only exception is the verse used for the third paradigm, which comes from Paul's letter to the Colossians (see Colossians 3:23). Jesus addressed the fact that we are ministers and that our work for Him is worship, however, when He taught that we are the light of the world, when He assured us that we will do the same works that He did and even greater ones, and when He told parables such as the one about the minas and the talents (see Luke 19:11–27).

Chapter 17: The Way Forward

1. Sign up for "Transformation on Demand" at www.transformourworld.org, which will allow you to watch transformation documentaries and access other instructional material. The online instructions to sign up are simple and self-guided.

2. I was greatly enlightened on this point by Bahadir Yahyagil, a brilliant marketplace minister who is also featured in our documentary DVD *Transformational Entrepreneurs*, available at https://transformourworld.org/transformationondemand/product/transform ational-entrepreneurs/.

3. For more on this subject, see Stephen Mitchell's *Anatolia: Land, Men, and Gods in Asia Minor Volume II: The Rise of the Church* (Clarendon Press, 1995).

Dr. Ed Silvoso is the founder and president of Harvest Evangelism Inc. and also of the Transform Our World Network, which is composed of thousands of pulpit and marketplace influencers across the globe. He is widely recognized as a visionary strategist and solid Bible teacher who specializes in nation and marketplace transformation.

Dr. Silvoso has been trained both in theology and business, and his work experience includes banking, hospital administration, financial services and church ministry. As a strategic thinker with a passion to equip ordinary people to do extraordinary things, he has spent his lifetime mining life-giving biblical principles for transformation and linking them to practical application for Christians so that they will see transformation impact their lives, families, spheres of influence and, ultimately, their cities and nations.

Dr. Silvoso's bestselling books on the topic of transformation have become groundbreaking classics. His DVD series *Transformation in the Marketplace with Ed Silvoso* provides tangible validation of the transformation principles at work by documenting prototypes now being developed on every continent.

Dr. Silvoso and his wife, Ruth, have four married daughters and twelve grandchildren. For more details on his life and ministry, see the Wikipedia article "Ed Silvoso" at http://en.wikipedia.org/wiki/Ed_Silvoso. You can also find Dr. Silvoso online at www.transformourworld.org or www.edsilvoso.com. Contact him at Edsilvoso@transformourworld .org, or visit him at

Facebook
www.facebook.com/transformourworld
www.facebook.com/EdSilvoso

Twitter
@transfrmourwrld
@edsilvoso

Instagram
EdSilvoso

More from Ed Silvoso

Visit edsilvoso.com to learn more about Ed, his ministry and his books.

The role of women in the Church is hotly debated, even today. Here Ed Silvoso offers his response to this issue, persuasively presenting the Bible's portrayal of women as powerful adversaries of the devil. There is no doubt that women have a pivotal place in God's plan for Satan's ruin. And there is no doubt that we, the united Body of Christ, will triumph in His name.

Women: God's Secret Weapon

God loves us and has a unique blueprint for our lives, but it's up to us to live it out. Mingling stories and biblical anecdotes with practical advice, Silvoso shows how God intervenes to transform people and nations today. As he helps you discover your own specific purpose, you'll learn that God has great things planned for you!

Transformation

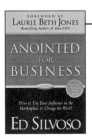

In this bestselling book, Ed Silvoso invites the Church to engage with the heart of our cities: the marketplace. With biblical examples and extraordinary true stories, he shows us how to knock down the perceived wall between commercial pursuit and service to God—and participate in an unparalleled marketplace transformation.

Anointed for Business